# THE NEW
# CLARENDON SHAKESPEARE

Under the general editorship of

**R. E. C. HOUGHTON, M.A.**

*Emeritus Fellow, St. Peter's College, Oxford*

Edited by

THE NEW CLARENDON SHAKESPEARE

# RICHARD III

Edited by

### R. E. C. HOUGHTON, M.A.
Sometime Fellow and Tutor of
St. Peter's College, Oxford

OXFORD
AT THE CLARENDON PRESS

*Oxford University Press, Ely House, London W.1*

GLASGOW NEW YORK TORONTO MELBOURNE WELLINGTON
CAPE TOWN SALISBURY IBADAN NAIROBI DAR ES SALAAM LUSAKA ADDIS ABABA
BOMBAY CALCUTTA MADRAS KARACHI LAHORE DACCA
KUALA LUMPUR SINGAPORE HONG KONG TOKYO

FIRST PUBLISHED 1965
REPRINTED 1968 (WITH CORRECTIONS)
1969, 1970

PRINTED IN GREAT BRITAIN

# CONTENTS

# LIST OF ILLUSTRATIONS

# INTRODUCTION

*Richard the Third* is not one of the greatest of Shakespeare's plays. It is not comparable for depth and subtlety of character-drawing or for poetic power with either the Roman history plays or with the later tragedies; and if we compare it only with other plays written before the turn of the century and ignore comedy, it has neither the lyric sweetness of *Romeo and Juliet* nor the humour and variety of the two plays on *Henry IV*. Nevertheless it is still a play which has much to offer both young and old: to the younger reader it presents, like *Julius Caesar*, dramatic qualities that are easily grasped, and brings to life an obscure and confused period of medieval history (however distorted the picture of its titular hero); to the older reader it reveals the great dramatist of the future first emerging from the welter of the chronicle history play; while to the professional scholar it furnishes the problem of deciding the relative importance to its author of contemporary ideas of history and morality as against more mercenary considerations of box-office appeal, and at the same time a text of which the precise form and derivation is unusually puzzling. The ordinary reader may be surprised to hear that *Richard III* has been dubbed by a respected modern scholar 'a very religious play', since it is its more obvious dramatic qualities that have always made the play a favourite on the stage. It was the play in which Garrick first won fame, and of which Olivier made what is perhaps the most widely known Shakespearian film.

## DATE AND POSITION IN SHAKESPEARE'S WORK

The date of the writing and first production of *Richard III* almost certainly lies between 1591 and 1593, and later rather than earlier within these limits. It was first printed in 1597, and occurs in the list of Shakespeare's plays given by Meres in 1598. A diary of 1601 records Burbage as having acted the name-part 'on a time'. But these facts do not show how much *earlier* the play was; whereas both its subject and its style connect it closely with the three parts of *Henry VI*. The last of these was acted not later than 1592, since Greene who died in that September quotes from it; and it is highly probable that our play followed fairly closely after it, in 1592 or 1593. If this is so, it may have come just before the first comedy, *The Comedy of Errors*, and the first tragedy, *Titus Andronicus*. Thus Shakespeare would have begun his career as a dramatist by writing plays on English history; and 'there is no certain evidence that any popular dramatist before Shakespeare wrote a play based on English history' (F. P. Wilson).

The First Folio arranged the plays on English history together, even if, like *Richard II* and *Richard III*, they might also be considered as tragedies; and it printed them in historical order from *King John* to *Henry VIII*. But it is important for the student to distinguish clearly between the position of a play in the dramatist's career and its chronological position in English history. For Shakespeare did not write his plays entirely according to the order of the events portrayed, but in two groups, of which the first written dealt with later history. *Richard III* depicts the end of the Wars of the Roses in 1485, and is thus, apart from *Henry VIII* at the end of his career, the nearest to the dramatist's own day in subject. A few years later he went back to Richard II, and then added the two parts of *Henry IV*, and *Henry V*. Thus the earlier written tetralogy of *Henry VI* to *Richard III* deals with the later century, the fifteenth. The dynastic wars which are called after the badges of the rival houses had only ended about

a century before Shakespeare wrote our play, and the confusion and bloodshed was not too distant a memory in the
country to heighten the fear of renewed anarchy if the
succession were again to be in doubt. The Tudor settle-
ment and its alternative was a live topic in the reign of the
grand-daughter of Henry VII.

When about 1590 Shakespeare came up to London from
Stratford-on-Avon, possibly after a few years as a country
schoolmaster, he found the stage recently invigorated by
the so-called 'university wits', especially Kyd and Marlowe. Kyd's *Spanish Tragedy* was produced before 1590,
and, although its Shakespearian connexions are more
clearly with *Hamlet* than with *Richard III*, its use of
ghosts forms one link between the plays of Seneca, the
Latin dramatist, and the scene in our play before the battle
of Bosworth. An even more prominent feature of Senecan
tragedy, and of Kyd's play, was the theme of revenge,
which was to dominate so much of Elizabethan tragedy.
In Shakespeare it looms largest in *Titus Andronicus* and
*Hamlet*; but in the form of Nemesis or Divine Judgement
on sin and pride it is a main thread in *Richard III*. Whereas Kyd had written his best-known play by 1590, Marlowe's *Edward II* and (probably) *Dr. Faustus* were still to
come. But Marlowe had produced *Tamburlaine* and *The
Jew of Malta*, in both of which plays he had concentrated
the interest on one character, and that as much villain as
hero. Indeed the Jew is even more of a self-confessed
villain than Richard, of the type called 'Machiavellian',
from the somewhat unscrupulous advice given in the
treatise on statesmanship, *Il Principe*, by Machiavelli
(1513). Marlowe used often to be thought to be part
author of the *Henry VI* plays, but there was no positive
evidence of this, and in fact the newer view is that Shakespeare was Marlowe's predecessor in the English history
play, and that *Edward II* is indebted to Shakespeare. But

this still leaves Marlowe some precedence both in the development of blank verse and in the type of villain-hero. Of this kind is the Aaron of *Titus Andronicus*, now normally ascribed to Shakespeare at about the same date as our play. But neither Aaron nor the Jew of Malta has the vigour, variety, or humour of Richard the Third. And here Shakespeare probably owed more to the humorous treatment of the Devil in the old Miracle plays, and to the Vice of the Morality plays, who is actually referred to at III. i. 82. For there *is* something diabolical about Richard's humour. But nothing that modern criticism has found to say about the antecedents of our play in earlier drama need detract from the originality of the impression made by Shakespeare's first full-scale character creation. Even the scholar who has most fully elaborated the intention of the history plays 'to show the working out of God's will in English history' admits that 'it does not detract from the importance of Richard in the process'. In fact 'Richard as Machiavel and Richard as the chosen victim of Nemesis are only moderately convincing. On the other hand, Richard as an actor is convincing enough; and in this side of his hero's personality I think Shakespeare was very much interested' (E. K. Chambers). There is no character in this play into whom the writer could put much of himself, even as much as he was soon to put into Richard II; but there are a fairly large number of references to the stage or to acting which serve to reveal the young dramatist's preoccupations. It is only when we contrast the poetry and psychology of Richard III with that of a later villain-hero, Macbeth, that we appreciate the full difference between superb melodrama and genuine tragedy.

Many of those who use this edition of *Richard III* will not yet be in a position to compare it with the plays of Shakespeare's predecessors to which reference has been made above; but if they are studying this play with any care they should read as much as possible of the three parts of *Henry VI* which preceded it and with which it is closely linked. The First Part covers a period of thirty-one years from the death of Henry V in 1422, and is almost wholly concerned with the wars in France, Talbot who dies at the end (in 1453) being the chief character. But even in this part we have already a reference to civil war, in Bedford's words

> Henry the Fifth! thy ghost I invocate:
> Prosper this realm; keep it from civil broil. (I. i. 53)

We may also draw attention to the scene invented by Shakespeare which shows the origin of the white and red rose symbols (II. iv), and the point at which Richard Plantagenet, father of Richard III, is created Duke of York (III. i). The Second Part begins with the arrival of Queen Margaret in England in 1445 and covers the succeeding ten years, down to the victory of York at the first battle of St. Albans, where his son, the later Richard III, is made to appear, although he was in reality only three years old (v. ii). There is also in this part some treatment of the requirements of kingship, a theme running through all the English history plays. The Third Part carries the Wars of the Roses to the murder of Henry VI in 1471, and deserves the special attention of the student of *Richard III*. A few of the more notable incidents may be singled out: Richard urges his father to break his oath to Henry VI (I. ii. 22–34); Clifford murders Rutland, York's third son, illustrating the new pitch of barbarity to which civil war has come (I. iii); the battle of Wakefield, in which the 'she-wolf of France' taunts York after putting a paper-crown on his head, and finally joins in stabbing him. She asks the father

> Where's that valiant crook-back'd prodigy,
> Dicky your boy?

and is herself hailed as 'a tiger's heart wrapp'd in a
woman's hide'—a line which Greene adapted to an attack
on Shakespeare himself (I. iv); Henry's soliloquy desiring
a quiet life followed by the entry of 'a Son that has killed
his Father' with the dead body, and then of 'a Father
that has killed his Son' (II. v); Gloucester revealing his
future designs (as Richard III) in a soliloquy in which he
claims to know how 'to set the murderous Machiavel to
school' (III. ii. 124–end); Warwick's proposal to marry his
daughter Anne to Margaret's young Prince Edward (III.
iii); the beginning of the quarrel between the new King
Edward's brothers and his queen (IV. i); the reference to
Richmond as 'England's hope' (IV. vi. 67); the murder
of Prince Edward (v. v. 38–40); Henry VI's prophecy of
Richard's cruelty; and, finally, his own murder at Richard's
hand (v. vi. 35–55 and 61–93).

Most of this historical background may already have
been obtained from a study of English medieval history,
but only the perusal of the *Henry VI* plays themselves will
enable the student to appreciate the progress made in
*Richard III* from dramatized history to the unified impression of true drama. Nothing could be more striking
than the fine metaphor with which our play opens:

> Now is the winter of our discontent
> Made glorious summer by this sun of York—

If all were like this we might imagine that the poet had
reached maturity overnight; for there is little or nothing
of this order of poetry in *Henry VI*. But of course he has
not. In its own way Clarence's dream is fine (T. S. Eliot
once said of it that 'the best of Seneca has here been ab-
sorbed into English'). But in general the style of *Richard
III* is more remarkable for 'patterning' than for deeper
poetical qualities; and the best example of this patterned
speech had already come in *3 Henry VI* (II. v. 1–54). If,

however, we extend the word 'style' to its widest sense we can add as a new feature the amount of dramatic irony in the play. The language is a curious mixture of the rhetorical and artificial with passages of something more homely and direct, like the short scene IV. v. The contrast is seen most strikingly in I. iv where Clarence's dream is followed by the talk of the murderers—the only use of prose in this play (80 lines out of some 3,600); and again in IV. iv in the contrast of Richard's speech after the entry of Catesby and Ratcliff with what has preceded. But, for all its unevenness and much rhetorical artificiality, the style of the play must be allowed to show much 'linguistic vitality'.

## THE SOURCES

The immediate source for the play of *Richard III* lay in what we should call the history books current in Shakespeare's day. Of these the one he used most, and for other plays besides this, was Holinshed's *Chronicles* (to abbreviate a title occupying several lines), which was first published in 1577, followed in 1586–7 by a second edition which Shakespeare possessed (see Commentary at V. iii. 325). But Holinshed had incorporated most of the work of Hall (Halle) published thirty years earlier (1548) under the following title (spelling modernized):

The Union of the two Noble and Illustrious Families of Lancaster and York being long in continued dissension for the crown of this noble realm with all the acts done in both the times of the prince, both of the one lineage and of the other, beginning at the time of King Henry the Fourth, the first author of this dissension, and so successively proceeding to the reign of the high and prudent Prince King Henry the Eighth, the indubitable flower and very heir of both the said lineages.

Hall's Chronicle actually covers the period from 1398 to 1485, the same as that covered by Shakespeare's two groups of plays, and the text upon which he preaches is made still more explicit in a long opening sentence about the 'mischief of intestine division' as to which 'especially this noble realm of England can apparently declare and make demonstration'; so that when it is said that the real hero of Shakespeare's history plays is England good precedent may be found in Hall, as well as for the obvious moral of the evils of civil war. The editor of the older Clarendon Press edition of this play felt justified in almost completely filling his introduction with fifty pages from Hall. But since so much of the matter is common to Holinshed and Hall we can only be sure which the dramatist was using on the comparatively few occasions where the matter comes in only one of the two, some of which occasions will be found in the Commentary. Let it suffice to say in this place that all the historical matter of our play which is not noted as an invention of Shakespeare's comes in either Hall or Holinshed, usually in both.

But behind both Hall and Holinshed there stands a greater man and writer, Sir Thomas More, Lord Chancellor under Henry VIII, and beheaded in 1535 by his master's tyranny. Many years before his death More had left unfinished *The History of King Richard the Third*, and this work is the ultimate source of most that concerns Richard in the play down to IV. iv, since it was incorporated by Hall and Holinshed. More is one of the best writers of early modern English prose, and has been claimed to be a pillar of the arch connecting modern English with the Old English of pre-conquest days. His *Richard III* is one of the earliest examples of historical biography in English literature; and it may have been More's example that helped Shakespeare to move on from the anecdotal type of history to the centrality of one character (although it must in fairness be admitted that Talbot in *1 Henry VI* had been saluted by Nash as a heroical figure), and to grasp something of the tragic idea of Greek drama, 'the feeling of fate hanging over blind men who can see what is happening to others but are unconscious of their own danger' (R. W. Chambers, whose *Thomas More* is a moving story finely told). And it may just be noted here that Shakespeare is now generally thought to have contributed 147 lines in his own hand to the anonymous Elizabethan play *Sir Thomas More* (first printed in the nineteenth century).

There was one other ultimate source which Shakespeare is unlikely to have known at first hand, the *Anglia Historia* of Polydore Vergil, an Italian humanist who was in England from 1502, and began to produce his history in 1534. It is he who first recounts the supposed dream of Richard before Bosworth, and ascribes it to a 'conscience guilty of hainous offences'.

So much for the prose sources and professed history writers. But something must be added about poetical sources, or influences, in which some of the same material had been handled from a mainly moral point of view. About thirty years before *Richard III* was acted there had appeared in two parts a poem much read at the time called *A Mirror for Magistrates* (1559), which recounted the fall of twenty illustrious figures in history, mostly English. The only one of these 'tragedies' which Shakespeare can be *shown* to have read is the eighteenth, by Baldwin, which is entitled 'How George Plantagenet, third son of the Duke of York, was by his brother King Edward wrongfully imprisoned and by his brother Richard miserably murdered'. It includes these lines:

> A prophecy was found, which seyd a G
> Of Edwardes children should destruccion be

which are echoed in I. i. 39–40 (cf. also the Commentary on I. i. 50). But Shakespeare had almost certainly read also

the Induction by Sackville, which recounts how Sorrow
led the poet to the realm of the dead (cf. Clarence's dream).
The *Mirror*, however, is less important as a direct source
than as one embodiment of contemporary thought, which
has received much more attention in recent times than
from earlier critics. The sixteenth century was much
interested in history, less from a speculative point of view,
or as intellectual entertainment, than as a source of lessons
for the present. And the same applied to tragedy. For
example, in the preface to his translation of the *Orlando
Furioso* (1591) Sir John Harington not only claimed that
'the reading of a good Heroicall Poeme may make a man
both wiser and honester', but also that 'Tragedies well
handled be a most worthie kind of Poesie', and added as
an instance

that that was played at St John's in Cambridge, of Richard the
3, would move (I thinke) Phalaris the tyraunt, and terrifie all
tyrannous minded men from following their foolish ambitious
humours, seeing how his ambition made him kill his brother,
his nephew, his wife, beside infinit others, and, last of all, after
a short and troublesome raigne, to end his miserable life, and
to have his body harried after his death.

So also, twenty years earlier, Richard had been used as an
example of tyranny in a political pamphlet; and the preface to the *Mirror* proclaimed that its object was to serve
as a warning where men might see vice 'as in a looking-
glass' and 'with how grievous plagues vices are punished'.
Even the dry chronicler Holinshed added moral comments,
such as this on the murder of Prince Edward at Tewkesbury: 'for the which cruel act the more part of the doers
in their latter day drank of the like cup, by the righteous
justice and due punishment of God' (cf. i. iii. 20). Shakespeare and his contemporaries knew their Bibles, their
Old Testament at least as well as their New, and they
could already read in the Geneva version of 1560 words

which were often to be on the lips of preachers: 'Vengeance is mine, saith the Lord, I will repay'. The Elizabethan public came to the theatre not only for the thrill that melodrama always gives an unsophisticated audience, but also to find their moral and religious sense satisfied by the condign punishment inflicted on the transgressors of God's laws.

The quotation from Harington given above leads us finally to the mention of two other plays on the subject of Richard III, one of which certainly preceded Shakespeare's, although there is no reason to think he knew of it. That is an academic play in Latin, *Ricardus Tertius*, performed at Cambridge in 1579 and still surviving. The other, called the *True Tragedie of Richard the Third*, was printed in 1594, and has usually been considered a corrupt text of a play which was acted before Shakespeare's. If that were the case it would have been possible that, as Dover Wilson maintained, Shakespeare knew an earlier form of the *True Tragedie*, and owed something of his framework to it. But the form in which it now survives is lame stuff, and the following lines about Richard will be quite enough for most people:

> A man ill-shap'd, crooked backed, lame armed withall,
> Valiantly minded, but tyrannous in authoritie,
> So during the minoritie of the young Prince
> He is made Lord Protector over the Realme.

Another passage ends twelve out of sixteen lines with the word 'revenge'; which makes us thankful that Shakespeare was so moderate in his use of rhetorical patterning. The most recent view, that the *True Tragedie* is a corrupt pirated version of Shakespeare's work, would of course remove it altogether from the consideration of the Sources; but the present editor finds it difficult to believe that the *True Tragedie* is this, since it introduces not only new matter but even new characters.

## THE HISTORICAL SETTING OF THE PLAY

Those who are reasonably familiar with English medieval history can ignore this section of the Introduction; but others who have never worked through it, or have left their schooldays long behind, may find even the following slight sketch useful. Further information and reminders as to historical personages will be found in the Commentary at various points. Edward III, who reigned for fifty years from 1327 to 1377, 'had seven sons' (as Shakespeare says in *2 Henry VI*, II. ii. 10), and it was the rivalry between the descendants of some of these sons that gave rise to the Wars of the Roses. The House of Lancaster was descended from John of Gaunt, Duke of Lancaster, *fourth* son of Edward III, and its emblem was a red rose. The House of York was descended from his *fifth* son, Edmund, Duke of York, but through marriage was able to assert the claim of the *third* son, Lionel, Duke of Clarence. Its emblem was a white rose.

Edward III was succeeded by his grandson Richard II, son of his eldest son, the Black Prince, who died one year before his father. Richard II proved a weak king, as readers of Shakespeare's play will know, and was deposed in 1399 by Henry Bolingbroke, son of Gaunt. His seizure of the throne, whatever the provocation, set a precedent for the dynastic struggle which tore the country apart for most of the fifteenth century. Henry IV and Henry V (1413–22) were strong men, who, in spite of revolts, held to and strengthened their position; but Henry VI, who succeeded as a child, was never the man to rule in those turbulent days; which gave the rival house an opportunity to assert its claims (read *3 Henry VI*, II. vi. 11–203). Richard, Duke of York, had held a limited Protectorate during an illness of Henry VI, and in 1455 took up arms, and, supported by Warwick among others, won the first battle of St. Albans, but in 1460, after claiming the crown, was defeated and killed at Wakefield by the Lancastrians, led by Queen Margaret. Fortune was soon reversed at Mortimer's Cross and the second battle of St. Albans, and Edward, son of Richard, Duke of York, was declared king (1461–83). A few years later war was resumed, Warwick now changing to the Lancastrian side, and Henry VI was momentarily restored (1470). In 1471 Edward regained his position by the battle of Tewkesbury in which Margaret was defeated and her son, Prince Edward of Lancaster, killed. Our play opens shortly after the death of Henry VI in 1471, and ends in 1485, thus compressing events over fourteen years into the 'two hours traffic of our stage', or a little longer.

## THE REAL RICHARD

No previous edition of the play seems to have touched on the credibility of its hero. Its derivation from the version of history current in the dramatist's day has already been summarized, and more details of Shakespeare's use of More, Hall, and Holinshed will be given in the Commentary. But it seems right to include at least some hints that Richard may be the most maligned king in English history, if only because the genius of Shakespeare has fixed in all our minds a picture that may well be a gross libel on an unfortunate man. 'Shakespeare's Richard is nothing but a royal gangster who had been presented to him ready-made by the Tudor historians' (V. B. Lamb, *The Betrayal of Richard III*, 1959). Even More may have blackened his portrait in order to attack indirectly the non-moral statecraft of the sixteenth century.

But doubts as to the truth of the accepted portrait are no new thing. Defence of Richard began in the seventeenth century with Buck's *History of Richard III*,

continued in the eighteenth with the better-known Horace
Walpole's *Historic Doubts on Richard III* (1768), and was
the subject of periodical controversy in the later nineteenth century. But the fullest and most impartial
investigation came recently with P. Kendall's biography
of *Richard the Third* (1955), a book which makes rewarding
reading for anyone who can find time for it. Kendall has
laid aside the emotional heat which had enveloped the
subject, and, ignoring the Tudor tradition, has based his
biography 'almost entirely upon source material contemporary with Richard's day'. It is clearly impossible
to summarize it here, but a few points may be abstracted
from it: the only stain certainly left on Richard's character is his treatment of Hastings; Richard was no more
responsible than Edward IV for the death of Henry VI;
Richard had spent three years of his boyhood with Anne
at Middleham Castle, and the marriage 'seems to have
been a happy one'; there is no evidence for Richard having
plotted the death of Clarence; Edward had appointed
Richard Protector of the Realm; his sons were found to be
illegitimate through his pre-contract with Lady Butler
before he married their mother; Richard's kingship had
been legitimized by a *Titulus Regius* of Parliament; there
was nothing sinister in the young princes being lodged in
the Tower, which was not yet of bloody memory; the
fate of the princes is still a mystery (and even More
does not commit himself to Richard's guilt). But perhaps
the strongest evidence brought forward to redeem the
reputation of Richard is the work he did in the north
of England as the king's representative, and the high
regard in which he was always held by the city of York.
In short there seems to be nothing we know of Richard
before he became king to confirm the 'bloody boar' of
tradition.

Why, then, the reader will ask at once, has tradition

handed down so different a picture? An answer may lie
in the deliberate creation of a fictitious picture by Henry
VII and his archbishop of Canterbury, Morton. Morton was
Richard's enemy, handed over for safe keeping to Buckingham, with whom, it is supposed, he began to concoct a view
of Richard as a monster so acceptable to his supplanter
Henry VII. This view is supposed to have been partly
imbibed by the young More when a page in the house of
Morton (and this is the weakest link in the argument, on
account of More's youth), so that, later on, when More
took over from Polydore Vergil the moral pattern of
history he found Richard ready to his hand for the
portrait of 'the Bad Prince', so much more effective from
a literary point of view than a more neutral or uncertain
portrait. To quote the conclusion of Kendall's book:

The forceful moral pattern of Vergil, the vividness of More,
the fervour of Hall, and the dramatic exuberance of Shakespeare have endowed the Tudor myth with a vitality that is
one of the wonders of the world. What a tribute this is to art!
what a misfortune this is for history!

It is only fair to add that by no means all medieval
historians would go all the way with Kendall in his re-
habilitation of Richard, on the ground that the 'Tudor
myth' could hardly have gained sway without some
foundation in fact.

(Many readers would enjoy a short detective story by
J. Tey, *The Daughter of Time* (1951) [i.e. Truth], which
shows that the verdict on Richard as to the murder of the
Princes can only be 'non-proven'.)

## THE TEXT OF *RICHARD III*

By 'the text' of the play we mean here the exact form
of words which the author finally intended should be
spoken on the stage, just as in the case of a book we should

mean that form of words which the writer finally desired should go out to the world in print. The authority for the text of a play of Shakespeare lies either in the Folio alone (the collected edition of his plays produced after his death by his friends Heming and Condell in 1623), or in that, plus any separate printed editions of particular plays that may have preceded it in Quarto form. When we have Quarto editions (Q and QQ) as well as the Folio (F), the chief problem for a textual editor is to determine both in general and in each particular case whether to follow F or Q. And 'no Good Quarto differs so much from its Folio counterpart as that of *Richard III*' (Alexander in 1929). There are in all the plays of Shakespeare many places where F, or both F and Q, have been corrected by editors as to spelling, lineation, attribution of speeches, &c., which are generally agreed and printed in all modern texts, and such things are rarely mentioned in the Commentary to this edition. There are other places where the correction or improvement is less certain, more particularly where the readings of both F and Q seem possible. It has, for example, been reckoned that in *Richard III* the text of Alexander's modern *Tudor Shakespeare* differs in a thousand places from that of the most authoritative collected edition of the last century—the (old) Cambridge text. In some plays, for instance *King Lear*, a fair critic (i.e. one who does not start from the prejudice that one or other is always right) has to admit that sometimes F and sometimes Q appears to offer a reading more likely to be right. In *Richard III* the general relationship of F and Q was long in dispute, and some editors (e.g. Aldis Wright, Herford, and Ridley) took Q as the basis of their text, whereas others (e.g. Craig in the *Oxford Shakespeare* and the *Arden* edition of this play) relied chiefly on F. But since the work of J. C. Patrick (published in 1936) it has come to be generally admitted by textual experts that F is the more authoritative text of *Richard III*, since the first Quarto (not published till 1597) was made up from actors' memories of parts (a 'reported text'), although it is better than many of what are called the 'Bad Quartos'. F is most commonly supposed to have been actually printed from a corrected copy of Q 6 (there were six Q editions before the Folio), though a few eminent critics of the text think it was from Q 3.

Since the basis of all plays in the *New Clarendon Shakespeare* series is the Oxford collected edition we start with a text favourable to F. But since the text of *Richard III* is more disputed than that of most plays of Shakespeare, the editor has ventured to change the Oxford edition somewhat more than usual, and a list of those changes follows. A few of them are in the direction of regularizing the metre. This is an early play of Shakespeare's, and most of the verse is very regular, even stiff at times. When therefore this regularity is broken by what might easily be an actor's or even a printer's addition, regularity has been restored. (In these cases we follow the authority of Dr. Alice Walker, as recorded in the new *Cambridge Shakespeare*.)

|      |      |     |                                                   |
|------|------|-----|---------------------------------------------------|
| I.   | i.   | 49  | 'O!' omitted                                      |
|      |      | 84  | 'I' omitted.                                       |
|      |      | 88  | 'an't' for 'an' (Q and F 'and').                  |
|      |      | 95  | 'kin' for 'kindred'.                              |
|      | iii. | 273 | attribution changed.                              |
|      | iv.  | 26  | 'ingots' for 'anchors'.                           |
|      |      | 46  | 'sour' for 'grim'.                                |
| II.  | i.   | 82  | attribution changed.                              |
|      |      | 91  | 'but' for 'and'.                                  |
|      |      | 99  | 'requests' for 'request'st'.                      |
|      | ii.  | 46  | 'ne'er changing night' for 'perpetual rest'.      |
| III. | v.   | 55  | 'hear' for 'heard'.                              |
| IV.  | iii. | 31  | 'after-supper' hyphened.                          |

iv. 349 'vail' for 'wail'.
    535 'tidings, yet' for 'news, but yet'.
v. iii. 177–8 part of s.d. omitted.
    187 'What!' omitted.
    188 'Wherefore' omitted.
    210 'Ratcliff' omitted.

## THE PLOT OF THE PLAY

I. i. Richard explains himself, confessing his grudge against Nature for his physical deformity, and his jealous designs against his elder brother, Clarence. He pretends to Clarence that it is the Queen's relatives who have procured his imprisonment.

I. ii. Anne is accompanying the funeral procession of her father-in-law, the late King Henry VI, and cursing Richard as his murderer, when he starts to woo her with flattery.

I. iii. Elizabeth, wife of the reigning king, Edward IV, bewails his illness to her son and her brother, and reveals her fears of Richard. Richard attacks Elizabeth, and, later, the old Queen Margaret, widow of Henry VI, who has been prophesying revenge. Richard again confesses his villainy to the audience, and interviews the men he is sending to murder Clarence.

I. iv. Clarence relates his foreboding dreams to Brakenbury, Keeper of the Tower, where he is imprisoned. After arguing with his murderers, he is dispatched by one of them.

II. i. The King reconciles the noblemen Hastings and Buckingham to his wife's relatives. Richard hypocritically pretends to a similar reconciliation. Edward regrets his consent to the death of Clarence.

II. ii. The Duchess of York, mother of the King and Richard, appears with Clarence's children, and hears from

Elizabeth of Edward's death.  Richard decides to go and escort his son, young Edward, from Ludlow to London.

II. iii.  Some citizens of London voice their fear for the land with a child as ruler.

II. iv.  The Queen hears that Richard and Buckingham have imprisoned her son and brother, and herself takes sanctuary.

III. i.  Richard welcomes Prince Edward to London, and his younger brother from sanctuary, and plays with them. Buckingham asks Catesby to sound Hastings as to his support for Richard seizing the throne.

III. ii.  Stanley (*alias* Derby) sends a message to Hastings proposing flight.  Hastings, sounded by Catesby, rebuts the idea of disloyalty to the legitimate heir of Edward IV. Stanley follows up his message in person, and expresses his fear of Richard.

III. iii.  The Queen's relatives at Pomfret are taken to execution.

III. iv.  At a Council in the Tower Richard picks a quarrel with Hastings and orders his execution.

III. v.  Richard and Buckingham excuse themselves to the Mayor of London on the ground that Hastings was plotting against them.  Buckingham undertakes to throw doubt upon the legitimacy of Edward IV and his children.

III. vi.  A Scrivener has copied out an indictment of Hastings, but doubts its truth.

III. vii.  Richard's hypocrisy reaches its climax when he appears between two bishops and affects reluctance to accept the crown.

IV. i.  Queen Elizabeth is prevented by Richard's orders from visiting her children, the Princes, in the Tower. Anne reveals her unhappiness as Richard's wife.

IV. ii.  Richard, now crowned, hints to Buckingham his desire to be rid of Prince Edward; but, not finding him compliant, gets Tyrrell to undertake the murder.  He refuses to listen to Buckingham's request that he should be given the earldom of Hereford and its possessions which had been previously promised him.

IV. iii. Richard learns of the death of the Princes in the Tower, and also of gathering opposition.

IV. iv. In this long scene Queen Margaret joins in the lamentations of Queen Elizabeth and the Duchess of York, mother of Edward IV. The women upbraid Richard as he comes marching past them. He now proposes to marry Elizabeth, daughter of Edward IV's queen, and asks her mother's favour. Finally Richard hears of Richmond's landing to lead the forces rallying against him.

IV. v. Stanley sends a message of support to Richmond, whom he dare not join openly since Richard holds his son as a hostage.

V. i. Buckingham, led to execution, admits he has deserved his fate

V. ii. We meet Richmond now arrived near Tamworth.

V. iii. The rival commanders are seen preparing for the next day's battle. Richmond sleeps with a good conscience, while Richard sees the ghosts of his victims. Both address their followers.

V. iv. Richard calls desperately for another horse.

V. v. Richmond has killed Richard, and now proclaims the union of the rival houses, and roses, in his marriage to Elizabeth.

# DRAMATIS PERSONAE

KING EDWARD THE FOURTH
EDWARD, Prince of Wales; afterwards
    King Edward the Fifth, ⎫
RICHARD, Duke of York, ⎬ Sons to the King.
GEORGE, Duke of Clarence,
RICHARD, Duke of Gloucester,
    afterwards King Richard the ⎬ Brothers to the King.
    Third,
A young Son of Clarence.
HENRY, Earl of Richmond; afterwards King Henry the Seventh.
CARDINAL BOURCHIER, Archbishop of Canterbury.
THOMAS ROTHERHAM, Archbishop of York.
JOHN MORTON, Bishop of Ely.
DUKE OF BUCKINGHAM.
DUKE OF NORFOLK.
EARL OF SURREY, his Son.
EARL RIVERS, Brother to King Edward's Queen.
MARQUESS OF DORSET, and LORD GREY, her Sons.
EARL OF OXFORD.
LORD HASTINGS.
LORD STANLEY, called also EARL OF DERBY.
LORD LOVEL.
SIR THOMAS VAUGHAN.
SIR RICHARD RATCLIFF.
SIR WILLIAM CATESBY.
SIR JAMES TYRRELL.
SIR JAMES BLOUNT.
SIR WALTER HERBERT.
SIR ROBERT BRAKENBURY, Lieutenant of the Tower.
SIR WILLIAM BRANDON.
CHRISTOPHER URSWICK, a Priest.
Another Priest.
Lord Mayor of London. Sheriff of Wiltshire.
TRESSEL and BERKELEY, Gentlemen attending on Lady Anne.

ELIZABETH, Queen of King Edward the Fourth.

MARGARET, Widow of King Henry the Sixth.

DUCHESS OF YORK, Mother to King Edward the Fourth, Clarence, and Gloucester.

LADY ANNE, Widow of Edward, Prince of Wales, Son to King Henry the Sixth; afterwards married to the Duke of Gloucester.

LADY MARGARET PLANTAGENET, a young Daughter of Clarence.

Lords, and other Attendants; two Gentlemen, a Pursuivant, Scrivener, Citizens, Murderers, Messengers, Ghosts of those murdered by Richard the Third, Soldiers, &c.

SCENE.—England.

3. The White Boar of the House of York.

# THE TRAGEDY OF
# KING RICHARD THE THIRD

## ACT I

### *Scene I.* LONDON. A STREET

*Enter* GLOUCESTER.

*Gloucester.* Now is the winter of our discontent
Made glorious summer by this sun of York;
And all the clouds that lour'd upon our house
In the deep bosom of the ocean buried.
Now are our brows bound with victorious wreaths;    5
Our bruised arms hung up for monuments;
Our stern alarums changed to merry meetings;
Our dreadful marches to delightful measures.
Grim-visag'd war hath smooth'd his wrinkled front;
And now,—instead of mounting barbed steeds,    10
To fright the souls of fearful adversaries,—
He capers nimbly in a lady's chamber
To the lascivious pleasing of a lute.
But I, that am not shap'd for sportive tricks,

The letter [*N*] in the footnotes indicates that a *further* note on that
line, not necessarily on the same word(s), will be found in the Commentary.

2 **sun of York:** Edward IV [*N*].     3 **lour'd upon:** hung
heavily over.     4 **buried:** are buried (sc. 'are' from 'is' of l. 1).
6 **bruised:** metre requires that the last syllable should be sounded.
**monuments:** memorials, records.     7 **alarums:** calls to arms
(Italian *all'arme*).     8 **measures:** dances.     9 **front:** forehead
(War personified).     10 **barbed:** armed (French *barde* =horse-
armour).     11 **fearful:** terrified (*not* terrible).     12 **He:** war, i.e.
the warrior.     13 **To . . . lute:** at the pleasure of, i.e. keeping
time with, a voluptuous lute (a kind of guitar).     14 **sportive
tricks:** the amusements of peace, such as dancing.

Nor made to court an amorous looking-glass;                    15
I, that am rudely stamp'd, and want love's majesty
To strut before a wanton ambling nymph;
I, that am curtail'd of this fair proportion,
Cheated of feature by dissembling nature,
Deform'd, unfinish'd, sent before my time                    20
Into this breathing world, scarce half made up,
And that so lamely and unfashionable
That dogs bark at me, as I halt by them;
Why, I, in this weak piping time of peace,
Have no delight to pass away the time,                    25
Unless to see my shadow in the sun
And descant on mine own deformity:
And therefore, since I cannot prove a lover,
To entertain these fair well-spoken days,
I am determined to prove a villain,                    30
And hate the idle pleasures of these days.
Plots have I laid, inductions dangerous,
By drunken prophecies, libels, and dreams,
To set my brother Clarence and the king
In deadly hate the one against the other:                    35

---

15 **amorous**: suitable for lovers' use [N].          16 **stamp'd**: formed (by nature).          **want**: lack.          17 **To strut**: so as to (be able to) strut.          **ambling**: mincing (see *Hamlet* III. i. 150–4) [N].          18 **curtail'd**: (accent on first) cut short, deprived.          **this fair proportion**: such symmetry as a lover needs ('love's majesty' l. 16).          19 **feature**: good bodily form.          **dissembling**: deceiving (i.e. covering up my real quality).          21 **breathing**: living.          **made up**: finished.          22 **unfashionable**: unfashionably [N].          23 **halt**: limp.          24 **Why**: resumes the 'I' of l. 16 and l. 18.          **piping**: the shepherd's pipe suggests peace.          27 **descant**: elaborate (a musical metaphor).          29 **entertain**: while away.          **well-spoken days**: days for fair words, smooth speeches.          30 **determinéd**: cf. bruiséd (l. 6).          31 **hate**: scorn.          32 **inductions dangerous**: mischievous preparations.          33 **libels**: defamatory notices or pamphlets [N].

And if King Edward be as true and just
As I am subtle, false, and treacherous,
This day should Clarence closely be mew'd up,
About a prophecy, which says, that G
Of Edward's heirs the murderer shall be.                    40
Dive, thoughts, down to my soul: here Clarence comes.

*Enter* CLARENCE, *guarded, and* BRAKENBURY.

Brother, good day: what means this armed guard
That waits upon your Grace?
  *Clarence.*                        His majesty,
Tendering my person's safety, hath appointed
This conduct to convey me to the Tower.                    45
  *Gloucester.* Upon what cause?
  *Clarence.*                        Because my name is George.
  *Gloucester.* Alack! my lord, that fault is none of yours;
He should, for that, commit your godfathers.
Belike his majesty hath some intent
That you should be new-christen'd in the Tower.                    50
But what's the matter, Clarence? may I know?
  *Clarence.* Yea, Richard, when I know; for I protest
As yet I do not: but, as I can learn,
He hearkens after prophecies and dreams;
And from the cross-row plucks the letter G,                    55
And says a wizard told him that by G
His issue disinherited should be;
And, for my name of George begins with G,

36 i.e. and therefore unlikely to suspect me.    **38 mew'd up:**
imprisoned.    **39 About:** on account of [N].    **41 Dive . . .
soul:** let my secret thoughts be hidden.    **44 Tendering . . .
safety:** being concerned for the safety of my life [N].    **45 conduct:** escort (cf. 'safe-conduct').    **46 Upon:** in consequence of,
for.    **48 commit:** i.e. to prison.    **49 Belike:** probably.    **50 new-
christened:** newly christened [N].    **53 as:** as far as.    **54 hearkens
after:** listens to.    **55 cross-row:** alphabet [N].    **58 for:**
because.

It follows in his thought that I am he.
These, as I learn, and such like toys as these,                    60
Have mov'd his highness to commit me now.

  *Gloucester.* Why, this it is, when men are rul'd by women:
'Tis not the king that sends you to the Tower;
My Lady Grey, his wife, Clarence, 'tis she
That tempers him to this extremity.                    65
Was it not she and that good man of worship,
Anthony Woodville, her brother there,
That made him send Lord Hastings to the Tower,
From whence this present day he is deliver'd?
We are not safe, Clarence; we are not safe.                    70

  *Clarence.* By heaven, I think there is no man secure
But the queen's kindred and night-walking heralds
That trudge betwixt the king and Mistress Shore.
Heard you not what a humble suppliant
Lord Hastings was to her for his delivery?                    75

  *Gloucester.* Humbly complaining to her deity
Got my lord chamberlain his liberty.
I'll tell you what; I think it is our way,
If we will keep in favour with the king,
To be her men and wear her livery:                    80
The jealous o'er-worn widow and herself,
Since that our brother dubb'd them gentlewomen,
Are mighty gossips in our monarchy.

  *Brakenbury.* Beseech your Graces both to pardon me;

---

60 **toys**: trifles, pieces of silliness.    62 **this it is**: this is what comes of it.    65 **tempers**: moulds (like wax).    **extremity**: extreme measures [N].    66 **of worship**: honourable. 67 **Woodville**: pronounce 'Woodeville'.    **her brother there**: that brother of hers [N].    72 **heralds**: messengers.    76 **deity**: sarcastic, like our 'high and mighty'.    77 **my lord chamberlain**: i.e. Hastings.    78 **our way**: the best course for us. 80 **men**: servants.    81 **widow**: i.e. the Queen.    83 **gossips**: (vulgarly) familiar with one another [N].    84 **Beseech**: I beg [N].

His majesty hath straitly given in charge          85
That no man shall have private conference,
Of what degree soever, with your brother.

*Gloucester.* Even so; an't please your worship, Braken-
  bury,
You may partake of anything we say:
We speak no treason, man: we say the king          90
Is wise and virtuous, and his noble queen
Well struck in years, fair, and not jealous;
We say that Shore's wife hath a pretty foot,
A cherry lip, a bonny eye, a passing-pleasing tongue;
And that the queen's kin are made gentlefolks.     95
How say you, sir? can you deny all this?

*Brakenbury.* With this, my lord, myself have nought
  to do.

*Gloucester.* Naught to do with Mistress Shore! I tell thee,
  fellow,
He that doth naught with her, excepting one,
Were best to do it secretly, alone.                100

*Brakenbury.* What one, my lord?

*Gloucester.* Her husband, knave. Wouldst thou betray
  me?

*Brakenbury.* I beseech your Grace to pardon me; and
  withal
Forbear your conference with the noble duke.       104

*Clarence.* We know thy charge, Brakenbury, and will
  obey.

---

85 **straitly**: strictly (biblical).    **given in charge**: commanded.
87 **Of what degree**: with 'no man'.    88 **an't**: if it.    89 **partake
of**: share, i.e. hear.    92 **Well struck**: advanced (cf. 'stricken' in
Luke i. 7 and 18).    **jealous**: trisyllabic (F. *jealious*).    94 **passing**: pre-eminently.    98–99 **naught**: something wicked,
naughty.    **one**: i.e. the King.    100 **Were best**: would be well
advised.    103 **withal**: moreover [*N*].    104 **Forbear**:
give up.    105 **thy charge**: the orders you have received.

*Gloucester.* We are the queen's abjects, and must obey.
Brother, farewell: I will unto the king;
And whatsoe'er you will employ me in,
Were it to call King Edward's widow sister,
I will perform it to enfranchise you.                    110
Meantime, this deep disgrace in brotherhood
Touches me deeper than you can imagine.
   *Clarence.* I know it pleaseth neither of us well.
   *Gloucester.* Well, your imprisonment shall not be
       long;
I will deliver you, or else lie for you:                    115
Meantime, have patience.
   *Clarence.*                    I must perforce: farewell.

             [*Exeunt* CLARENCE, BRAKENBURY, *and* Guard.

   *Gloucester.* Go, tread the path that thou shalt ne'er
       return,
Simple, plain Clarence! I do love thee so
That I will shortly send thy soul to heaven,
If heaven will take the present at our hands.                    120
But who comes here? the new-deliver'd Hastings!

                    *Enter* HASTINGS.

   *Hastings.* Good time of day unto my gracious lord!
   *Gloucester.* As much unto my good lord chamberlain!
Well are you welcome to this open air.
How hath your lordship brook'd imprisonment?                    125
   *Hastings.* With patience, noble lord, as prisoners must:
But I shall live, my lord, to give them thanks
That were the cause of my imprisonment.

---

106 **abjects**: cast-offs [*N*].    107 **unto**: go to.    109 **widow**:
the Queen, cf. 81 [*N*].    110 **enfranchise**: set free.    111 **in
brotherhood**: i.e. which affects me as your brother.    115 **lie**:
in prison; but implying, for the audience, 'tell lies about you'.
121 **new-deliver'd**: newly released (from prison).    125 **brook'd**:
endured.

**1. Richard III, a sixteenth-century copy of a
lost contemporary painting**

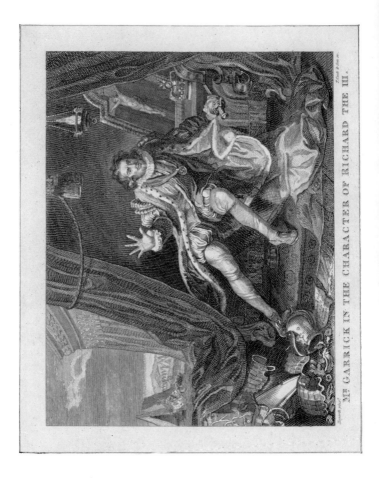

Mr GARRICK IN THE CHARACTER OF RICHARD THE III.

*Gloucester.* No doubt, no doubt; and so shall Clarence too;
For they that were your enemies are his,                    130
And have prevail'd as much on him as you.

*Hastings.* More pity that the eagles should be mew'd,
While kites and buzzards prey at liberty.

*Gloucester.* What news abroad?

*Hastings.* No news so bad abroad as this at home;         135
The king is sickly, weak, and melancholy,
And his physicians fear him mightily.

*Gloucester.* Now by Saint Paul, this news is bad indeed.
O! he hath kept an evil diet long.
And over-much consum'd his royal person:                   140
'Tis very grievous to be thought upon.
What, is he in his bed?

*Hastings.*                   He is.

*Gloucester.* Go you before, and I will follow you.

[*Exit* HASTINGS.

He cannot live, I hope; and must not die
Till George be pack'd with post-horse up to heaven.        145
I'll in, to urge his hatred more to Clarence,
With lies well steel'd with weighty arguments;
And, if I fail not in my deep intent,
Clarence hath not another day to live:
Which done, God take King Edward to his mercy,             150
And leave the world for me to bustle in!
For then I'll marry Warwick's youngest daughter.

---

131 **prevail'd . . . you:** had as much power over him as they had
over you.        132 **mew'd:** shut up (in a cage).        137 **fear
him:** fear for him.        139 **diet:** way of life (the proper meaning of
the Greek word).        140 **consum'd:** wasted away (with self-
indulgence).        145 **with post-horse:** hastily (like a traveller
using relays of post-horses).        146 **urge:** incite, press on.
147 **steel'd:** pointed and/or strengthened.        151 **bustle:**
bustle about (modern slang sense).        152 **daughter:** Anne.

What though I kill'd her husband and her father,
The readiest way to make the wench amends
Is to become her husband and her father:                    155
The which will I; not all so much for love
As for another secret close intent,
By marrying her, which I must reach unto.
But yet I run before my horse to market:
Clarence still breathes; Edward still lives and reigns:     160
When they are gone, then must I count my gains.   [*Exit.*

### *Scene II.* LONDON. ANOTHER STREET

*Enter the corpse of* KING HENRY THE SIXTH, *borne in an
    open coffin; Gentlemen bearing halberds to guard it;
    and* LADY ANNE, *as mourner.*

*Anne.* Set down, set down your honourable load,
If honour may be shrouded in a hearse,
Whilst I awhile obsequiously lament
The untimely fall of virtuous Lancaster.
Poor key-cold figure of a holy king!                         5
Pale ashes of the house of Lancaster!
Thou bloodless remnant of that royal blood!
Be it lawful that I invocate thy ghost,
To hear the lamentations of poor Anne,
Wife to thy Edward, to thy slaughter'd son,                 10
Stabb'd by the selfsame hand that made these wounds!

153 **husband**: Prince Edward.          **father**: (in law) Henry VI
(cf. I. ii. 11) [*N*].          155 i.e. replace them both.          157 **close**:
concealed (strengthens 'secret') [*N*].          158 **By marrying her**:
take after 'unto'.          159 **my . . . market**: go too fast, count
my chickens before they are hatched.          2 i.e. If a dead King retains
his royal honour.          **hearse**: coffin.          3 **obsequiously**: as befits
a funeral (L. *exsequiae*).          5 **key-cold**: proverbial for as cold as
iron (can be) [*N*].          8 **Be it**: counts as one syllable (cf. 15 and 21).
**invocate**: strengthened form of 'invoke' (L. *invocare*) [*N*].
11 **selfsame hand**: i.e. Richard's.

Lo, in these windows that let forth thy life,
I pour the helpless balm of my poor eyes.
O! cursed be the hand that made these holes;
Cursed the heart that had the heart to do it!          15
Cursed the blood that let this blood from hence!
More direful hap betide that hated wretch,
That makes us wretched by the death of thee,
Than I can wish to adders, spiders, toads,
Or any creeping venom'd thing that lives!          20
If ever he have child, abortive be it,
Prodigious, and untimely brought to light,
Whose ugly and unnatural aspect
May fright the hopeful mother at the view;
And that be heir to his unhappiness!          25
If ever he have wife, let her be made
More miserable by the death of him
Than I am made by my young lord and thee!
Come, now towards Chertsey with your holy load,
Taken from Paul's to be interred there;          30
And still, as you are weary of the weight,
Rest you, whiles I lament King Henry's corse.

[*The* Bearers *take up the corpse and advance.*

*Enter* GLOUCESTER.

*Gloucester.* Stay, you that bear the corse, and set it down.
*Anne.* What black magician conjures up this fiend,

---

12 **windows**: i.e. the wounds.          13 **helpless**: unavailing.
16 **blood**: life *or* passion, temper.     **let**: drew forth [*N*].          17 **hap**:
chance, fate.          20 **venom'd**: venomous.          21 **abortive**:
unnatural.          22 **Prodigious**: monstrous.          23 **aspect**: (accent
on last).          24 **at the view**: where she sees it.          25 **that be**:
let the child be.     **unhappiness**: evil nature, power of doing mischief.
28 **by** (the deaths) **of**: [*N*].          30 **interred**: buried.          31 **still,
as**: whenever.          32 **whiles**: whilst.          33 **corse**: corpse (old
French *cors*).          34 **this fiend**: i.e. Gloucester.

To stop devoted charitable deeds?                                35

   *Gloucester.* Villains! set down the corse; or, by Saint Paul,
I'll make a corse of him that disobeys.

   *First Gentleman.* My lord, stand back, and let the coffin
    pass.

   *Gloucester.* Unmanner'd dog! stand thou when I com-
    mand:

Advance thy halberd higher than my breast,                       40
Or, by Saint Paul, I'll strike thee to my foot,
And spurn upon thee, beggar, for thy boldness.

               *[The* Bearers *set down the coffin.*

   *Anne.* What! do you tremble? are you all afraid?
Alas! I blame you not; for you are mortal,
And mortal eyes cannot endure the devil.                         45
Avaunt! thou dreadful minister of hell,
Thou hadst but power over his mortal body,
His soul thou canst not have: therefore, be gone.

   *Gloucester.* Sweet saint, for charity, be not so curst.

   *Anne.* Foul devil, for God's sake hence, and trouble us
    not;                                                    50

For thou hast made the happy earth thy hell,
Fill'd it with cursing cries and deep exclaims.
If thou delight to view thy heinous deeds,
Behold this pattern of thy butcheries.
O! gentlemen; see, see! dead Henry's wounds                      55
Open their congeal'd mouths and bleed afresh.
Blush, blush, thou lump of foul deformity,
For 'tis thy presence that exhales this blood
From cold and empty veins, where no blood dwells:

---

   **35 devoted . . . deeds:** deeds of devoted charity.       **39 Unmanner'd:** unmannerly.     **40 advance:** raise.    **halberd:** a
kind of pike [*N*].      **46 Avaunt!:** away, forward! (French *avant*).
**49 curst:** shrewish, spiteful.     **52 exclaims:** exclamation.
**54 pattern:** example [*N*].     **56 congeal'd:** that had coagulated,
closed over [*N*].    **58 exhales:** draws forth.

Thy deed, inhuman and unnatural, 60
Provokes this deluge most unnatural.
O God! which this blood mad'st, revenge his death;
O earth! which this blood drink'st, revenge his death;
Either heaven with lightning strike the murderer dead,
Or earth, gape open wide, and eat him quick, 65
As thou dost swallow up this good king's blood,
Which his hell-govern'd arm hath butchered!

*Gloucester.* Lady, you know no rules of charity,
Which renders good for bad, blessings for curses.

*Anne.* Villain, thou know'st no law of God nor man: 70
No beast so fierce but knows some touch of pity.

*Gloucester.* But I know none, and therefore am no beast.

*Anne.* O! wonderful, when devils tell the truth.

*Gloucester.* More wonderful when angels are so angry.
Vouchsafe, divine perfection of a woman, 75
Of these supposed evils, to give me leave,
By circumstance, but to acquit myself.

*Anne.* Vouchsafe, diffus'd infection of a man,
For these known evils, but to give me leave,
By circumstance, to curse thy cursed self. 80

*Gloucester.* Fairer than tongue can name thee, let me have
Some patient leisure to excuse myself.

*Anne.* Fouler than heart can think thee, thou canst make
No excuse current, but to hang thyself.

*Gloucester.* By such despair I should accuse myself. 85

*Anne.* And by despairing shouldst thou stand excus'd

---

64 **Either:** metrically a monosyllable.     65 **quick:** alive (cf.
'the quick and the dead').     67 **butchered:** accented -ed.
71 **No beast:** sc. there is.     77 **circumstance:** a detailed account.
78 **diffus'd . . . man:** a man spreading poison far and wide (phrase
coined to balance 'divine . . . woman' in 75) [*N*].     81–82 **let me
. . . myself:** i.e. be patient with me while I excuse myself (transferred
epithet, cf. I. i. 15).     84 **current:** pass current, appear valid.
**but . . . thyself:** i.e. that is the only action of yours which would
be excusable.     86 **despairing:** i.e. that act of despair.

For doing worthy vengeance on thyself.
Which didst unworthy slaughter upon others.
  *Gloucester.*  Say that I slew them not.
  *Anne.*                    Then say they were not slain:
But dead they are, and, devilish slave, by thee.      90
  *Gloucester.*  I did not kill your husband.
  *Anne.*                    Why, then he is alive.
  *Gloucester.*  Nay, he is dead; and slain by Edward's hand.
  *Anne.*  In thy foul throat thou liest: Queen Margaret saw
Thy murderous falchion smoking in his blood;
The which thou once didst bend against her breast,    95
But that thy brothers beat aside the point.
  *Gloucester.*  I was provoked by her slanderous tongue,
That laid their guilt upon my guiltless shoulders.
  *Anne.*  Thou was provoked by thy bloody mind,
That never dreamt on aught but butcheries.            100
Didst thou not kill this king?
  *Gloucester.*  I grant ye.
  *Anne.*  Dost grant me, hedgehog? Then, God grant me
    too
Thou mayst be damned for that wicked deed!
O! he was gentle, mild, and virtuous.                 105
  *Gloucester.*  The fitter for the King of heaven, that hath
    him.
  *Anne.*  He is in heaven, where thou shalt never come.
  *Gloucester.*  Let him thank me, that help'd to send him
    thither;
For he was fitter for that place than earth.
  *Anne.*  And thou unfit for any place but hell.        110

---

   87 **worthy:** suitable, deserved.      89 **Say:** suppose.      **Then
say:** you might as well suppose.      92 **Edward's:** i.e. King
Edward's [*N*].      95 **bend:** aim, turn (from 'bending' a bow to
shoot).      96 **But that:** i.e. and would have struck her if . . . had
not.      98 **their:** that of my brothers.      102 **I grant ye:** I
admit it to you.

*Gloucester.* Yes, one place else, if you will hear me
   name it.

*Anne.* Some dungeon.

*Gloucester.*              Your bed-chamber.

*Anne.* Ill rest betide the chamber where thou liest!

*Gloucester.* So will it, madam, till I lie with you.

*Anne.* I hope so.

*Gloucester.*      I know so. But, gentle Lady Anne,   115
To leave this keen encounter of our wits,
And fall somewhat into a slower method,
Is not the causer of the timeless deaths
Of these Plantagenets, Henry and Edward,
As blameful as the executioner?               120

*Anne.* Thou wast the cause, and most accurs'd effect.

*Gloucester.* Your beauty was the cause of that effect;
Your beauty, that did haunt me in my sleep
To undertake the death of all the world,
So might I live one hour in your sweet bosom.   125

*Anne.* If I thought that, I tell thee, homicide,
These nails should rend that beauty from my cheeks.

*Gloucester.* These eyes could not endure that beauty's
   wrack;
You should not blemish it if I stood by:
As all the world is cheered by the sun,        130
So I by that; it is my day, my life.

*Anne.* Black night o'ershade thy day, and death thy life!

*Gloucester.* Curse not thyself, fair creature; thou art both.

*Anne.* I would I were, to be reveng'd on thee.

*Gloucester.* It is a quarrel most unnatural,     135
To be reveng'd on him that loveth thee.

*Anne.* It is a quarrel just and reasonable,

---

117 **slower:** more deliberate, leaving this quick repartee.   121
**effect:** (probably) effecter, doer (choice of word owing to 'cause and
effect').     134 **were ... thee:** i.e. were your 'day', your 'life', so
that I could make you suffer from unrequited love.

To be reveng'd on him that kill'd my husband.

*Gloucester.* He that bereft thee, lady, of thy husband,

Did it to help thee to a better husband.                    140

*Anne.* His better doth not breath upon the earth.

*Gloucester.* He lives that loves thee better than he could.

*Anne.* Name him.

*Gloucester.*          Plantagenet.

*Anne.*                    Why, that was he.

*Gloucester.* The selfsame name, but one of better nature.

*Anne.* Where is he?

*Gloucester.*          Here. [*She spitteth at him.*] Why
dost thou spit at me?                                        145

*Anne.* Would it were mortal poison, for thy sake!

*Gloucester.* Never came poison from so sweet a place.

*Anne.* Never hung poison on a fouler toad.

Out of my sight! thou dost infect mine eyes.

*Gloucester.* Thine eyes, sweet lady, have infected mine.  150

*Anne.* Would they were basilisks, to strike thee dead!

*Gloucester.* I would they were, that I might die at once;

For now they kill me with a living death.

Those eyes of thine from mine have drawn salt tears,

Sham'd their aspects with store of childish drops;          155

These eyes, which never shed remorseful tear;

No, when my father York and Edward wept

To hear the piteous moan that Rutland made

When black-fac'd Clifford shook his sword at him;

Nor when thy warlike father like a child,                   160

Told the sad story of my father's death,

And twenty times made pause to sob and weep,

---

149 **infect:** pollute.     150 **infected:** i.e. with love.     151
**basilisks:** fabulous reptile [*N*].     152 **at once:** once and for all.
153 **living death:** death while I am alive.     155 **Sham'd their
aspécts:** shamed their looks, i.e. made me ashamed to look up.
156 **These eyes:** picked up, grammatically, in 165.     157 **No:**
not even.

That all the standers-by had wet their cheeks,
Like trees bedash'd with rain: in that sad time
My manly eyes did scorn an humble tear;                   165
And what these sorrows could not thence exhale,
Thy beauty hath, and made them blind with weeping.
I never sued to friend nor enemy;
My tongue could never learn sweet smoothing words;
But, now thy beauty is propos'd my fee,                   170
My proud heart sues, and prompts my tongue to speak.

       *[She looks scornfully at him.*

Teach not thy lip such scorn, for it was made
For kissing, lady, not for such contempt.
If thy revengeful heart cannot forgive,
Lo! here I lend thee this sharp-pointed sword;            175
Which if thou please to hide in this true breast,
And let the soul forth that adoreth thee,
I lay it open to the deadly stroke,
And humbly beg the death upon my knee.

 *[He lays his breast open: she offers at it with his sword.*

Nay, do not pause; for I did kill King Henry;            180
But 'twas thy beauty that provoked me.
Nay, now dispatch; 'twas I that stabb'd young Edward;

       *[She again offers at his breast.*

But 'twas thy heavenly face that set me on.

        *[She lets fall the sword.*

Take up the sword again, or take up me.

 *Anne.* Arise, dissembler: though I wish thy death,   185
I will not be thy executioner.

 *Gloucester.* Then bid me kill myself, and I will do it.

 *Anne.* I have already.

---

163 **That**: so that.  166 **exhale**: see 58.  169 **smoothing**:
flattering (cf. 'smooth someone down').  170 **my fee**: or my
reward.  179–80 *s.d. offers at*: threatens [*N*].  182 **dispatch**:
make haste (cf. I. iii. 341).  184 **take up me**: (probably) raise
me from my knees (with your hand).  185 **dissembler**:
deceiver, hypocrite (cf. I. i. 19).

*Gloucester.* That was in thy rage:
Speak it again, and, even with the word,
This hand, which for thy love did kill thy love,  190
Shall, for thy love, kill a far truer love:
To both their deaths shalt thou be accessary
  *Anne.* I would I knew thy heart.
  *Gloucester.* 'Tis figur'd in my tongue.
  *Anne.* I fear me both are false.  195
  *Gloucester.* Then never man was true.
  *Anne.* Well, well, put up your sword.
  *Gloucester.* Say, then, my peace is made.
  *Anne.* That shalt thou know hereafter.
  *Gloucester.* But shall I live in hope?  200
  *Anne.* All men, I hope, live so.
  *Gloucester.* Vouchsafe to wear this ring.
  *Anne.* To take is not to give. [*She puts on the ring.*
  *Gloucester.* Look how my ring encompasseth thy finger,
Even so thy breast encloseth my poor heart;  205
Wear both of them, for both of them are thine.
And if thy poor devoted servant may
But beg one favour at thy gracious hand,
Thou dost confirm his happiness for ever.
  *Anne.* What is it?  210
  *Gloucester.* That it may please you leave these sad
    designs
To him that hath most cause to be a mourner,
And presently repair to Crosby-place;
Where, after I have solemnly interr'd
At Chertsey monastery this noble king,  215
And wet his grave with my repentant tears,

---

190 **thy love:** see 182.    191 **a far truer love:** i.e. myself.
192 **accessary:** assistant.    194 **figur'd:** represented (truly).
204 **Look how:** just as.    212 **him:** i.e. myself.    213 **presently:** at once.    216 **wet:** wetted.

I will with all expedient duty see you:
For divers unknown reasons, I beseech you,
Grant me this boon.

*Anne.* With all my heart; and much it joys me too          220
To see you are become so penitent.
Tressel and Berkeley, go along with me.

*Gloucester.* Bid me farewell.

*Anne.*                                          'Tis more than you deserve;
But since you teach me how to flatter you,
Imagine I have said farewell already.          225

> [*Exeunt* LADY ANNE, TRESSEL, *and* BERKELEY.

*Gloucester.* Sirs, take up the corse.

*Gentleman.* Towards Chertsey, noble lord?

*Gloucester.* No, to White-Friars; there attend my coming.

> [*Exeunt all but* GLOUCESTER.

Was ever woman in this humour woo'd?
Was ever woman in this humour won?          230
I'll have her; but I will not keep her long.
What! I, that kill'd her husband, and his father,
To take her in her heart's extremest hate;
With curses in her mouth, tears in her eyes,
The bleeding witness of her hatred by;          235
Having God, her conscience, and these bars against me,
And nothing I to back my suit withal
But the plain devil and dissembling looks,
And yet to win her, all the world to nothing!
Ha!          240

217 **expedient duty**: swift homage.          218 **unknown**: secret.
220 **joys**: pleases.          222 **Tressel and Berkeley**: unknown.
223 **'Tis**: that (i.e. to fare well) is.          231 **Keep her**: i.e. as my
wife.          232-3 **What . . . To take**: Fancy! To think that I should
take.          235 **witness . . . hatred**: i.e. evidence of the justice of
her hatred.          **by**: close at hand.          236 **these bars**: (probably)
my physical deformities (cf. 252).          237 **I**: take with 'having'.
**withal**: with.          238 **the plain devil**: merely the devil.          239 **all
. . . to nothing**: when the odds were all against me.

Hath she forgot already that brave prince,
Edward, her lord, whom I, some three months since,
Stabb'd in my angry mood at Tewksbury?
A sweeter and a lovelier gentleman,
Fram'd in the prodigality of nature,                            245
Young, valiant, wise, and, no doubt, right royal,
The spacious world cannot again afford:
And will she yet abase her eyes on me,
That cropp'd the golden prime of this sweet prince,
And made her widow to a woeful bed?                             250
On me, whose all not equals Edward's moiety?
On me, that halt and am mis-shapen thus?
My dukedom to a beggarly denier
I do mistake my person all this while:
Upon my life, she finds, although I cannot,                     255
Myself to be a marvellous proper man.
I'll be at charges for a looking-glass,
And entertain a score or two of tailors,
To study fashions to adorn my body:
Since I am crept in favour with myself,                         260
I will maintain it with some little cost.
But first I'll turn yon fellow in his grave,
And then return lamenting to my love.
Shine out, fair sun, till I have bought a glass,               264
That I may see my shadow as I pass.                  [*Exit*

245 **in the prodigality of nature**: when nature was in a generous mood.          246 **right royal**: as we say 'every inch a king' [*N*].
247 **afford**: provide, produce.          248 **abase ... on me**: lower ... to me.          249 i.e. cut him down in the sunny springtime of life.
251 **moiety**: half, part [*N*].          252 **halt**: cf. I. i. 23.          253 The construction is 'I wager my ... that ...' (cf. 239) **denier**: a copper coin worth a tenth of a penny (derived from L. *denarius*).
254 **mistake**: misjudge.          256 **marvellous proper**: wonderfully handsome.          257 **be at charges for**: go to the expense of, buy.
258 **entertain**: engage.          262 **in**: into.          263 **lamenting**: i.e. professing sorrow.

## *Scene III.* London. A Room in the Palace

*Enter* QUEEN ELIZABETH, LORD RIVERS, *and* LORD GREY.

*Rivers.*  Have patience, madam: there's no doubt his majesty

Will soon recover his accustom'd health.

*Grey.*  In that you brook it ill, it makes him worse:

Therefore, for God's sake, entertain good comfort,

And cheer his Grace with quick and merry words.        5

*Queen Elizabeth.*  If he were dead, what would betide on me?

*Grey.*  No other harm but loss of such a lord.

*Queen Elizabeth.*  The loss of such a lord includes all harms.

*Grey.*  The heavens have bless'd you with a goodly son,

To be your comforter when he is gone.                  10

*Queen Elizabeth.*  Ah! he is young; and his minority

Is put into the trust of Richard Gloucester,

A man that loves not me, nor none of you.

*Rivers.*  Is it concluded he shall be protector?

*Queen Elizabeth.*  It is determin'd, not concluded yet:   15

But so it must be if the king miscarry.

### *Enter* BUCKINGHAM *and* STANLEY.

*Grey.*  Here come the Lords of Buckingham and Stanley.

*Buckingham.*  Good time of day unto your royal Grace!

*Stanley.*  God make your majesty joyful as you have been!

*Queen Elizabeth.*  The Countess Richmond, good my Lord of Stanley,                                          20

To your good prayer will scarcely say amen.

---

3 **brook:** bear.          4 **entertain good comfort:** take heart.
5 **quick:** lively (cf. I. ii. 65).        6 **betide on:** happen to.     11
**his minority:** he while a minor.        15 **determin'd:** decided.
**concluded:** formally, legally recorded [*N*].        16 **miscarry:**
euphemism for 'die'.        18 See Commentary at I. i. 122.

Yet, Stanley, notwithstanding she's your wife,
And loves not me, be you, good lord, assur'd
I hate not you for her proud arrogance.

*Stanley.* I do beseech you, either not believe     25
The envious slanders of her false accusers;
Or, if she be accus'd on true report,
Bear with her weakness, which, I think, proceeds
From wayward sickness, and no grounded malice.

*Queen Elizabeth.* Saw you the king to-day, my Lord of
     Stanley?     30

*Stanley.* But now the Duke of Buckingham and I
Are come from visiting his majesty.

*Queen Elizabeth.* What likelihood of his amendment,
     lords?

*Buckingham.* Madam, good hope; his Grace speaks
     cheerfully.

*Queen Elizabeth.* God grant him health! did you confer
     with him?     35

*Buckingham.* Ay, madam: he desires to make atonement
Between the Duke of Gloucester and your brothers,
And between them and my lord chamberlain;
And sent to warn them to his royal presence.

*Queen Elizabeth.* Would all were well! But that will
     never be.     40
I fear our happiness is at the highest.

     *Enter* GLOUCESTER, HASTINGS, *and* DORSET.

*Gloucester.* They do me wrong, and I will not endure it:
Who are they that complain unto the king,
That I, forsooth, am stern and love them not?
By holy Paul, they love his Grace but lightly     45

---

25 **not believe:** don't believe.      26 **envious:** malicious.
29 **wayward sickness:** sickness producing waywardness.
**grounded:** permanent, deeply-seated.     31 **But now:** just now.
33 **amendment:** recovery.      35 **confer:** have conference.
36 **atonement:** at-one-ment, reconciliation.     38 **lord chamberlain:** see I. i. 77.     39 **warn:** summon.

That fill his ears with such dissentious rumours.
Because I cannot flatter and speak fair,
Smile in men's faces, smooth, deceive, and cog,
Duck with French nods and apish courtesy,
I must be held a rancorous enemy.                             50
Cannot a plain man live and think no harm,
But thus his simple truth must be abus'd
By silken, sly, insinuating Jacks?
  *Grey.* To whom in all this presence speaks your Grace?
  *Gloucester.* To thee, that hast nor honesty nor grace.    55
When have I injur'd thee? when done thee wrong?
Or thee? or thee? or any of your faction?
A plague upon you all! His royal person,—
Whom God preserve better than you would wish!—
Cannot be quiet scarce a breathing-while,                    60
But you must trouble him with lewd complaints.
  *Queen Elizabeth.* Brother of Gloucester, you mistake the
    matter.
The king, on his own royal disposition,
And not provok'd by any suitor else,
Aiming, belike, at your interior hatred,                     65
That in your outward action shows itself
Against my children, brothers, and myself,
Makes him to send; that thereby he may gather
The ground of your ill-will, and so remove it.
  *Gloucester.* I cannot tell; the world is grown so bad     70

46 **dissentious**: causing dissension, quarrelsome.    48 **smooth**:
flatter (cf. I. ii. 169). **cog**: cheat.    49 **Duck**: bow. **apish**: imitative
(since monkeys are proverbial for mimicry) [*N*].    53 **Jacks**:
fellows (contemptuous).    54 **this presence**: those present
(especially at court).    60 **scarce**: scarcely, hardly.    61 **lewd**:
vile, worthless (cf. 'lewd fellows of the baser sort', Acts xvii. 5).
64 **else**: (the word is not needed) i.e. anyone else, any suitor.
65 **Aiming, belike, at**: in view, probably, of.    **interior**: inward,
concealed.    68 **Makes him to send**: the fact that the King
guesses your hatred . . . causes him to send (a sense construction).
70 **I cannot tell**: I don't know what to say.

That wrens make prey where eagles dare not perch:
Since every Jack became a gentleman
There's many a gentle person made a Jack.
   *Queen Elizabeth.* Come, come, we know your meaning,
    brother Gloucester;
You envy my advancement and my friends'.        75
God grant we never may have need of you!
   *Gloucester.* Meantime, God grants that we have need of
    you:
Our brother is imprison'd by your means,
Myself disgrac'd, and the nobility
Held in contempt; while great promotions       80
Are daily given to ennoble those
That scarce, some two days since, were worth a noble.
   *Queen Elizabeth.* By him that rais'd me to this careful
    height
From that contented hap which I enjoy'd,
I never did incense his majesty       85
Against the Duke of Clarence, but have been
An earnest advocate to plead for him.
My lord, you do me shameful injury,
Falsely to draw me in these vile suspects.
   *Gloucester.* You may deny that you were not the mean   90
Of my Lord Hastings' late imprisonment.
   *Rivers.* She may, my lord; for—
   *Gloucester.* She may, Lord Rivers! why, who knows
    not so?
She may do more, sir, than denying that:

   **71 make prey:** prey on others [*N*].        **72 Jack:** common man.
**73 gentle person:** gentleman (cf. 'gently born').       **75 my
friends':** that of my friends.      **77 have need of you:** are in
distress because of you.     **82 a noble:** a gold coin (chosen for
pun with 'ennoble').     **83 careful:** bringing care, anxious.
**84 hap:** state.     **89 in ... suspects:** into ... suspicion.     **90** i.e.
you may deny (my accusation) and say you were not ... (double
negative).     **mean:** means.

She may help you to many fair preferments,                95
And then deny her aiding hand therein,
And lay those honours on your high desert.
What may she not? She may,—ay, marry, may she,—
  *Rivers.* What, marry, may she?                99
  *Gloucester.* What, marry, may she! marry with a king,
A bachelor, a handsome stripling too.
I wis your grandam had a worser match.
  *Queen Elizabeth.* My Lord of Gloucester, I have too long
    borne
Your blunt upbraiding and your bitter scoffs;
By heaven, I will acquaint his majesty                    105
Of those gross taunts that oft I have endur'd.
I had rather be a country servantmaid
Than a great queen, with this condition,
To be so baited, scorn'd, and stormed at:
Small joy have I in being England's queen.                110
       *Enter* QUEEN MARGARET, *behind.*
  *Queen Margaret.* [*Apart.*] And lessen'd be that small,
    God, I beseech him!
Thy honour, state, and seat is due to me.
  *Gloucester.* What! threat you me with telling of the king?
Tell him, and spare not: look, what I have said
I will avouch in presence of the king:                    115
I dare adventure to be sent to the Tower.
'Tis time to speak; my pains are quite forgot.
  *Queen Margaret.* [*Apart.*] Out, devil! I remember them
    too well:
Thou kill'dst my husband Henry in the Tower,

---

    97 **lay . . . on:** attribute . . . to.    98 **marry:** indeed (a mild
oath).    102 **I wis:** surely.    **worser:** worse.    106 **Of:** with.
108 **with this condition:** on these terms.    111 i.e. and may
even that small joy be lessened, I pray God [*N*].    112 **is due:**
rightly belong.    113 See 105.    115 **avouch:** affirm.
116 **adventure to be:** risk being.    117 **pains:** efforts, trouble;
see 121–5.

And Edward, my poor son, at Tewksbury.                    120
  *Gloucester.* Ere you were queen, ay, or your husband king,
I was a pack-horse in his great affairs,
A weeder-out of his proud adversaries,
A liberal rewarder of his friends;
To royalize his blood I spilt mine own.                   125
  *Queen Margaret.* Ay, and much better blood than his,
    or thine.
  *Gloucester.* In all which time you and your husband Grey
Were factious for the house of Lancaster;
And, Rivers, so were you. Was not your husband
In Margaret's battle at Saint Alban's slain?              130
Let me put in your minds, if you forget,
What you have been ere now, and what you are;
Withal, what I have been, and what I am.
  *Queen Margaret.* A murderous villain, and so still thou art.
  *Gloucester.* Poor Clarence did forsake his father, War-
    wick,                                                 135
Ay, and forswore himself,—which Jesu pardon!—
  *Queen Margaret.* Which God revenge!
  *Gloucester.* To fight on Edward's party for the crown;
And for his meed, poor lord, he is mew'd up.
I would to God my heart were flint, like Edward's;       140
Or Edward's soft and pitiful, like mine:
I am too childish-foolish for this world.
  *Queen Margaret.* Hie thee to hell for shame, and leave
    this world,

---

    120 see I. ii. 241–3.          122 **pack-horse:** beast of burden.
125 **royalize:** make royal.       127 **husband Grey:** i.e. Sir
John Grey, father of the Lord Grey now present.     128 **Were
factious for:** took the side of.    130 **In Margaret's battle:** fighting for Margaret [*N*].      133 **Withal:** and at the same time.
135 **father:** i.e. father-in-law.      136 **forswore himself:** broke
his oath (to fight on the Lancastrian side).      138 **party:** side.
139 **meed:** reward.    **mew'd:** shut.    142 **childish-foolish:**
of a childlike simplicity.

Thou cacodemon! there thy kingdom is.

*Rivers.* My Lord of Gloucester, in those busy days          145
Which here you urge to prove us enemies,
We follow'd then our lord, our lawful king;
So should we you, if you should be our king.

*Gloucester.* If I should be! I had rather be a pedlar.
Far be it from my heart the thought thereof!          150

*Queen Elizabeth.* As little joy, my lord, as you suppose
You should enjoy, were you this country's king,
As little joy, you may suppose in me
That I enjoy, being the queen thereof.

*Queen Margaret.* As little joy enjoys the queen there-
of;          155
For I am she, and altogether joyless.
I can no longer hold me patient.          [*Advancing.*
Hear me, you wrangling pirates, that fall out
In sharing that which you have pill'd from me!
Which of you trembles not that looks on me?          160
If not, that, I being queen, you bow like subjects,
Yet that, by you depos'd, you quake like rebels?
Ah! gentle villain, do not turn away.

*Gloucester.* Foul wrinkled witch, what makest thou in
my sight?

*Queen Margaret.* But repetition of what thou hast
marr'd;          165
That will I make before I let thee go.

---

144 **cacodemon:** evil spirit (two Greek words).          146 **urge:**
bring up, press upon us.          153 **in me:** in my case (picked up by
'That I enjoy').          157 **patient:** three syllables.          159 **sharing:** sharing out, distributing.          **pill'd:** taken (the same word as
'peel' = strip) [*N*].          161 **If not:** If the reason is not.          162 **Yet
that, by you depos'd:** then it is that, I have been deposed, you . . .
163 **gentle:** ironical for 'cruel'.          164 **makest . . . sight?:** are
you doing here?          165 i.e. I am only making repetition of, i.e.
reciting, your misdeeds [*N*].

*Gloucester.* Wert thou not banished on pain of death?

*Queen Margaret.* I was; but I do find more pain in banishment

Than death can yield me here by my abode.

A husband and a son thou owest to me;                         170

And thou, a kingdom; all of you, allegiance:

This sorrow that I have, by right is yours,

And all the pleasures you usurp are mine.

*Gloucester.* The curse my noble father laid on thee,

When thou didst crown his warlike brows with paper,          175

And with thy scorns drew'st rivers from his eyes;

And then, to dry them, gavest the duke a clout

Steep'd in the faultless blood of pretty Rutland;

His curses, then from bitterness of soul

Denounc'd against thee, are all fall'n upon thee;            180

And God, not we, hath plagu'd thy bloody deed.

*Queen Elizabeth.* So just is God, to right the innocent.

*Hastings.* O! 'twas the foulest deed to slay that babe,

And the most merciless, that e'er was heard of.              184

*Rivers.* Tyrants themselves wept when it was reported.

*Dorset.* No man but prophesied revenge for it.

*Buckingham.* Northumberland, then present, wept to see it.

*Queen Margaret.* What! were you snarling all before I came,

Ready to catch each other by the throat,

And turn you all your hatred now on me?                      190

Did York's dread curse prevail so much with heaven

---

167 **banished**: accent on last.        169 **by my abode**: if I stay
here.        170 **thou**: Richard.        171 **thou**: Queen Elizabeth.
174 **my ... father**: Richard Plantaganet, (3rd) Duke (177) of York,
cf. 191 [*N*].        176 **scorns**: scoffs, taunts.        177 **clout**: cloth,
rag.        178 **faultless**: innocent.        **pretty**: he was a boy of
twelve.        181 **plagu'd**: punished [*N*].        185 **Tyrants**: violent
men (not only 'rulers').        186 **No man but**: there was no man
who did not.        190 **all**: take with 'you'.

That Henry's death, my lovely Edward's death,
Their kingdom's loss, my woeful banishment,
Should all but answer for that peevish brat?
Can curses pierce the clouds and enter heaven?          195
Why then, give way, dull clouds, to my quick curses!
Though not by war, by surfeit die your king,
As ours by murder, to make him a king!
Edward, thy son, that now is Prince of Wales,
For Edward, my son, which was Prince of Wales,          200
Die in his youth by like untimely violence!
Thyself a queen, for me that was a queen,
Outlive thy glory, like my wretched self!
Long mayst thou live to wail thy children's loss,
And see another, as I see thee now,                     205
Deck'd in thy rights, as thou art stall'd in mine!
Long die thy happy days before thy death;
And, after many lengthen'd hours of grief,
Die neither mother, wife, nor England's queen!
Rivers, and Dorset, you were standers by,—             210
And so wast thou, Lord Hastings,—when my son
Was stabb'd with bloody daggers: God, I pray him,
That none of you may live your natural age,
But by some unlook'd accident cut off.

   *Gloucester.* Have done thy charm, thou hateful wither'd
     hag!                                              215

   *Queen Margaret.* And leave out thee? stay, dog, for thou
     shalt hear me.
If heaven have any grievous plague in store
Exceeding those that I can wish upon thee,

---

194 **but**: only, no more than.    **peevish**: conventional epithet
for a child.    196 **quick**: see l. 5 of this scene [*N*].    197 **die**:
let him die.    201 **like**: equally.    202 **for**: in return for.
206 **stall'd**: installed.    212 **God . . . him**: cf. l. 111.    214 **But**
(be) **by**.    **unlook'd**: unexpected.    215 **charm**: curse, incantation.    **hag**: witch.    216 **leave out**: am I to leave out.

O! let them keep it till thy sins be ripe,
And then hurl down their indignation 220
On thee, the troubler of the poor world's peace.
The worm of conscience still begnaw thy soul!
Thy friends suspect for traitors while thou livest
And take deep traitors for thy dearest friends!
No sleep close up that deadly eye of thine, 225
Unless it be while some tormenting dream
Affrights thee with a hell of ugly devils!
Thou elvish-mark'd, abortive, rooting hog!
Thou that wast seal'd in thy nativity
The slave of nature and the son of hell! 230
Thou slander of thy mother's heavy womb!
Thou loathed issue of thy father's loins!
Thou rag of honour! thou detested—

*Gloucester.* Margaret!

*Queen Margaret.* Richard!

*Gloucester.* Ha!

*Queen Margaret.* I call thee not.

*Gloucester.* I cry thee mercy then, for I did think 235
That thou hadst call'd me all these bitter names.

*Queen Margaret.* Why, so I did; but look'd for no reply.
O! let me make the period to my curse.

*Gloucester.* 'Tis done by me, and ends in 'Margaret'.

*Queen Elizabeth.* Thus have you breath'd your curse
against yourself. 240

---

219 **them**: the gods, heavenly powers.　222 **still**: continually.
223 **suspect**: may you suspect.　228 **elvish-mark'd**: marked
by (evil) fairies (at thy birth).　**abortive**: monstrous.　**rooting**:
destructive [*N*].　229 **seal'd**: stamped.　230 **slave of
nature**: contemptible [*N*].　231 **slander of**: disgrace to.
**heavy**: sad (in having born thee).　233 **rag of honour**: almost
= destitute of honour [*N*].　**Ha!**: What's that you say ? [*N*].
235 **I cry thee mercy**: I beg your pardon.　238 **make the
period to**: end.

*Queen Margaret.*  Poor painted queen, vain flourish of my
  fortune!
Why strew'st thou sugar on that bottled spider,
Whose deadly web ensnareth thee about?
Fool, fool! thou whet'st a knife to kill thyself.
The day will come that thou shalt wish for me          245
To help thee curse this poisonous bunch-back'd toad.
  *Hastings.*  False-boding woman, end thy frantic curse,
Lest to thy harm thou move our patience.
  *Queen Margaret.*  Foul shame upon you! you have all
  mov'd mine.
  *Rivers.*  Were you well serv'd, you would be taught your
  duty.                                                    250
  *Queen Margaret.*  To serve me well, you all should do me
  duty,
Teach me to be your queen, and you my subjects:
O! serve me well, and teach yourselves that duty.
  *Dorset.*  Dispute not with her, she is lunatic.
  *Queen Margaret.*  Peace! Master marquess, you are
  malapert:                                                255
Your fire-new stamp of honour is scarce current.
O! that your young nobility could judge
What 'twere to lose it, and be miserable!
They that stand high have many blasts to shake them,
And if they fall, they dash themselves to pieces.        260
  *Gloucester.*  Good counsel, marry: learn it, learn it,
  marquess.

---

241 **painted queen:** unreal, image of, a queen.  **vain...fortune:**
empty ornament of a rank which really belongs to me.          242
**strew'st thou sugar on:** feed, encourage.  **bottled spider ...
toad:** Richard, as swollen with venom, and hunchback [N].     246
**bunch-back'd:** with bunched-up shoulders, i.e. hunchback.
247 **False-boding:** prophesying falsely.       250 **well serv'd:**
treated as you deserve.        255 **malapert:** pert, impertinent.
256 i.e. your patent of nobility is as fresh as newly-minted coinage
not yet in circulation [N].

*Dorset.*  It touches you, my lord, as much as me.

*Gloucester.*  Ay, and much more; but I was born so high,
Our aery buildeth in the cedar's top,
And dallies with the wind, and scorns the sun.          265

*Queen Margaret.*  And turns the sun to shade; alas! alas!
Witness my son, now in the shade of death;
Whose bright out-shining beams thy cloudy wrath
Hath in eternal darkness folded up.
Your aery buildeth in our aery's nest:                   270
O God! that seest it, do not suffer it;
As it was won with blood, lost be it so!

*Gloucester.*  Peace, peace! for shame, if not for charity.

*Queen Margaret.*  Urge neither charity nor shame to me:
Uncharitably with me have you dealt,                     275
And shamefully my hopes by you are butcher'd.
My charity is outrage, life my shame;
And in that shame still live my sorrow's rage!

*Buckingham.*  Have done, have done.

*Queen Margaret.*  O princely Buckingham! I'll kiss thy
hand,                                                    280
In sign of league and amity with thee:
Now fair befall thee and thy noble house!
Thy garments are not spotted with our blood,
Nor thou within the compass of my curse.

*Buckingham.*  Nor no one here; for curses never pass   285
The lips of those that breathe them in the air.

*Queen Margaret.*  I will not think but they ascend the sky,
And there awake God's gentle-sleeping peace.
O Buckingham! take heed of yonder dog:

---

263 **much more:** i.e. as I stand higher.          264 **Our aery:**
eagle's brood, i.e. the royal house of York [N].          272 **so:** with
blood.          277 i.e. all the charity I get is outrage and my life is one
of shame.          281 **amity:** friendship.          286 **in:** into.
287–8 i.e. I refuse to think that curses do not rise up to God and stir
Him up to avenge wrongs.

Look, when he fawns, he bites; and when he bites     290
His venom tooth will rankle to the death:
Have not to do with him, beware of him;
Sin, death and hell have set their marks on him.
And all their ministers attend on him.

   *Gloucester.* What doth she say, my Lord of Bucking-
    ham?     295

   *Buckingham.* Nothing that I respect, my gracious lord.

   *Queen Margaret.* What! dost thou scorn me for my
    gentle counsel,
And soothe the devil that I warn thee from?
O! but remember this another day,
When he shall split thy very heart with sorrow,     300
And say poor Margaret was a prophetess.
Live each of you the subject to his hate,
And he to yours, and all of you to God's!     [*Exit.*

   *Hastings.* My hair doth stand on end to hear her
    curses.

   *Rivers.* And so doth mine. I muse why she's at liberty.

   *Gloucester.* I cannot blame her: by God's holy mother, 306
She hath had too much wrong, and I repent
My part thereof that I have done to her.

   *Queen Elizabeth.* I never did her any, to my knowledge.

   *Gloucester.* Yet you have all the vantage of her wrong. 310
I was too hot to do somebody good,
That is too cold in thinking of it now.
Marry, as for Clarence, he is well repaid;
He is frank'd up to fatting for his pains:
God pardon them that are the cause thereof!     315

---

   291 **venom**: venomous.     **rankle**: breed corruption, cause fester-
ing.     296 **respect**: am concerned with.     298 **soothe**: flatter
(cf. I. ii. 169).     305 **muse**: wonder.     310 **vantage**:
advantage, profit.     311 **hot**: eager.     **somebody**: i.e. Edward.
312 **That**: who.     **cold**: i.e. ungrateful.     314 **frank'd**: put in
a stall [*N*].

*Rivers.*  A virtuous and a Christian-like conclusion,
To pray for them that have done scath to us.
*Gloucester.*  So do I ever, [*Aside.*] being well-advis'd;
For had I curs'd now, I had curs'd myself.

*Enter* CATESBY.

*Catesby.*  Madam, his majesty doth call for you;  320
And for your Grace; and you, my noble lords.
*Queen Elizabeth.*  Catesby, I come. Lords, will you go
with me?
*Rivers.*  We wait upon your Grace.

[*Exeunt all but* GLOUCESTER.

*Gloucester.*  I do the wrong, and first begin to brawl.
The secret mischiefs that I set abroach  325
I lay unto the grievous charge of others.
Clarence, whom I, indeed, have cast in darkness,
I do beweep to many simple gulls;
Namely, to Stanley, Hastings, Buckingham;
And tell them 'tis the queen and her allies  330
That stir the king against the duke my brother.
Now they believe it; and withal whet me
To be reveng'd on Rivers, Vaughan, Grey;
But then I sigh, and, with a piece of scripture,
Tell them that God bids us do good for evil:  335
And thus I clothe my naked villany
With odd old ends stolen forth of holy writ,
And seem a saint when most I play the devil.

*Enter two* Murderers.

316–17 (cf. 335) presumably sarcastic.    **scath**: harm.
318 **well-advis'd**: wise.    324 **brawl**: complain about it [*N*].
325 **set abroach**: start up (metaphor from opening a barrel).
326 **grievous**: so as to hurt them (cf. I. i. 15).    327 **cast in darkness**: got imprisoned.    328 **beweep**: weep for.    **to**: in the hearing of.    **gulls**: simpletons [*N*].    329 **Namely**: especially (as regularly in Chaucer).    333 **Vaughan**: a disyllable.
337 **odd old ends**: various stale tags (cf. 'odds and ends').    **of holy writ**: from the Bible.

But soft! here come my executioners.
How now, my hardy, stout, resolved mates!                    340
Are you now going to dispatch this thing?
   *First Murderer.* We are, my lord; and come to have the
     warrant,
That we may be admitted where he is.
   *Gloucester.* Well thought upon; I have it here about me:
                         *[Gives the warrant.*
When you have done, repair to Crosby-place.                    345
But, sirs, be sudden in the execution,
Withal obdurate, do not hear him plead;
For Clarence is well-spoken, and perhaps
May move your hearts to pity, if you mark him.
   *First Murderer.* Tut, tut, my lord, we will not stand to
     prate;                    350
Talkers are no good doers: be assur'd
We go to use our hands and not our tongues.
   *Gloucester.* Your eyes drop millstones, when fools' eyes
     fall tears:
I like you, lads; about your business straight;
Go, go dispatch.                    355
   *First Murderer.* We will, my noble lord.        *[Exeunt.*

### Scene IV. THE SAME. THE TOWER

#### Enter CLARENCE and BRAKENBURY.

   *Brakenbury.* Why looks your Grace so heavily to-day?
   *Clarence.* O, I have pass'd a miserable night,
So full of ugly sights, of ghastly dreams,

---

340 **stout:** strong and brave.    **resolved:** determined.
342 **warrant:** permit.    345 **Crosby-place:** see I. ii. 213.
346 **sudden:** rapid.    347 **Withal obdurate:** and also tough.
349 **mark:** listen to.    353 i.e. let your eyes drop millstones (like
the metaphor of a 'stony' heart), cf. I. iv. 243.    **fall:** drop.
355 **dispatch:** make haste about it.    1 **heavily:** sad.

That, as I am a Christian faithful man,
I would not spend another such a night,      5
Though 'twere to buy a world of happy days,
So full of dismal terror was the time.

   *Brakenbury.* What was your dream, my lord? I pray
     you, tell me.

   *Clarence.* Methought that I had broken from the Tower,
And was embark'd to cross to Burgundy;      10
And in my company my brother Gloucester,
Who from my cabin tempted me to walk
Upon the hatches: thence we look'd toward England,
And cited up a thousand heavy times,
During the wars of York and Lancaster,      15
That had befall'n us. As we pac'd along
Upon the giddy footing of the hatches,
Methought that Gloucester stumbled; and, in falling,
Struck me, that thought to stay him, overboard,
Into the tumbling billows of the main.      20
Lord, Lord! methought what pain it was to drown:
What dreadful noise of water in mine ears!
What sights of ugly death within mine eyes!
Methought I saw a thousand fearful wracks;
A thousand men that fishes gnaw'd upon;      25
Wedges of gold, great ingots, heaps of pearl,
Inestimable stones, unvalu'd jewels,
All scatter'd in the bottom of the sea.
Some lay in dead men's skulls; and in those holes
Where eyes did once inhabit, there were crept,      30
As 'twere in scorn of eyes, reflecting gems,

---

4 **Christian faithful**: a faithful believer (in Christianity).
9 **broken from**: escaped from.      10 **Burgundy**: Flanders [*N*].
13 **hatches**: deck.      14 **cited up**: recalled.      17 **giddy**:
slippery.      19 **stay**: check, support.      20 **tumbling**: toss-
ing (the word is used again slightly differently in III. iv. 99).
24 **wracks**: wrecks [*N*].      27 **unvalu'd**: invaluable.      30 **inhabit**: dwell (often intransitive in Sh.) [*N*].

That woo'd the slimy bottom of the deep,
And mock'd the dead bones that lay scatter'd by.
  *Brakenbury.*  Had you such leisure in the time of death
To gaze upon these secrets of the deep?                    35
  *Clarence.*  Methought I had; and often did I strive
To yield the ghost; but still the envious flood
Stopt in my soul, and would not let it forth
To find the empty, vast, and wandering air;
But smother'd it within my panting bulk,                    40
Which almost burst to belch it in the sea.
  *Brakenbury.*  Awak'd you not with this sore agony?
  *Clarence.*  No, no, my dream was lengthen'd after life;
O! then began the tempest to my soul.
I pass'd, methought, the melancholy flood,                    45
With that sour ferryman which poets write of,
Unto the kingdom of perpetual night.
The first that there did greet my stranger soul,
Was my great father-in-law, renowned Warwick;
Who cried aloud, 'What scourge for perjury                    50
Can this dark monarchy afford false Clarence?'
And so he vanish'd: then came wandering by
A shadow like an angel, with bright hair
Dabbled in blood; and he shriek'd out aloud,
'Clarence is come,—false, fleeting, perjur'd Clarence,                    55
That stabb'd me in the field by Tewksbury;—
Seize on him! Furies, take him unto torment.'
With that, methought, a legion of foul fiends
Environ'd me, and howled in mine ears
Such hideous cries, that with the very noise                    60

37 **yield the ghost:** give up my spirit, i.e. die (cf. Matt. xxvii. 50).
**envious:** malicious, grudging me my wish.      38 **stopt in:** held
back (in my body).      40 **bulk:** frame.      45 **the melancholy
flood:** the river Styx [*N*].      46 **ferryman:** Charon [*N*].
48 **stranger:** wandering *or* newly arrived.      50 **perjury:** see
206–9 below.      53 **A shadow:** Prince Edward of Lancaster.
55 **fleeting:** unstable.      59 **Environ'd:** surrounded.

I trembling wak'd, and, for a season after,
Could not believe but that I was in hell,
Such terrible impression made my dream.
  *Brakenbury.*  No marvel, lord, though it affrighted you;
I am afraid, methinks, to hear you tell it.        65
  *Clarence.*  O Brakenbury! I have done these things
That now give evidence against my soul,
For Edward's sake; and see how he requites me.
O God! if my deep prayers cannot appease thee,
But thou wilt be aveng'd on my misdeeds,       70
Yet execute thy wrath on me alone:
O! spare my guiltless wife and my poor children.
I pray thee, gentle keeper, stay by me;
My soul is heavy, and I fain would sleep.
  *Brakenbury.*  I will, my lord. God give your Grace good
    rest!                     [CLARENCE *sleeps.*
Sorrow breaks seasons and reposing hours,     76
Makes the night morning, and the noon-tide night.
Princes have but their titles for their glories,
An outward honour for an inward toil;
And, for unfelt imaginations,         80
They often feel a world of restless cares:
So that, between their titles and low names,
There's nothing differs but the outward fame.

*Enter the two* Murderers.

  *First Murderer.*  Ho! who's here?       84
  *Brakenbury.*  What wouldst thou, fellow? and how
    cam'st thou hither?

---

61 **a season:** some time.     76 **seasons and reposing hours:**
the time usually devoted to rest and sleep.    78 **for:** as.
79 **for:** in return for.    80 **for unfelt imaginations:** instead of
what they hope to possess but have not realized.    82 **low names:**
common people.    83 **There's nothing differs:** there is no (real)
difference.    **fame:** reputation.

*First Murderer.* I would speak with Clarence, and I came
hither on my legs.

*Brakenbury.* What! so brief?

*Second Murderer.* 'Tis better, sir, than to be tedious.—
Let him see our commission, and talk no more.           90

      *[A paper is delivered to* BRAKENBURY, *who reads it.*

*Brakenbury.* I am, in this, commanded to deliver
The noble Duke of Clarence to your hands:
I will not reason what is meant hereby,
Because I will be guiltless of the meaning.
There lies the duke asleep, and there the keys.           95
I'll to the king; and signify to him
That thus I have resign'd to you my charge.

*First Murderer.* You may, sir; 'tis a point of wisdom:
fare you well.           *[Exit* BRAKENBURY.

*Second Murderer.* What! shall we stab him as he sleeps?

*First Murderer.* No; he'll say 'twas done cowardly,
when he wakes.

*Second Murderer.* When he wakes! why, fool, he shall
never wake till the judgment-day.           104

*First Murderer.* Why, then he'll say we stabbed him
sleeping.

*Second Murderer.* The urging of that word 'judgment'
hath bred a kind of remorse in me.

*First Murderer.* What! art thou afraid?           109

*Second Murderer.* Not to kill him, having a warrant for
it; but to be damn'd for killing him, from the which no
warrant can defend me.

*First Murderer.* I thought thou hadst been resolute.

---

  90 **him:** Brakenbury.    **commission:** mandate, authority.
93 **reason:** argue.    94 **meaning:** almost = 'consequences'[N].
97 **charge:** responsibility (for the prisoner).    **98 a point
of wisdom:** a sensible thing to do.    101 **cowardly:** an
adverb here.    108 **remorse:** compunction [N].    111 **damn'd:**
condemned (hereafter).

*Second Murderer.* So I am, to let him live.                    114

*First Murderer.* I'll back to the Duke of Gloucester, and tell him so.

*Second Murderer.* Nay, I prithee, stay a little: I hope my holy humour will change; it was wont to hold me but while one tells twenty.

*First Murderer.* How dost thou feel thyself now?          120

*Second Murderer.* Some certain dregs of conscience are yet within me.

*First Murderer.* Remember our reward when the deed's done.                    124

*Second Murderer.* 'Zounds! he dies: I had forgot the reward.

*First Murderer.* Where's thy conscience now?

*Second Murderer.* In the Duke of Gloucester's purse.

*First Murderer.* So when he opens his purse to give us our reward, thy conscience flies out.                    130

*Second Murderer.* 'Tis no matter; let it go: there's few or none will entertain it.

*First Murderer.* What if it come to thee again?

*Second Murderer.* I'll not meddle with it; it makes a man a coward; a man cannot steal, but it accuseth  135
him; a man cannot swear, but it checks him; a man cannot lie with his neighbour's wife, but it detects him: 'tis a blushing shamefast spirit, that mutinies in a man's bosom; it fills one full of obstacles; it made me once restore a purse of gold that I found; it beggars  140
any man that keeps it; it is turned out of all towns and cities for a dangerous thing; and every man that

117–18 **my holy humour**: this pious frame of mind.     119 **tells**: counts.          120 **now**: (after a short interval).          121 **Some certain**: just a few (one word is really otiose).          125 **Zounds!** **he dies**: then, of course, he must die [N].          132 **it**: my conscience. 133 **entertain it**: take it in, employ it.          138 **shamefast**: modest, bashful [N].          139 **fills . . . obstacles**: makes difficulties for a man.

4. Act I, Sc. ii. 149–50.

*Anne.* Out of my sight! thou dost infect mine eyes.
*Gloucester.* Thine eyes, sweet lady, have infected mine.
(Marius Goring and Yvonne Mitchell at Stratford-upon-Avon, 1953)

5. Act III, Sc. iv. 67.

*Richard.* Look how I am bewitched: behold mine arm
Is like a blasted sapling, withered up.

means to live well, endeavours to trust to himself and
live without it. 144

*First Murderer.* 'Zounds! it is even now at my elbow,
persuading me not to kill the duke.

*Second Murderer.* Take the devil in thy mind, and believe him not: he would insinuate with thee but to make
thee sigh.

*First Murderer.* Tut, I am strong-framed; he cannot
prevail with me. 151

*Second Murderer.* Spoke like a tall fellow that respects
his reputation. Come, shall we to this gear?

*First Murderer.* Take him over the costard with the hilts
of thy sword, and then throw him into the malmsey-butt
in the next room. 156

*Second Murderer.* O, excellent device! make a sop of
him.

*First Murderer.* Soft! he wakes.

*Second Murderer.* Strike! 160

*First Murderer.* No, we'll reason with him.

*Clarence.* Where art thou, keeper? give me a cup of
wine.

*First Murderer.* You shall have wine enough, my lord,
anon. 165

*Clarence.* In God's name, what art thou?

*First Murderer.* A man, as you are.

*Clarence.* But not, as I am, royal.

*First Murderer.* Nor you, as we are, loyal. 169

*Clarence.* Thy voice is thunder, but thy looks are humble.

---

143 **live well:** have a good time. 147 **Take:** catch.
148 **him:** the devil of conscience. **insinuate with:** worm his way into
[*N*]. 152 **tall:** brave (cf. our use of 'stout'). 153 **gear:** business.
154 **Take:** catch, i.e. hit. **costard:** head (slang, costard being properly a large, round apple). **hilts:** hilt. 155 **malmsey-butt:**
cask of malmsey wine [*N*]. 157 **sop:** something dipped in or
floated on a liquid. 161 **reason:** talk. 170 **thy looks
...humble:** you look like a man of low birth [*N*].

*First Murderer.* My voice is now the king's, my looks
   mine own.

*Clarence.* How darkly, and how deadly dost thou speak!
Your eyes do menace me: why look you pale?
Who sent you hither? Wherefore do you come?

*Both Murderers.* To, to, to—                                           175

*Clarence.* To murder me?

*Both Murderers.* Ay, ay.

*Clarence.* You scarcely have the hearts to tell me so,
And therefore cannot have the hearts to do it.
Wherein, my friends, have I offended you?                              180

*First Murderer.* Offended us you have not, but the king.

*Clarence.* I shall be reconcil'd to him again.

*Second Murderer.* Never, my lord; therefore prepare to
   die.

*Clarence.* Are you call'd forth from out a world of men
To slay the innocent? What is my offence?                             185
Where is the evidence that doth accuse me?
What lawful quest have given their verdict up
Unto the frowning judge? or who pronounc'd
The bitter sentence of poor Clarence' death?
Before I be convict by course of law,                                 190
To threaten me with death is most unlawful.
I charge you, as you hope to have redemption
By Christ's dear blood shed for our grievous sins,
That you depart and lay no hands on me;
The deed you undertake is damnable.                                    195

*First Murderer.* What we will do, we do upon command.

*Second Murderer.* And he that hath commanded is our
   king.

*Clarence.* Erroneous vassal! the great King of kings

---

172 **darkly**: in riddles.    184 i.e. Is it your special mission
in life . . .?    187 **quest**: jury, body of persons appointed to
hold an inquiry [N].    190 **convict**: convicted [N].    198
**Erroneous vassal!**: misguided wretch.

Hath in the table of his law commanded
That thou shalt do no murder: will you, then,                200
Spurn at his edict and fulfil a man's?
Take heed; for he holds vengeance in his hand,
To hurl upon their heads that break his law.
  *Second Murderer.* And that same vengeance doth he hurl
    on thee,
For false forswearing and for murder too:                    205
Thou didst receive the sacrament to fight
In quarrel of the house of Lancaster.
  *First Murderer.* And, like a traitor to the name of
    God,
Didst break that vow, and, with thy treacherous blade
Unripp'dst the bowels of thy sovereign's son.               210
  *Second Murderer.* Whom thou wast sworn to cherish
    and defend.
  *First Murderer.* How canst thou urge God's dreadful
    law to us,
When thou hast broke it in such dear degree?
  *Clarence.* Alas! for whose sake did I that ill deed?
For Edward, for my brother, for his sake:                    215
He sends you not to murder me for this;
For in that sin he is as deep as I.
If God will be avenged for the deed,
O! know you yet, he doth it publicly:
Take not the quarrel from his powerful arm;                  220
He needs no indirect or lawless course

---

199 **table of his law:** the ten Commandments, written on two tables
of stone (see Exodus xxxii. 15).     202 cf. 'To me belongeth vengeance' (Deuteronomy xxxii. 35).     205 **forswearing:** perjury
(so 'false' is strictly otiose); see I. iii. 135–8.     206 i.e. swear
at or after Mass [*N*].     207 **In quarrel of:** on the side of.
210 **Unripp'dst:** didst rip open.   **thy sovereign's son:** Edward,
son of Henry VI, cf. 226–7 below and note to I. i. 153.     212 **dreadful:** to be dreaded (cf. I. i. 8).     213 **dear:** extreme [*N*].     217 **deep:**
deeply involved.     221 **indirect:** unlawful *or* human [*N*].

To cut off those that have offended him.

 *First Murderer.* Who made thee then a bloody minister,
When gallant-springing, brave Plantagenet,
That princely novice, was struck dead by thee?  225

 *Clarence.* My brother's love, the devil, and my rage.

 *First Murderer.* Thy brother's love, our duty, and thy fault,
Provoke us hither now to slaughter thee.

 *Clarence.* If you do love my brother, hate not me;
I am his brother, and I love him well.  230
If you are hir'd for meed, go back again,
And I will send you to my brother Gloucester,
Who shall reward you better for my life
Than Edward will for tidings of my death.

 *Second Murderer.* You are deceiv'd, your brother Gloucester hates you.  235

 *Clarence.* O, no! he loves me, and he holds me dear:
Go you to him from me.

 *Both Murderers.*   Ay, so we will.

 *Clarence.* Tell him, when that our princely father
  York
Bless'd his three sons with his victorious arm,
And charg'd us from his soul to love each other,  240
He little thought of this divided friendship:
Bid Gloucester think on this, and he will weep.

 *First Murderer.* Ay, millstones; as he lesson'd us to
  weep.

 *Clarence.* O! do not slander him, for he is kind.

 *First Murderer.* Right;  245
As snow in harvest. Thou deceiv'st thyself:

---

 223 **minister**: agent.  224 **gallant-springing**: growing up
so promisingly [*N*].  225 **novice**: one entering on a new life (of
knighthood, cf. *3 Henry VI*, II. ii. 58).  226 **My brother's love**:
love for my brother (Edward IV).  227 **Thy brother's love**:
i.e. his love for you [*N*].  231 **meed**: reward.  243 **millstones**: not tears; see I. iii. 353.  245–6 i.e. Yes, as natural as
snow would be at harvest-time [*N*].

'Tis he that sends us to destroy you here.

*Clarence.* It cannot be; for he bewept my fortune,
And hugg'd me in his arms, and swore, with sobs,
That he would labour my delivery.                    250

*First Murderer.* Why, so he doth, when he delivers you
From this earth's thraldom to the joys of heaven.

*Second Murderer.* Make peace with God, for you must
    die, my lord.

*Clarence.* Hast thou that holy feeling in thy soul,
To counsel me to make my peace with God,             255
And art thou yet to thy own soul so blind,
That thou wilt war with God by murdering me?
O! sirs, consider, he that set you on
To do this deed, will hate you for the deed.         259

*Second Murderer.* What shall we do?

*Clarence.*                    Relent, and save your souls.

*First Murderer.* Relent! 'tis cowardly, and womanish.

*Clarence.* Not to relent is beastly, savage, devilish.
Which of you, if you were a prince's son,
Being pent from liberty, as I am now,
If two such murderers as yourselves came to you,     265
Would not entreat for life?
My friend, I spy some pity in thy looks;
O! if thine eye be not a flatterer,
Come thou on my side, and entreat for me,
As you would beg, were you in my distress:           270
A begging prince what beggar pities not?

*Second Murderer.* Look behind you, my lord.

*First Murderer.* [*Stabs him.*] Take that, and that: if all
    this will not do,

---

250 **labour:** work for, effect [*N*].      260 **Relent:** repent [*N*].
264 **pent:** shut away.          267 **My friend:** addressed to Second
Murderer.          268 i.e. if I am not mistaken in your looks.
273 [*Stabs him*] i.e. from behind.

I'll drown you in the malmsey-butt within.

[*Exit with the body.*

 *Second Murderer.* A bloody deed, and desperately dispatch'd!            275

How fain, like Pilate, would I wash my hands
Of this most grievous murder.

     *Re-enter first* Murderer.

 *First Murderer.* How now! what mean'st thou that
  thou help'st me not?

By heaven, the duke shall know how slack you have been.

 *Second Murderer.* I would he knew that I had sav'd his
  brother!            280

Take thou the fee, and tell him what I say;
For I repent me that the duke is slain.   [*Exit.*

 *First Murderer.* So do not I: go, coward as thou art.

Well, I'll go hide the body in some hole,
Till that the duke give order for his burial:  285
And when I have my meed, I will away;
For this will out, and here I must not stay.  [*Exit.*

 276 **Pilate**: see Matt. xxvii. 24 (referred to again, *Richard II*, IV.
i. 239).   287 **this**: murder.  **out**: get known (cf. proverb
'Murder will out').

# ACT II

## Scene I. LONDON. A ROOM IN THE PALACE

*Enter* KING EDWARD *sick*, QUEEN ELIZABETH, DORSET, RIVERS, HASTINGS, BUCKINGHAM, GREY, *and Others*.

*King Edward.* Why, so: now have I done a good day's work.
You peers, continue this united league:
I every day expect an embassage
From my Redeemer to redeem me hence;
And more in peace my soul shall part to heaven, 5
Since I have made my friends at peace on earth.
Rivers and Hastings, take each other's hand;
Dissemble not your hatred, swear your love.

*Rivers.* By heaven, my soul is purg'd from grudging hate;
And with my hand I seal my true heart's love. 10

*Hastings.* So thrive I, as I truly swear the like!

*King Edward.* Take heed, you dally not before your king;
Lest he that is the supreme King of kings
Confound your hidden falsehood, and award
Either of you to be the other's end. 15

*Hastings.* So prosper I, as I swear perfect love!

*Rivers.* And I, as I love Hastings with my heart!

*King Edward.* Madam, yourself are not exempt in this,
Nor you, son Dorset, Buckingham, nor you;
You have been factious one against the other. 20

1 **so:** good!    3 **embassage:** message [*N*].    4 **redeem:** deliver (as from a 'vale of woe'; but chosen for play on words).
5 **part:** depart.    8 i.e. Do not (merely) cover up hatred which you still hide in your hearts.    11 **thrive I:** may I thrive.
12 **dally:** trifle.    13 **supreme:** accent súpreme, as usually in Sh.
14 **award:** decree, appoint.    15 **be . . . end:** cause the other's destruction.    20 **factious:** quarrelsome (literally 'forming parties', cf. i. iii. 128).

Wife, love Lord Hastings, let him kiss your hand;
And what you do, do it unfeignedly.

    *Queen Elizabeth.* There, Hastings; I will never more
      remember
Our former hatred, so thrive I and mine!

    *King Edward.* Dorset, embrace him; Hastings, love lord
      marquess.                                 25

    *Dorset.* This interchange of love, I here protest,
Upon my part shall be inviolable.

    *Hastings.* And so swear I.             *[They embrace.*

    *King Edward.* Now, princely Buckingham, seal thou this
      league
With thy embracements to my wife's allies,       30
And make me happy in your unity.

    *Buckingham.* [*To the* QUEEN.] Whenever Buckingham
      doth turn his hate
Upon your Grace, but with all duteous love
Doth cherish you and yours, God punish me
With hate in those where I expect most love!       35
When I have most need to employ a friend,
And most assured that he is a friend,
Deep, hollow, treacherous, and full of guile,
Be he unto me! This do I beg of God,
When I am cold in love to you or yours.   *[They embrace.*

    *King Edward.* A pleasing cordial, princely Buckingham,
Is this thy vow unto my sickly heart.
There wanteth now our brother Gloucester here
To make the blessed period of this peace.

    *Buckingham.* And, in good time, here comes the noble
      duke.                                      45

---

25 **marquess**: the Marquess of Dorset.      29 cf. i. iii. 280 and
note there.     30 **embracements to**: embracings of.     33–34 **but
... doth**: and does not (syntax mixed) [*N*].     37 **And ... assured**: (accent on last) and feel most assured.     41 **cordial**: tonic,
restorative.     43 **wanteth**: is (only) lacking.     44 **period**:
conclusion (cf. i. iii. 238).     45 **in good time**: opportunely.

*Enter* GLOUCESTER.

*Gloucester.*  Good morrow to my sovereign king and
    queen;
And princely peers, a happy time of day!
  *King Edward.*  Happy, indeed, as we have spent the day.
Gloucester, we have done deeds of charity;
Made peace of enmity, fair love of hate,        50
Between these swelling wrong-incensed peers.
  *Gloucester.*  A blessed labour, my most sovereign lord.
Among this princely heap, if any here,
By false intelligence, or wrong surmise,
Hold me a foe;        55
If I unwittingly, or in my rage,
Have aught committed that is hardly borne
By any in this presence, I desire
To reconcile me to his friendly peace:
'Tis death to me to be at enmity;        60
I hate it, and desire all good men's love.
First, madam, I entreat true peace of you,
Which I will purchase with my duteous service;
Of you, my noble cousin Buckingham,
If ever any grudge were lodg'd between us;        65
Of you, Lord Rivers, and Lord Grey, of you,
That all without desert have frown'd on me;
Of you, Lord Woodvile, and Lord Scales, of you;
Dukes, earls, lords, gentlemen; indeed, of all.
I do not know that Englishman alive        70

47 **a happy . . . day**: see note to I. i. 122.    50 **of**: instead of.
51 **swelling**: with anger.    **wrong-incensed**: stirred up by
(fancied) wrongs (and so perhaps also 'wrongly').    53 **heap**:
company, body (*not* contemptuous in older use).    54 **intelligence**: information received.    57 **hardly borne**: resented.
58 **presence**: cf. I. iii. 54.    59 i.e. reconcile myself to him
and make a friendly peace with him.    67 **desert**: my deserving it.

With whom my soul is any jot at odds
More than the infant that is born to-night:
I thank my God for my humility.
   *Queen Elizabeth.* A holy day shall this be kept hereafter:
I would to God all strifes were well compounded.   75
My sovereign lord, I do beseech your highness
To take our brother Clarence to your grace.
   *Gloucester.* Why, madam, have I offer'd love for this,
To be so flouted in this royal presence?
Who knows not that the gentle duke is dead?   80

                                      [*They all start.*

You do him injury to scorn his corse.
   *Rivers.* Who knows not he is dead! who knows he is?
   *Queen Elizabeth.* All-seeing heaven, what a world is this!
   *Buckingham.* Look I so pale, Lord Dorset, as the rest?
   *Dorset.* Ay, my good lord; and no man in the presence   85
But his red colour hath forsook his cheeks.
   *King Edward.* Is Clarence dead? the order was revers'd.
   *Gloucester.* But he, poor man, by your first order died,
And that a winged Mercury did bear;
Some tardy cripple bore the countermand,   90
That came too lag to see him buried.
God grant that some, less noble and less loyal,
Nearer in bloody thoughts, but not in blood,
Deserve not worse than wretched Clarence did,
And yet go current from suspicion.   95

    **71 any jot:** in the least degree.    **at odds:** at variance.
**73 humility:** (perhaps) gentleness, willingness to be friends [*N*].
**75 compounded:** made up.       **77 to your grace:** (back)
into favour.    **78 offer'd love:** viz. in 58–59.    **85 no man:**
there is no one.        **89 winged Mercury:** speedy messenger
[*N*].        **91 lag:** slowly.        **93 Nearer in bloody thoughts:**
more murderously inclined (cf. I. iii. 330–1).    **blood:** kinship [*N*].
**95 go current:** pass along, our 'get away with it' (cf. I. ii. 84).    **from:**
free from.

*Enter* STANLEY.

*Stanley.* A boon, my sovereign, for my service done!

*King Edward.* I prithee, peace: my soul is full of sorrow.

*Stanley.* I will not rise, unless your highness hear me.

*King Edward.* Then say at once, what is it thou requests.

*Stanley.* The forfeit, sovereign, of my servant's life;  100
Who slew to-day a riotous gentleman
Lately attendant on the Duke of Norfolk.

*King Edward.* Have I a tongue to doom my brother's death,
And shall that tongue give pardon to a slave?
My brother kill'd no man, his fault was thought;  105
And yet his punishment was bitter death.
Who sued to me for him? who, in my wrath,
Kneel'd at my feet, and bade me be advis'd?
Who spoke of brotherhood? who spoke of love?
Who told me how the poor soul did forsake  110
The mighty Warwick, and did fight for me?
Who told me, in the field at Tewksbury,
When Oxford had me down, he rescu'd me,
And said, 'Dear brother, live, and be a king'?
Who told me, when we both lay in the field  115
Frozen almost to death, how he did lap me
Even in his garments; and did give himself,
All thin and naked, to the numb cold night?
All this from my remembrance brutish wrath
Sinfully pluck'd, and not a man of you  120
Had so much grace to put it in my mind.
But when your carters or your waiting-vassals

100 **The forfeit . . . life:** the life of my servant which he has deserved to forfeit.          105 **thought:** mere thought [*N*].          108 **be advis'd:** be cautious, think again.          116 **lap:** wrap.          118 **thin:** thinly clad.          121 **to put:** as to put.          122 **carters . . . waiting-vassals:** i.e. your lowest servants.

Have done a drunken slaughter, and defac'd
The precious image of our dear Redeemer,
You straight are on your knees for pardon, pardon;    125
And I, unjustly too, must grant it you;
But for my brother not a man would speak,
Nor I, ungracious, speak unto myself
For him, poor soul. The proudest of you all
Have been beholding to him in his life.                130
Yet none of you would once beg for his life.
O God! I fear, thy justice will take hold
On me and you and mine and yours for this.
Come, Hastings, help me to my closet. O! poor Clarence!
            *Exeunt* KING EDWARD, QUEEN, HASTINGS, RIVERS,
                                DORSET, *and* GREY.
  *Gloucester.* This is the fruit of rashness. Mark'd you not
How that the guilty kindred of the queen         136
Look'd pale when they did hear of Clarence' death?
O! they did urge it still unto the king:
God will revenge it. Come, lords; will you go
To comfort Edward with our company?              140
  *Buckingham.* We wait upon your Grace.      [*Exeunt.*

### Scene II. The Same. A Room in the Palace

*Enter the* DUCHESS OF YORK, *with a Son and Daughter of*
                        CLARENCE.

  *Boy.* Good grandam, tell us, is our father dead?
  *Duchess.* No, boy.
  *Daughter.* Why do you wring your hands, and beat your
        breast.
And cry—'O Clarence  my unhappy son?'
  *Boy.* Why do you look on us, and shake your head,    5

124 **image:** i.e. a man [N].        130 **beholding:** indebted.
134 **closet:** private room [N].     135 **This:** viz. repentance,
regret.

And call us orphans, wretches, castaways,
If that our noble father be alive?
*Duchess.*  My pretty cousins, you mistake me much;
I do lament the sickness of the king,
As loath to lose him, not your father's death;                10
It were lost sorrow to wail one that's lost.
*Boy.*  Then, grandam, you conclude that he is dead.
The king mine uncle is to blame for it:
God will revenge it; whom I will importune
With earnest prayers all to that effect.                      15
*Daughter.*  And so will I.
*Duchess.*  Peace, children, peace! the king doth love you
well:
Incapable and shallow innocents,
You cannot guess who caus'd your father's death.
*Boy.*  Grandam, we can; for my good uncle Gloucester  20
Told me, the king, provok'd to 't by the queen,
Devis'd impeachments to imprison him:
And when my uncle told me so, he wept,
And pitied me, and kindly kiss'd my cheek;
Bade me rely on him, as on my father,                         25
And he would love me dearly as his child.
*Duchess.*  Ah! that deceit should steal such gentle shape,
And with a virtuous vizard hide deep vice.
He is my son, ay, and therein my shame,
Yet from my dugs he drew not this deceit.                     30
*Boy.*  Think you my uncle did dissemble, grandam?
*Duchess.*  Ay, boy.
*Boy.*  I cannot think it. Hark! what noise is this?

8 **cousins**: used loosely here for grandchildren.        12 **conclude**:
decide.        15 **prayers**: (two syllables).        18 **Incapable**: i.e.
of understanding.        22 **impeachments**: official accusations.
26 **And** (said) **he**.        27 **steal ... shape**: falsely take upon it an
appearance of gentleness.        28 **vizard**: vizor, mask.        30 **dugs**:
breasts [*N*].        31 **dissemble**: deceive us, cover up his real feeling.
33 **think**: believe.

*Enter* QUEEN ELIZABETH, *distractedly*: RIVERS *and*
                DORSET *following her.*

*Queen Elizabeth.* Oh! who shall hinder me to wail and
    weep,
To chide my fortune, and torment myself?                    35
I'll join with black despair against my soul,
And to myself become an enemy.
    *Duchess.* What means this scene of rude impatience?
    *Queen Elizabeth.* To make an act of tragic violence:
Edward, my lord, thy son, our king, is dead!              40
Why grow the branches now the root is wither'd?
Why wither not the leaves that want their sap?
If you will live, lament: if die, be brief,
That our swift-winged souls may catch the king's;
Or, like obedient subjects, follow him                      45
To his new kingdom of ne'er changing night.
    *Duchess.* Ah! so much interest have I in thy sorrow
As I had title in thy noble husband.
I have bewept a worthy husband's death,
And liv'd with looking on his images;                       50
But now two mirrors of his princely semblance
Are crack'd in pieces by malignant death,
And I for comfort have but one false glass,
That grieves me when I see my shame in him.
Thou art a widow; yet thou art a mother,                    55
And hast the comfort of thy children left thee:
But death hath snatch'd my husband from mine arms,
And pluck'd two crutches from my feeble limbs,
Clarence and Edward. O! what cause have I—

**34 hinder me to wail:** prevent me from wailing.        **38 impatience:** (four syllables).          **39 make:** (perhaps) complete [*N*].
**42 want:** are deprived of.      **43 brief:** quick about it.      **48 title:**
rights (legal term like 'interest in').          **50 images:** likenesses,
i.e. children.          **51 semblance:** appearance.          **53 one false
glass:** Richard, who does not give me a true image of him.

Thine being but a moiety of my grief—                    60
To overgo thy plaints, and drown thy cries!

*Boy.* Ah, aunt, you wept not for our father's death;
How can we aid you with our kindred tears?

*Daughter.* Our fatherless distress was left unmoan'd;
Your widow-dolour likewise be unwept.                    65

*Queen Elizabeth.* Give me no help in lamentation;
I am not barren to bring forth complaints:
All springs reduce their currents to mine eyes,
That I, being govern'd by the watery moon,
May send forth plenteous tears to drown the world!       70
Ah! for my husband, for my dear Lord Edward!

*Children.* Ah! for our father, for our dear Lord Clarence!

*Duchess.* Alas! for both, both mine, Edward and
    Clarence!

*Queen Elizabeth.* What stay had I but Edward? and
    he's gone.

*Children.* What stay had we but Clarence? and he's
    gone.                                                75

*Duchess.* What stays had I but they? and they are gone.

*Queen Elizabeth.* Was never widow had so dear a loss.

*Children.* Were never orphans had so dear a loss.

*Duchess.* Was never mother had so dear a loss.

Alas! I am the mother of these griefs:                   80
Their woes are parcell'd, mine are general.
She for an Edward weeps, and so do I;
I for a Clarence weep, so doth not she:

---

60 **moiety**: part.    61 **overgo**: outdo.        62 **aunt**: to Queen
Elizabeth (and cf. 21–22).        66 **lamentation**: the -ion is two
syllables, as usual.    67 **to bring forth**: in producing.    **complaints**: lamentations.        68 (may) **All springs reduce**: bring
back, concentrate.    69 **I**: i.e. like the sea, whose tides are
governed by the moon (therefore called watery).    77 **dear**: keen
(see commentary at I. iv. 215).        81 **parcell'd**: individual,
proper to each of them.    **general**: include all the others (as she
proceeds to show) [*N*].

These babes for Clarence weep, and so do I;
I for an Edward weep, so do not they:                     85
Alas! you three, on me, threefold distress'd,
Pour all your tears; I am your sorrow's nurse,
And I will pamper it with lamentation.

   *Dorset.*  Comfort, dear mother: God is much displeas'd
That you take with unthankfulness his doing.              90
In common worldly things 'tis call'd ungrateful
With dull unwillingness to repay a debt
Which with a bounteous hand was kindly lent;
Much more to be thus opposite with heaven,
For it requires the royal debt it lent you.              95

   *Rivers.*  Madam, bethink you, like a careful mother,
Of the young prince your son: send straight for him;
Let him be crown'd; in him your comfort lives.
Drown desperate sorrow in dead Edward's grave,
And plant your joys in living Edward's throne.           100

   *Enter* GLOUCESTER, BUCKINGHAM, STANLEY, HASTINGS,
             RATCLIFF, *and Others.*

   *Gloucester.*  Sister, have comfort: all of us have cause
To wail the dimming of our shining star;
But none can cure their harms by wailing them.
Madam, my mother, I do cry you mercy;
I did not see your Grace: humbly on my knee               105
I crave your blessing.

   *Duchess.*  God bless thee! and put meekness in thy mind,
Love, charity, obedience, and true duty.

   *Gloucester.*  Amen; [*Aside.*] and make me die a good old
         man!
That is the butt-end of a mother's blessing;             110

   89 **mother:** Elizabeth.        94 **be opposite with:** quarrel with.
95 **For:** because (cf. I. i. 58).        96 **Madam:** to Elizabeth.
100 **plant:** i.e. where they may grow and flourish.        101 **Sister:** i.e.
sister-in-law; see I. i. 109.        104 **cry you mercy:** beg your pardon.
110 **butt-end:** conclusion (literally, the square end of a plank).

I marvel that her Grace did leave it out.

*Buckingham.*  You cloudy princes and heart-sorrowing
   peers,
That bear this heavy mutual load of moan,
Now cheer each other in each other's love:
Though we have spent our harvest of this king,     115
We are to reap the harvest of his son.
The broken rancour of your high-swoln hearts,
But lately splinter'd, knit, and join'd together,
Must gently be preserv'd, cherish'd, and kept:
Me seemeth good, that, with some little train,    120
Forthwith from Ludlow the young prince be fetch'd
Hither to London, to be crown'd our king.

*Rivers.*  Why with some little train, my Lord of Buckingham?

*Buckingham.*  Marry, my lord, lest, by a multitude,
The new-heal'd wound of malice should break out;   125
Which would be so much the more dangerous,
By how much the estate is green and yet ungovern'd;
Where every horse bears his commanding rein,
And may direct his course as please himself,
As well the fear of harm, as harm apparent,    130
In my opinion, ought to be prevented.

*Gloucester.*  I hope the king made peace with all of us;
And the compact is firm and true in me.

112 **cloudy**: melancholy, like a dull day.     113 **mutual**:
common.   **moan**: sorrow.    114 **in each other's love**: by
affection for one another.    115 **spent**: used up.    117 **The
broken rancour**: the breach caused by ill-feeling (like a poisoned
wound that had broken open; cf. 125).    118 **splinter'd**: joined
with splints [N].    119 the subject of the verb is the whole idea of
117–18, not 'rancour'.    120 **Me seemeth good**: it seems good to
me.    123 emphasize 'little' [N].    127 **estate**: administration
(of the realm) [N].    128 **bears . . . rein**: i.e. controls its own
course.    129 **as please**: as it pleases.    130 **apparent**:
clear, obvious.    133 **compact**: accent on last syllable, as usual
in Sh.

*Rivers.* And so in me; and so, I think, in all:
Yet, since it is but green, it should be put   135
To no apparent likelihood of breach,
Which haply by much company might be urg'd:
Therefore I say with noble Buckingham,
That it is meet so few should fetch the prince.

 *Hastings.* And so say I.        140

 *Gloucester.* Then be it so; and go we to determine
Who they shall be that straight shall post to Ludlow.
Madam, and you my mother, will you go
To give your censures in this business?

    [*Exeunt all except* BUCKINGHAM *and* GLOUCESTER.

 *Buckingham.* My lord, whoever journeys to the prince, 145
For God's sake, let not us two stay at home:
For by the way I'll sort occasion,
As index to the story we late talk'd of,
To part the queen's proud kindred from the prince.

 *Gloucester.* My other self, my counsel's consistory,  150
My oracle, my prophet! My dear cousin,
I, as a child, will go by thy direction.
Towards Ludlow then, for we'll not stay behind.

             [*Exeunt.*

## Scene III. The Same. A Street

*Enter two* Citizens, *meeting.*

 *First Citizen.* Good morrow, neighbour: whither away
so fast?

 *Second Citizen.* I promise you, I scarcely know myself:
Hear you the news abroad?

---

135 **green**: new (cf. 127).   137 i.e. to which a large train of
followers might perhaps be a temptation.  144 **censures**: opinions.
147 **sort occasion**: find opportunity.  148 **index**: prologue [*N*].
150 **consistory**: council-chamber, and so here adviser.  2 **promise**: assure.

*First Citizen.*                    Ay; that the king is dead.

*Second Citizen.* Ill news, by'r lady; seldom comes the
better;

I fear, I fear, 'twill prove a giddy world.                    5

*Enter a third* Citizen.

*Third Citizen.* Neighbours, God speed!

*First Citizen.*                    Give you good morrow, sir.

*Third Citizen.* Doth the news hold of good King Edward's
death?

*Second Citizen.* Ay, sir, it is too true; God help the while!

*Third Citizen.* Then, masters, look to see a troublous
world.

*First Citizen.* No, no; by God's good grace, his son shall
reign.                    10

*Third Citizen.* Woe to that land that's govern'd by
a child!

*Second Citizen.* In him there is a hope of government,

That in his nonage council under him,

And in his full and ripen'd years himself,

No doubt, shall then and till then govern well.                    15

*First Citizen.* So stood the state when Henry the Sixth

Was crown'd at Paris but at nine months old.

*Third Citizen.* Stood the state so? no, no, good friends,
God wot;

For then this land was famously enrich'd

With politic grave counsel; then the king                    20

Had virtuous uncles to protect his Grace.

---

4 **by'r lady:** by our Lady (the Virgin Mary).          **seldom comes
the better:** (an old proverb) things seldom improve.          5 **giddy:**
insecure, dangerous.          6 **Give you:** God give you.          7 **hold:**
hold good.          8 **the while:** the present time [*N*].          13 **nonage:**
minority (not (L. *non*) of age) [*N*].          16 **Henry:** metrically three
syllables [*N*].          19 **famously:** gloriously [*N*].          20 **counsel:**
advice given by (good) councillors.          21 **uncles:** viz. the Dukes
of Bedford and Gloucester (see *Henry VI*).

*First Citizen.* Why, so hath this, both by his father and
    mother.

*Third Citizen.* Better it were they all came by his father,
Or by his father there were none at all;
For emulation, who shall now be nearest,     25
Will touch us all too near, if God prevent not.
O! full of danger is the Duke of Gloucester!
And the queen's sons and brothers haught and proud;
And were they to be rul'd, and not to rule,
This sickly land might solace as before.     30

*First Citizen.* Come, come, we fear the worst; all will be
    well.

*Third Citizen.* When clouds are seen, wise men put on
    their cloaks;
When great leaves fall, then winter is at hand;
When the sun sets, who doth not look for night?
Untimely storms make men expect a dearth.     35
All may be well; but, if God sort it so,
'Tis more than we deserve, or I expect.

*Second Citizen.* Truly, the hearts of men are full of fear:
You cannot reason almost with a man
That looks not heavily and full of dread.     40

*Third Citizen.* Before the days of change, still is it so:
By a divine instinct men's minds mistrust
Ensuing danger; as, by proof, we see
The waters swell before a boisterous storm.
But leave it all to God. Whither away?     45

*Second Citizen.* Marry, we were sent for to the justices.

*Third Citizen.* And so was I: I'll bear you company.

                          *[Exeunt.*

---

26 **touch ... near**: involve us all.     28 **haught**: haughty.
30 **solace**: take comfort.     36 **sort**: ordain, arrange.     39 **cannot reason almost**: can hardly talk with anyone.     41 **still**:
always.     42–43 **mistrust ensuing danger**: fear that danger
is coming.     **proof**: experience.     44 **waters**: of the sea.
46 **Marry**: metrically one syllable, as in III. iv. 56 [*N*].

## *Scene IV.* The Same. A Room in the Palace

*Enter the* ARCHBISHOP OF YORK, *the young* DUKE OF YORK,
QUEEN ELIZABETH, *and the* DUCHESS OF YORK.

*Archbishop.* Last night, I hear, they lay at Northampton;
At Stony-Stratford they do rest to-night:
To-morrow, or next day, they will be here.

*Duchess.* I long with all my heart to see the prince.
I hope he is much grown since last I saw him.                    5

*Queen Elizabeth.* But I hear no; they say my son of York
Hath almost overta'en him in his growth.

*York.* Ay, mother, but I would not have it so.

*Duchess.* Why, my young cousin, it is good to grow.

*York.* Grandam, one night, as we did sit at supper,            10
My uncle Rivers talk'd how I did grow
More than my brother: 'Ay,' quoth my uncle Gloucester
'Small herbs have grace, great weeds do grow apace:'
And since, methinks, I would not grow so fast,
Because sweet flowers are slow and weeds make haste.            15

*Duchess.* Good faith, good faith, the saying did not hold
In him that did object the same to thee:
He was the wretched'st thing when he was young,
So long a-growing, and so leisurely,
That, if his rule were true, he should be gracious.             20

*Archbishop.* And so, no doubt, he is, my gracious madam.

*Duchess.* I hope he is; but yet let mothers doubt.

*York.* Now, by my troth, if I had been remember'd,
I could have given my uncle's grace a flout,
To touch his growth nearer than he touch'd mine.               25

*Duchess.* How, my young York? I prithee, let me hear it.

9 **cousin:** i.e. grandchild (cf. II. i. 64, Commentary).     14 **since:**
since then (adverb, not conjunction).          20 **gracious:** full of
grace, kind and generous.          23 **had been remember'd:** had
remembered (so in *A.Y.L.I.* III. v. 131).          24 **flout:** gibe, sarcasm.
25 **To touch:** so as to touch, that would have reflected on.

*York.* Marry, they say my uncle grew so fast,
That he could gnaw a crust at two hours old:
'Twas full two years ere I could get a tooth.
Grandam, this would have been a biting jest.                30
  *Duchess.* I prithee, pretty York, who told thee this?
  *York.* Grandam, his nurse.
  *Duchess.* His nurse! why, she was dead ere thou wast
    born.
  *York.* If 'twere not she, I cannot tell who told me.
  *Queen Elizabeth.* A parlous boy: go to, you are too
    shrewd.                                                  35
  *Archbishop.* Good madam, be not angry with the child.
  *Queen Elizabeth.* Pitchers have ears.

*Enter a* Messenger.

  *Archbishop.* Here comes a messenger. What news?
  *Messenger.* Such news, my lord, as grieves me to report.
  *Queen Elizabeth.* How doth the prince?
  *Messenger.*                    Well, madam, and in health.40
  *Duchess.* What is thy news?
  *Messenger.* Lord Rivers and Lord Grey are sent to
    Pomfret.
With them Sir Thomas Vaughan, prisoners.
  *Duchess.* Who hath committed them?
  *Messenger.*                             The mighty dukes,
Gloucester and Buckingham.
  *Archbishop.*                    For what offence?         45
  *Messenger.* The sum of all I can I have disclos'd:
Why or for what the nobles were committed
Is all unknown to me, my gracious lord.
  *Queen Elizabeth.* Ah me! I see the ruin of my house!
The tiger now hath seiz'd the gentle hind;                  50

---

27–28 cf. IV. iv. 49.          **35 parlous**: dangerously precocious
(parlous = perilous).    **shrewd**: sharp, mischievous.    **37 Pitchers**:
jugs, i.e. children [*N*].          **46 can**: know (its older meaning).

Insulting tyranny begins to jet
Upon the innocent and aweless throne:
Welcome, destruction, death, and massacre!
I see, as in a map, the end of all.
  *Duchess.* Accursed and unquiet wrangling days,    55
How many of you have mine eyes beheld!
My husband lost his life to get the crown,
And often up and down my sons were toss'd,
For me to joy and weep their gain and loss:
And being seated, and domestic broils    60
Clean over-blown, themselves, the conquerors,
Make war upon themselves; brother to brother,
Blood to blood, self against self: O! preposterous
And frantic outrage, end thy damned spleen;
Or let me die, to look on death no more.    65
  *Queen Elizabeth.* Come, come, my boy; we will to
    sanctuary.
Madam, farewell.
  *Duchess.*       Stay, I will go with you.
  *Queen Elizabeth.* You have no cause.
  *Archbishop.* [*To the* QUEEN.] My gracious lady, go;
And thither bear your treasure and your goods.
For my part, I'll resign unto your Grace    70
The seal I keep: and so betide to me
As well I tender you and all of yours!
Come; I'll conduct you to the sanctuary.     [*Exeunt.*

---

51 **jet**: encroach [*N*].       52 **awcless**: unreverenced.
54 **as in a map**: as if set out clearly in front of me.    55 **unquiet wrangling days**: days of unquiet wrangling.    63 **preposterous**: unnatural [*N*].    64 **spleen**: hatred, malice, out-
breaks of passion (cf. v. iii. 351).    65 **to**: so as to.    66 **to
sanctuary**: take sanctuary [*N*].    71–72 **so betide ... as**: may
it be well with me according as.    **tender**: care for (cf. I. i. 44) [*N*].

# ACT III

## Scene I. The Same. A Street

*The Trumpets sound. Enter the* PRINCE OF WALES,
GLOUCESTER, BUCKINGHAM, CATESBY, CARDINAL
BOURCHIER, *and Others.*

*Buckingham.* Welcome, sweet prince, to London, to
your chamber.
*Gloucester.* Welcome, dear cousin, my thoughts'
sovereign;
The weary way hath made you melancholy.
  *Prince.* No, uncle; but our crosses on the way
Have made it tedious, wearisome, and heavy:     5
I want more uncles here to welcome me.
  *Gloucester.* Sweet prince, the untainted virtue of your
years
Hath not yet div'd into the world's deceit:
No more can you distinguish of a man
Than of his outward show; which, God he knows,     10
Seldom or never jumpeth with the heart.
Those uncles which you want were dangerous;
Your Grace attended to their sugar'd words,
But look'd not on the poison of their hearts:
God keep you from them, and from such false friends!   15
  *Prince.* God keep me from false friends! but they were
none.

---

1 **chamber**: residence [*N*].
object of all my thoughts [*N*].
on me).   6 **want**: miss [*N*].
innocent to know the wickedness of men.   **div'd into**: sounded
the depths of.   9 **distinguish**: discern.   10 **Than ... show**:
what shows on the surface [*N*].   11 **jumpeth with**: agrees
with.   13 **sugar'd**: pleasant, flattering (like 'honeyed').
  2 **my thoughts' sovereign**:
  4 **crosses**: troubles (inflicted
  7–8 i.e. you are too young and

*Gloucester.* My lord, the Mayor of London comes to
greet you.

   *Enter* the Lord Mayor *and his Train.*

*Mayor.* God bless your Grace with health and happy
days!

*Prince.* I thank you, good my lord; and thank you all.
I thought my mother and my brother York   20
Would long ere this have met us on the way:
Fie! what a slug is Hastings, that he comes not
To tell us whether they will come or no.

   *Enter* HASTINGS.

*Buckingham.* And in good time here comes the sweating
 lord.
*Prince.* Welcome, my lord. What, will our mother
 come?   25
*Hastings.* On what occasion, God he knows, not I,
The queen your mother, and your brother York,
Have taken sanctuary: the tender prince
Would fain have come with me to meet your Grace,
But by his mother was perforce withheld.   30
*Buckingham.* Fie! what an indirect and peevish course
Is this of hers! Lord Cardinal, will your Grace
Persuade the queen to send the Duke of York
Unto his princely brother presently?
If she deny, Lord Hastings, go with him,   35
And from her jealous arms pluck him perforce.
*Cardinal.* My Lord of Buckingham, if my weak oratory
Can from his mother win the Duke of York,
Anon expect him here; but if she be obdurate

---

22 **slug**: sluggard.  26 **occasion**: provocation.  30 **perforce**: forcibly.  31 **indirect**: wrong, unjustifiable. **peevish**:
tiresome.  32 **Cardinal**: the Archbishop of Canterbury.
35 **deny**: refuse.  39 **Anon**: at once. **obdurate to**: obstinate
in resisting.

To mild entreaties, God in heaven forbid                    40
We should infringe the holy privilege
Of blessed sanctuary! not for all this land
Would I be guilty of so great a sin.
  *Buckingham.* You are too senseless-obstinate, my lord,
Too ceremonious and traditional:                    45
Weigh it but with the grossness of this age,
You break not sanctuary in seizing him.
The benefit thereof is always granted
To those whose dealings have deserved the place
And those who have the wit to claim the place:                    50
This prince hath neither claim'd it, nor deserv'd it;
And therefore, in mine opinion, cannot have it:
Then, taking him from thence that is not there,
You break no privilege nor charter there.
Oft have I heard of sanctuary men,                    55
But sanctuary children ne'er till now.
  *Cardinal.* My lord, you shall o'er-rule my mind for once.
Come on, Lord Hastings, will you go with me?
  *Hastings.* I go, my lord.                    59
  *Prince.* Good lords, make all the speedy haste you may.
          [*Exeunt* CARDINAL BOURCHIER *and* HASTINGS.
Say, uncle Gloucester, if our brother come,
Where shall we sojourn till our coronation?
  *Gloucester.* Where it seems best unto your royal self.
If I may counsel you, some day or two
Your highness shall repose you at the Tower:                    65
Then where you please, and shall be thought most fit
For your best health and recreation.

---

    **44 senseless-obstinate:** foolishly obstinate [*N*].     **45 cere-
monious and traditional:** standing on (paying attention to) cere-
mony and custom.     **46** i.e. If you consider the matter in the
light of modern freedom in such matters (**grossness:** lack of
scruple).     **50 wit:** understanding.     **66 and** (in the place
which) **shall be thought.**

*Prince.* I do not like the Tower, of any place:
Did Julius Cæsar build that place, my lord?
  *Buckingham.* He did, my gracious lord, begin that
    place, 70
Which, since, succeeding ages have re-edified.
  *Prince.* Is it upon record, or else reported
Successively from age to age, he built it?
  *Buckingham.* Upon record, my gracious lord.
  *Prince.* But say, my lord, it were not register'd, 75
Methinks the truth should live from age to age,
As 'twere retail'd to all posterity,
Even to the general all-ending day.
  *Gloucester.* [*Aside.*] So wise so young, they say, do never
    live long.
  *Prince.* What say you uncle? 80
  *Gloucester.* I say, without characters, fame lives long.
[*Aside.*] Thus, like the formal Vice, Iniquity,
I moralize two meanings in one word.
  *Prince.* That Julius Cæsar was a famous man;
With what his valour did enrich his wit, 85
His wit set down to make his valour live:
Death makes no conquest of this conqueror,
For now he lives in fame, though not in life.
I'll tell you what, my cousin Buckingham,—
  *Buckingham.* What, my gracious lord? 90
  *Prince.* An if I live until I be a man,
I'll win our ancient right in France again,
Or die a soldier, as I liv'd a king.

---

68 **I do ... place:** I like the Tower least of anywhere.    72 **re-córd:** written testimony.    75 **register'd:** recorded.    77 **re-tail'd:** reported (cf. IV. iv. 336).    79 **never:** read as 'ne'er' [*N*].
81 **charácters:** writing.    82 **formal:** well known, traditional [*N*].    83 i.e. play on the words 'live(s) long' (**moralize** = draw out the hidden meaning).    85 **With what:** that with which [*N*].    91 **An if:** (simply) if.

*Gloucester.* [*Aside.*] Short summers lightly have a forward spring.

*Enter* YORK, HASTINGS, *and* CARDINAL BOURCHIER.

*Buckingham.* Now, in good time, here comes the Duke of
York.                                                          95
*Prince.* Richard of York! how fares our loving brother?
*York.* Well, my dread lord; so must I call you now.
*Prince.* Ay, brother, to our grief, as it is yours:
Too late he died that might have kept that title,
Which by his death hath lost much majesty.                   100
*Gloucester.* How fares our cousin, noble Lord of York?
*York.* I thank you, gentle uncle. O, my lord,
You said that idle weeds are fast in growth:
The prince my brother hath outgrown me far.
*Gloucester.* He hath, my lord.
*York.*                         And therefore is he idle?    105
*Gloucester.* O, my fair cousin, I must not say so.
*York.* Then he is more beholding to you than I.
*Gloucester.* He may command me as my sovereign;
But you have power in me as in a kinsman.
*York.* I pray you, uncle, give me this dagger.             110
*Gloucester.* My dagger, little cousin? with all my heart.
*Prince.* A beggar, brother?
*York.* Of my kind uncle, that I know will give;
And, being but a toy, which is no grief to give.
*Gloucester.* A greater gift than that I'll give my cousin. 115
*York.* A greater gift! O, that's the sword to it.
*Gloucester.* Ay, gentle cousin, were it light enough.

94 **lightly**: commonly.     **forward**: early.     97 **dread**:
revered.     99 **late**: lately, recently (so that our grief is strong).
100 **Which**: the title 'King'.     103 **You said**: see II. iv. 13.
**idle**: useless.     107 **beholding**: indebted.     109 **in me**: over
me.     114 **And . . . toy**: especially when I am only begging
something of trifling value [*N*].

*York.* O, then, I see you'll part but with light gifts;
In weightier things you'll say a beggar nay.
  *Gloucester.* It is too weighty for your Grace to wear. 120
  *York.* I weigh it lightly, were it heavier.
  *Gloucester.* What! would you have my weapon, little
    lord?
  *York.* I would, that I might thank you as you call me.
  *Gloucester.* How?
  *York.* Little.                                            125
  *Prince.* My Lord of York will still be cross in talk.
Uncle, your Grace knows how to bear with him.
  *York.* You mean, to bear me, not to bear with me:
Uncle, my brother mocks both you and me.
Because that I am little, like an ape,                            130
He thinks that you should bear me on your shoulders.
  *Buckingham.* With what a sharp-provided wit he reasons!
To mitigate the scorn he gives his uncle,
He prettily and aptly taunts himself:
So cunning and so young is wonderful.                            135
  *Gloucester.* My lord, will 't please you pass along?
Myself and my good cousin Buckingham
Will to your mother, to entreat of her
To meet you at the Tower and welcome you.
  *York.* What! will you go unto the Tower, my lord? 140
  *Prince.* My Lord Protector needs will have it so.
  *York.* I shall not sleep in quiet at the Tower.
  *Gloucester.* Why, what would you fear?
  *York.* Marry, my uncle Clarence' angry ghost:
My grandam told me he was murder'd there.                        145

---

118 **light**: the dagger is (*a*) light to carry and (*b*) of small value.
119 **weightier**: contains the same play.          121 i.e. I should find
it light to carry even if it were heavier than it is [*N*].          126 **will
still be cross**: is always perverse.          132 **sharp-provided**:
ready-sharpened.          133 **scorn**: taunt.          136 **pass along**:
move on (towards the Tower).          138 **Will**: will go.

*Prince.*  I fear no uncles dead.
*Gloucester.*  Nor none that live, I hope.
*Prince.*  An if they live, I hope, I need not fear.
But come, my lord; and, with a heavy heart,
Thinking on them go I unto the Tower.                    150

> [*Sennet.  Exeunt all but* GLOUCESTER, BUCKINGHAM,
> *and* CATESBY.

*Buckingham.*  Think you, my lord, this little prating York
Was not incensed by his subtle mother
To taunt and scorn you thus opprobriously?
*Gloucester.*  No doubt, no doubt: O! 'tis a parlous boy;
Bold, quick, ingenious, forward, capable:                155
He's all the mother's, from the top to toe.
*Buckingham.*  Well, let them rest.  Come hither, Catesby;
thou art sworn
As deeply to effect what we intend
As closely to conceal what we impart.
Thou know'st our reasons urg'd upon the way:             160
What think'st thou?  is it not an easy matter
To make William Lord Hastings of our mind,
For the instalment of this noble duke
In the seat royal of this famous isle?
*Catesby.*  He for his father's sake so loves the prince  165
That he will not be won to aught against him.
*Buckingham.*  What think'st thou then of Stanley?  what
will he?
*Catesby.*  He will do all in all as Hastings doth.

147 **Nor . . . live**: and none that live either.        148 **fear**: (here)
fear for them (cf. I. i. 137) [*N*].                150–1 *s.d. Sennet*: a set of
notes on a trumpet.        152 **incenséd**: fired, i.e. set on.
154 **parlous**: see II. iv. 35.        155 **forward**: precocious (cf. 94
of this scene).        **capable**: intelligent (cf. II. ii. 18).        157
**let them rest**: don't let us worry about them any more [*N*].
159 **closely**: probably with 'conceal' rather than 'sworn'.  163
**this noble duke**: the duke of Gloucester.  164 **seat royal**: throne.

*Buckingham.*  Well then, no more but this: go, gentle
    Catesby,
And, as it were far off, sound thou Lord Hastings,        170
How he doth stand affected to our purpose;
And summon him to-morrow to the Tower,
To sit about the coronation.
If thou dost find him tractable to us,
Encourage him, and tell him all our reasons:             175
If he be leaden, icy-cold, unwilling,
Be thou so too, and so break off the talk,
And give us notice of his inclination;
For we to-morrow hold divided councils,
Wherein thyself shalt highly be employ'd.                180
   *Gloucester.*  Commend me to Lord William: tell him,
    Catesby,
His ancient knot of dangerous adversaries
To-morrow are let blood at Pomfret Castle;
And bid my lord, for joy of this good news,
Give Mistress Shore one gentle kiss the more.            185
   *Buckingham.* Good Catesby, go, effect this business soundly.
   *Catesby.*  My good lords both, with all the heed I can.
   *Gloucester.*  Shall we hear from you, Catesby, ere we sleep?
   *Catesby.*  You shall, my lord.                       189
   *Gloucester.*  At Crosby-place, there shall you find us both.
                              [*Exit* CATESBY.
   *Buckingham.*  Now, my lord, what shall we do if we
    perceive
Lord Hastings will not yield to our complots?

---

170 **far off**: (More's phrase) without committing us.      171 **doth
stand affected**: is disposed.        173 **sit about**: deliberate about.
174 **tractable to us**: amenable to our designs.       179 **divided**:
separate [*N*].         182 **knot**: gang.        183 **are let blood**:
will have their blood shed (euphemism from 'bleeding').       185
**Mistress Shore**: see I. i. 73.   186 **effect**: perform.     190 **Crosby-
place**: see I. ii. 213.          192 **complots**: strong form of 'plots'.

*Gloucester.* Chop off his head; something we will de-
    termine:
And, look, when I am king, claim thou of me
The earldom of Hereford, and all the moveables      195
Whereof the king my brother stood possess'd.
    *Buckingham.* I'll claim that promise at your Grace's
        hand.
    *Gloucester.* And look to have it yielded with all kindness.
Come, let us sup betimes, that afterwards              199
We may digest our complots in some form.      [*Exeunt.*


### Scene II. The Same. Before Lord Hastings' House

#### *Enter a* Messenger.

*Messenger.* [*Knocking.*] My lord! my lord!
*Hastings.* [*Within.*] Who knocks?
*Messenger.* One from the Lord Stanley.
*Hastings.* [*Within.*] What is't o'clock?
*Messenger.* Upon the stroke of four.                    5


#### *Enter* HASTINGS.

*Hastings.* Cannot my Lord Stanley sleep these tedious
    nights?
*Messenger.* So it appears by that I have to say.
First, he commends him to your noble self.
    *Hastings.* What then?
    *Messenger.* Then certifies your lordship, that this night 10
He dreamt the boar had razed off his helm:
Besides, he says there are two councils held;

---

193 **something**: i.e. some charge against him.        196 **stood**:
was (cf. 171) [*N*].              200 **digest**: arrange (with a quibble on
the usual sense).        10 **certifies**: he assures.        11 **the boar**:
Richard, see Commentary I. iii. 228.              **razéd**: pulled off.
**helm**: helmet [*N*].        12 **held**: to be held; see III. i. 179.

And that may be determin'd at the one
Which may make you and him to rue at the other.
Therefore he sends to know your lordship's pleasure,      15
If you will presently take horse with him,
And with all speed post with him toward the north,
To shun the danger that his soul divines.

*Hastings.* Go, fellow, go, return unto thy lord;
Bid him not fear the separated councils:                  20
His honour and myself are at the one,
And at the other is my good friend Catesby;
Where nothing can proceed that toucheth us
Whereof I shall not have intelligence.
Tell him his fears are shallow, wanting instance:         25
And for his dreams, I wonder he's so fond
To trust the mockery of unquiet slumbers.
To fly the boar before the boar pursues,
Were to incense the boar to follow us
And make pursuit where he did mean no chase.              30
Go, bid thy master rise and come to me;
And we will both together to the Tower,
Where, he shall see, the boar will use us kindly.

*Messenger.* I'll go, my lord, and tell him what you say.
                                                   [*Exit.*

*Enter* CATESBY.

*Catesby.* Many good morrows to my noble lord.            35
*Hastings.* Good morrow, Catesby; you are early stirring.
What news, what news, in this our tottering state?
*Catesby.* It is a reeling world, indeed, my lord;
And I believe will never stand upright
Till Richard wear the garland of the realm.               40
*Hastings.* How! wear the garland! dost thou mean the
    crown?

16 **presently**: at once.      18 **divines**: foresees.      21 **His**
**honour**: i.e. Stanley.      25 **wanting instance**: lacking cause.
26 **for**: as for.      26–27 **fond to**: foolish as to.

*Catesby.*  Ay, my good lord.

*Hastings.*  I'll have this crown of mine cut from my
shoulders
Before I'll see the crown so foul misplac'd.
But canst thou guess that he doth aim at it?                45

*Catesby.*  Ay, on my life; and hopes to find you forward
Upon his party for the gain thereof:
And thereupon he sends you this good news,
That this same very day your enemies,
The kindred of the queen, must die at Pomfret.             50

*Hastings.*  Indeed, I am no mourner for that news,
Because they have been still my adversaries;
But that I'll give my voice on Richard's side,
To bar my master's heirs in true descent,
God knows I will not do it, to the death.                  55

*Catesby.*  God keep your lordship in that gracious mind!

*Hastings.*  But I shall laugh at this a twelvemonth hence,
That they which brought me in my master's hate,
I live to look upon their tragedy.
Well, Catesby, ere a fortnight make me older,              60
I'll send some packing that yet think not on 't.

*Catesby.*  'Tis a vile thing to die, my gracious lord,
When men are unprepar'd and look not for it.

*Hastings.*  O monstrous, monstrous!  and so falls it out
With Rivers, Vaughan, Grey; and so 'twill do              65
With some men else, who think themselves as safe
As thou and I; who, as thou know'st, are dear
To princely Richard and to Buckingham.

*Catesby.*  The princes both make high account of you;

43 i.e. I'd rather lose my life than see . . . .        46 **forward:**
eager.      47 **party:** side.      52 **still:** always.      53 **that:** as to the
idea that.    **voice:** vote, support.          54 i.e. so as to exclude the
rightful heirs of Edward IV.      55 **to the death:** even if opposing
it costs me my life (for '*the* death' cf. I. ii. 179).      58–59 i.e. that I
am still alive to look upon the tragedy of those who . . . (the Queen's
relatives).          61 **send . . . packing:** get rid of.

[*Aside.*] For they account his head upon the bridge. 70
   *Hastings.* I know they do, and I have well deserv'd it.

#### *Enter* STANLEY.

Come on, come on; where is your boar-spear, man?
Fear you the boar, and go so unprovided?
   *Stanley.* My lord, good morrow; good morrow, Catesby:
You may jest on, but by the holy rood, 75
I do not like these several councils, I.
   *Hastings.* My lord, I hold my life as dear as you do yours;
And never, in my days, I do protest,
Was it so precious to me as 'tis now.
Think you, but that I know our state secure, 80
I would be so triumphant as I am?
   *Stanley.* The lords at Pomfret, when they rode from London,
Were jocund and suppos'd their state was sure,
And they indeed had no cause to mistrust;
But yet you see how soon the day o'ercast. 85
This sudden stab of rancour I misdoubt;
Pray God, I say, I prove a needless coward!
What, shall we toward the Tower? the day is spent.
   *Hastings.* Come, come, have with you. Wot you what, my lord?
To-day the lords you talk of are beheaded. 90
   *Stanley.* They, for their truth, might better wear their heads,

---

70 **the bridge**: London Bridge (where traitors' heads were hung up *high*).     73 **unprovided**: unprepared.     75 **rood**: cross (cf. 'rood-screen' in churches).     76 **several**: separate.     **I ... I**: the second emphasizes the first.     83 **state**: position. 85 **o'ercast**: became cloudy.     86 **This ... rancour**: i.e. Richard's vengeance on the Queen's party.     **misdoubt**: suspect.     88 **the day is spent**: time is getting on [*N*].     89 **have with you**: let us be going     **Wot you what?**: do you know the news?     91 **for their truth**: as regards their loyalty (to the throne).

Than some that have accus'd them wear their hats.
But come, my lord, let's away.

*Enter a* Pursuivant.

*Hastings.*  Go on before; I'll talk with this good fellow.
[*Exeunt* STANLEY *and* CATESBY.

How now, sirrah! how goes the world with thee?      95
*Pursuivant.*  The better that your lordship please to ask.
*Hastings.*  I tell thee, man, 'tis better with me now
Than when I met thee last where now we meet:
Then was I going prisoner to the Tower,
By the suggestion of the queen's allies;                   100
But now, I tell thee,—keep it to thyself,—
This day those enemies are put to death,
And I in better state than e'er I was.
*Pursuivant.*  God hold it to your honour's good content!
*Hastings.*  Gramercy, fellow: there, drink that for me.  105
[*Throws him his purse.*
*Pursuivant.*  God save your lordship.              [*Exit.*

*Enter a* Priest.

*Priest.*  Well met, my lord; I am glad to see your honour.
*Hastings.*  I thank thee, good Sir John, with all my heart.
I am in your debt for your last exercise;
Come the next Sabbath, and I will content you.      110

*Enter* BUCKINGHAM.

*Buckingham.*  What, talking with a priest, lord chamberlain?
Your friends of Pomfret, they do need the priest:

---

92 **wear their hats:** keep their (high) position, i.e. Richard [*N*].
93–94 *s.d. Pursuivant:* (strictly) the attendant on a herald.      99
see I. i. 66–68.        100 **suggestion:** instigation, plotting.      104
**hold it:** keep it (for you).        105 **Gramercy:** many thanks (Fr.
*grand merci*).        109 **exercise:** sermon [*N*].        110 **content:**
satisfy, i.e. reward.

Your honour hath no shriving work in hand.

*Hastings.* Good faith, and when I met this holy man,
The men you talk of came into my mind.                    115
What, go you toward the Tower?

*Buckingham.* I do, my lord; but long I shall not stay:
I shall return before your lordship thence.

*Hastings.* Nay, like enough, for I stay dinner there.

*Buckingham.* [*Aside.*] And supper too, although thou
   know'st it not.                                        120
Come, will you go?

*Hastings.*                I'll wait upon your lordship. [*Exeunt.*


## Scene III. Pomfret. Before the Castle

*Enter* RATCLIFF, *with halberds, carrying* RIVERS, GREY, *and*
                    VAUGHAN *to death.*

*Rivers.* Sir Richard Ratcliff, let me tell thee this:
To-day shalt thou behold a subject die
For truth, for duty, and for loyalty.

*Grey.* God bless the prince from all the pack of you!
A knot you are of damned blood-suckers.                    5

*Vaughan.* You live that shall cry woe for this hereafter.

*Ratcliff.* Dispatch; the limit of your lives is out.

*Rivers.* O Pomfret, Pomfret! O thou bloody prison!
Fatal and ominous to noble peers!
Within the guilty closure of thy walls                     10
Richard the Second here was hack'd to death;
And, for more slander to thy dismal seat,

---

113 **shriving work:** confessing and getting shriven (absolved).
120 **supper:** i.e. your last meal before your long sleep (death).
3 **truth:** see 91 of previous scene, and cf. 21 of this scene.    4
**bless:** protect.      **pack:** conspiring gang (since 'pack' could mean
'plot' then).      5 **knot:** see III. i. 182.      **blood-suckers:** blood-
thirsty men.      7 **Dispatch:** prepare for death.      **limit:** term,
assigned period.      10 **closure:** enclosure.      12 **slander:**
scandal, disgrace.      **seat:** site.

We give thee up our guiltless blood to drink.

*Grey.* Now Margaret's curse is fall'n upon our heads,
When she exclaim'd on Hastings, you, and I,                    15
For standing by when Richard stabb'd her son.

*Rivers.* Then curs'd she Richard, then curs'd she Buck-
 ingham,
Then curs'd she Hastings: O! remember, God,
To hear her prayer for them, as now for us;
And for my sister and her princely sons,                       20
Be satisfied, dear God, with our true blood,
Which, as thou know'st, unjustly must be spilt.

*Ratcliff.* Make haste; the hour of death is expiate.

*Rivers.* Come, Grey, come, Vaughan; let us here embrace:
And take our leave until we meet in heaven.     [*Exeunt.*


## Scene IV. LONDON. THE TOWER

BUCKINGHAM, STANLEY, HASTINGS, *the* BISHOP OF ELY,
RATCLIFF, LOVEL, *and Others, sitting at a table.* Officers
of the Council *attending.*

*Hastings.* My lords, at once: the cause why we are met
Is to determine of the coronation:
In God's name, speak, when is the royal day?

*Buckingham.* Are all things ready for that royal time?

*Stanley.* It is; and wants but nomination.                   5

*Ely.* To-morrow then I judge a happy day.

*Buckingham.* Who knows the Lord Protector's mind
 herein?
Who is most inward with the noble duke?

---

14 **Margaret's curse**: see I. iii. 111–303.  15 **I**: loose grammar
for 'me'.  19 **for them**: with regard to, i.e. against.  20 **my
sister**: Queen Elizabeth.  23 **expiate(d)**: terminated, fully
arrived [N].  1 **at once**: let us get to business.  2 **determine of**: decide about.  **the coronation**: of Edward V.
5 **nomination**: naming (of the day) [N].  8 **inward**: intimate.

*Ely.*  Your Grace, we think, should soonest know his mind.

*Buckingham.*  We know each other's faces; for our hearts,
He knows no more of mine that I of yours;                    11
Nor I of his, my lord, than you of mine.
Lord Hastings, you and he are near in love.

*Hastings.*  I thank his Grace, I know he loves me well;
But, for his purpose in the coronation,                    15
I have not sounded him, nor he deliver'd
His gracious pleasure any way therein:
But you, my noble lords, may name the time;
And in the duke's behalf I'll give my voice,
Which, I presume, he'll take in gentle part.                    20


*Enter* GLOUCESTER.

*Ely.*  In happy time, here comes the duke himself.

*Gloucester.*  My noble lords and cousins all, good morrow.
I have been long a sleeper; but, I trust,
My absence doth neglect no great design,
Which by my presence might have been concluded.                    25

*Buckingham.*  Had you not come upon your cue, my lord,
William Lord Hastings had pronounc'd your part,
I mean, your voice, for crowning of the king.

*Gloucester.*  Than my Lord Hastings no man might be
    bolder:
His lordship knows me well, and loves me well.                    30
My Lord of Ely, when I was last in Holborn,
I saw good strawberries in your garden there;
I do beseech you send for some of them.

*Ely.*  Marry, and will, my lord, with all my heart.    [*Exit.*

*Gloucester.*  Cousin of Buckingham, a word with you.    35
                              [*Takes him aside.*

---

10 **for**: as for [*N*].       16 **deliver'd**: signified.       24 **neglect**:
cause to be neglected.       26 **upon your cue**: just at the right
moment [*N*].       28 **voice**: vote (cf. III. ii. 53).       34 **Marry,
and will**: I certainly will.

Catesby hath sounded Hastings in our business,
And finds the testy gentleman so hot,
That he will lose his head ere give consent
His master's child, as worshipfully he terms it,
Shall lose the royalty of England's throne.      40
    *Buckingham.* Withdraw yourself a while; I'll go with
      you.            [*Exeunt* GLOUCESTER *and* BUCKINGHAM.
    *Stanley.* We have not yet set down this day of triumph.
To-morrow, in my judgment, is too sudden;
For I myself am not so well provided
As else I would be, were the day prolong'd.      45

           *Re-enter* BISHOP OF ELY.

    *Ely.* Where is my lord, the Duke of Gloucester?
I have sent for these strawberries.
    *Hastings.* His Grace looks cheerfully and smooth this
      morning:
There's some conceit or other likes him well,
When that he bids good morrow with such spirit.      50
I think there's never a man in Christendom
Can lesser hide his hate or love than he;
For by his face straight shall you know his heart.
    *Stanley.* What of his heart perceiv'd you in his face
By any livelihood he show'd to-day?      55
    *Hastings.* Marry, that with no man here he is offended;
For, were he, he had shown it in his looks.

       *Re-enter* GLOUCESTER *and* BUCKINGHAM.

    *Gloucester.* I pray you all, tell me what they deserve
That do conspire my death with devilish plots

37 **testy**: irritable. reverentially.
44 **provided**: prepared. use, e.g. Ezekiel xii. 22). Commentary on I. i. 22. **well**: takes his fancy. of 'lively') [*N*].

39 **worshipfully**: paying him all honour,
42 **triumph**: pomp, public rejoicing.
45 **prolong'd**: postponed (a Biblical
48 **cheerfully and smooth**: see
49 **conceit**: thought.      **likes him**
55 **livelihood**: animation (cf. our use

Of damned witchcraft, and that have prevail'd          60
Upon my body with their hellish charms?
*Hastings.* The tender love I bear your Grace, my lord,
Makes me most forward in this princely presence
To doom th' offenders, whosoe'er they be:
I say, my lord, they have deserved death.              65
*Gloucester.* Then be your eyes the witness of their evil.
Look how I am bewitch'd; behold mine arm
Is like a blasted sapling, wither'd up:
And this is Edward's wife, that monstrous witch
Consorted with that harlot strumpet Shore,             70
That by their witchcraft thus have marked me.
*Hastings.* If they have done this thing, my noble lord,—
*Gloucester.* If! thou protector of this damned strumpet,
Talk'st thou to me of ifs? Thou art a traitor:
Off with his head! now, by Saint Paul, I swear,        75
I will not dine until I see the same.
Lovel and Ratcliff, look that it be done:
The rest, that love me, rise, and follow me.
               [*Exeunt all but* HASTINGS, RATCLIFF, *and* LOVEL.
*Hastings.* Woe, woe, for England! not a whit for me;
For I, too fond, might have prevented this.             80
Stanley did dream the boar did raze his helm;
And I did scorn it, and disdain'd to fly.
Three times to-day my foot-cloth horse did stumble,
And startled when he looked upon the Tower,
As loath to bear me to the slaughter-house.            85
O! now I need the priest that spake to me:
I now repent I told the pursuivant,
As too triumphing, how mine enemies

63 **this princely presence**: the presence of these princes (Richard
and Buckingham).        70 **Consorted with**: in league with.        79
**not ... me**: I am not pitying myself.        80 **fond**: foolish.    **prevented**: anticipated (in both senses of the word).        81 see III. ii. 11.
83 **foot-cloth**: i.e. normally quiet [*N*].        87 see III. ii. 97, &c.
88 **too**: too much.

To-day at Pomfret bloodily were butcher'd
And I myself secure in grace and favour.                    90
O Margaret, Margaret! now thy heavy curse
Is lighted on poor Hastings' wretched head.
 *Ratcliff.* Come, come, dispatch; the duke would be at
  dinner:
Make a short shrift, he longs to see your head.
 *Hastings.* O momentary grace of mortal man,     95
Which we more hunt for than the grace of God!
Who builds his hope in air of your good looks,
Lives like a drunken sailor on a mast;
Ready with every nod to tumble down
Into the fatal bowels of the deep.                         100
 *Lovel.* Come, come, dispatch; 'tis bootless to exclaim.
 *Hastings.* O bloody Richard! miserable England!
I prophesy the fearfull'st time to thee
That ever wretched age hath look'd upon.
Come, lead me to the block; bear him my head:     105
They smile at me who shortly shall be dead.     [*Exeunt.*

## Scene V. LONDON. THE TOWER WALLS

*Enter* GLOUCESTER *and* BUCKINGHAM, *in rotten armour,*
  *marvellous ill-favoured.*

 *Gloucester.* Come, cousin, canst thou quake, and change
  thy colour,
Murder thy breath in middle of a word,
And then again begin, and stop again,
As if thou wert distraught and mad with terror?     4

---

91–92 see I. iii. 211–14.   **93 dispatch:** cf. I. iii. 355.
**94 shrift:** shriving, confession (and absolution) [N].  **95 momentary grace:** short-lived favour.  **97 in air:** in the air, i.e. on the aery foundation.  **your:** men's.  **106 who:** the antecedent is 'they', not 'who'. Buckingham was one such.  *s.d. rotten:* rusty.  **2 murder:** cut short.  **4 distraught:** distracted.

*Buckingham.* Tut! I can counterfeit the deep tragedian,
Speak and look back, and pry on every side,
Tremble and start at wagging of a straw,
Intending deep suspicion: ghastly looks
Are at my service, like enforced smiles;
And both are ready in their offices,                          10
At any time, to grace my stratagems.
But what! is Catesby gone?
  *Gloucester.* He is; and, see, he brings the mayor along.

     *Enter the* Lord Mayor, *and* CATESBY.
*Buckingham.* Lord Mayor,—
*Gloucester.* Look to the drawbridge there!
*Buckingham.*                              Hark! a drum.     15
*Gloucester.* Catesby, o'erlook the walls.
*Buckingham.* Lord Mayor, the reason we have sent,—
*Gloucester.* Look back, defend thee; here are enemies.
*Buckingham.* God and our innocency defend and guard
  us!

    *Enter* LOVEL *and* RATCLIFF, *with* HASTINGS' *head.*
*Gloucester.* Be patient, they are friends, Ratcliff and
  Lovel.                                                       20
  *Lovel.* Here is the head of that ignoble traitor,
The dangerous and unsuspected Hastings.
  *Gloucester.* So dear I lov'd the man, that I must weep.
I took him for the plainest harmless creature
That breath'd upon the earth a Christian;                     25
Made him my book, wherein my soul recorded
The history of all her secret thoughts:

5 **counterfeit**: imitate.        **deep**: skilled, profound in his art [*N*].
7 **wagging**: moving (the phrase was proverbial).        8 **Intending**: pretending or (merely) signifying.        9 **enforced**: artificial,
put on.        10 **offices**: appointed function.        16 **o'erlook**:
look to, inspect.        24 **plainest harmless**: most sincere and
harmless [*N*].        26 **Made . . . book**: trusted him completely
('book' = notebook).

So smooth he daub'd his vice with show of virtue,
That, his apparent open guilt omitted,
I mean his conversation with Shore's wife,                    30
He liv'd from all attainder of suspect.

    *Buckingham.* Well, well, he was the covert'st shelter'd traitor
That ever liv'd.
Would you imagine, or almost believe,—
Were 't not that by great preservation                    35
We live to tell it,—that the subtle traitor
This day had plotted, in the council-house,
To murder me and my good Lord of Gloucester?

    *Mayor.*  Had he done so?                    39

    *Gloucester.*  What! think you we are Turks or infidels?
Or that we would, against the form of law,
Proceed thus rashly in the villain's death,
But that the extreme peril of the case,
The peace of England and our person's safety,
Enforc'd us to this execution?                    45

    *Mayor.*  Now, fair befall you! he deserv'd his death;
And your good Graces both have well proceeded,
To warn false traitors from the like attempts.
I never look'd for better at his hands,
After he once fell in with Mistress Shore.                    50

    *Buckingham.*  Yet had we not determin'd he should die,
Until your lordship came to see his end;
Which now the loving haste of these our friends,
Something against our meaning, hath prevented:
Because, my lord, we would have had you hear                    55

    28 **daub'd:** covered over.    29 **apparent:** manifest.
30 **conversation:** familiarity (cf. III. i. 185).    31 **from ... suspect:**
free from all taint of suspicion.    32 **covert'st:** most secret.
**shelter'd:** hidden.    34 **almost:** even, indeed.    35 **pre-**
**servation:** the mercy of God in saving our lives.    40 **infidels:**
unbelievers, heathens [*N*].    42 **rashly:** hastily, i.e. without
waiting for due legal process.    53 **Which:** i.e. his end.    54
**prevented:** anticipated, caused prematurely [*N*].

The traitor speak, and timorously confess
The manner and the purpose of his treason;
That you might well have signified the same
Unto the citizens, who haply may
Misconster us in him, and wail his death.                    60
  *Mayor.* But, my good lord, your Grace's word shall serve,
As well as I had seen and heard him speak:
And do not doubt, right noble princes both,
But I'll acquaint our duteous citizens
With all your just proceedings in this cause.                65
  *Gloucester.* And to that end we wish'd your lordship here,
To avoid the censures of the carping world.
  *Buckingham.* But since you come too late of our intent,
Yet witness what you hear we did intend:
And so, my good Lord Mayor, we bid farewell.                 70
                          [*Exit* Lord Mayor.
  *Gloucester.* Go, after, after, cousin Buckingham.
The mayor towards Guildhall hies him in all post:
There, at your meetest vantage of the time,
Infer the bastardy of Edward's children:
Tell them how Edward put to death a citizen,                 75
Only for saying he would make his son
Heir to the crown; meaning indeed his house.
Which by the sign thereof was termed so.
Moreover, urge his hateful luxury
And bestial appetite in change of lust;                      80
Which stretch'd unto their servants, daughters, wives,

60 **Misconster . . . him**: misconstrue, misunderstand our treatment of him ('in him' = in his case).        62 **as I**: as if I.        65
**cause**: case.        68 **of our intent**: for our purpose.        69 **witness**: bear witness to.        72 **post**: speed (cf. I. i. 145).        73 **at
your . . . time**: taking advantage of any opportunity.        74
**Infer**: suggest, bring up, see III. vii. 5, &c.        **bastardy**: illegitimacy
[*N*].        78 **sign**: i.e. like an inn-sign today ('The Crown').
79 **luxury**: licence, lechery.        80 **change of lust**: changing the
object of his desires.

Even where his raging eye or savage heart
Without control lusted to make a prey.
Nay, for a need, thus far come near my person:
Tell them, when that my mother went with child          85
Of that insatiate Edward, noble York
My princely father then had wars in France;
And, by true computation of the time,
Found that the issue was not his begot;
Which well appeared in his lineaments,                  90
Being nothing like the noble duke my father.
Yet touch this sparingly, as 'twere far off;
Because, my lord, you know my mother lives.
  *Buckingham.* Doubt not, my lord, I'll play the orator
As if the golden fee for which I plead                   95
Were for myself: and so, my lord, adieu.
  *Gloucester.* If you thrive well, bring them to Baynard's
    Castle;
Where you shall find me well accompanied
With reverend fathers and well-learned bishops.         99
  *Buckingham.* I go; and towards three or four o'clock
Look for the news that the Guildhall affords.        [*Exit.*
  *Gloucester.* Go, Lovel, with all speed to Doctor Shaw;
[*To* CATESBY.] Go thou to Friar Penker; bid them both
Meet me within this hour at Baynard's Castle.

                [*Exeunt* LOVEL *and* CATESBY.
Now will I in, to take some privy order,                105
To draw the brats of Clarence out of sight;
And to give notice that no manner person
Have any time recourse unto the princes.            [*Exit.*

---

   84 **for a need**: if necessary.       **come ... person**: bring me in
personally.     86 **insatiate**: insatiable.     89 **his begot**:
begotten by him.    91 **Being ... like**: since he did not resemble.
95 **the golden fee**: i.e. the crown.     98 **accompanied with**:
attended by.    101 **news**: (scans as two syllables).    102 **Doctor**: i.e. of divinity [*N*].       105 **take ... order**: make private
arrangements.     107 **manner person**: manner of person.

## Scene VI. The Same. A Street

*Enter a* Scrivener.

*Scrivener.* Here is the indictment of the good Lord
  Hastings;
Which in a set hand fairly is engross'd,
That it may be to-day read o'er in Paul's:
And mark how well the sequel hangs together.
Eleven hours I have spent to write it over,     5
For yesternight by Catesby was it sent me.
The precedent was full as long a-doing;
And yet within these five hours Hastings liv'd,
Untainted, unexamin'd, free, at liberty.
Here's a good world the while! Who is so gross     10
That cannot see this palpable device?
Yet who so bold but says he sees it not?
Bad is the world; and all will come to naught,
When such ill dealing must be seen in thought.     [*Exit.*

## Scene VII. The Same. The Court of Baynard's Castle

*Enter* Gloucester *and* Buckingham, *meeting.*

*Gloucester.* How now, how now! what say the citizens?
*Buckingham.* Now, by the holy mother of our Lord,

1 *Scrivener*: a scribe or writer of legal documents.     2 **set hand:**
the proper style of writing.     **engross'd:** written out large (gross),
i.e. in legal form.     3 **Paul's:** St. Paul's cathedral [*N*].     4 **the
sequel:** what follows.     7 **precedent:** the rough copy, original.
9 **Untainted:** without a stain upon his character (cf. III. v. 31).
**unexamin'd:** i.e. legally.     10 **Here's ... the while!:** it's
a fine world we are now living in! (sarcastic).     **gross:** stupid,
fat-witted [*N*].     11 **palpable device:** obvious piece of trickery.
12 **but says:** as not to say (i.e. pretend).     14 **in thought:** (only)
and not even protested at.     1 **How now:** well! (exclamation of
impatience).

The citizens are mum, say not a word.

    *Gloucester*. Touch'd you the bastardy of Edward's
    children?

    *Buckingham*. I did; with his contract with Lady Lucy,   5
And his contract by deputy in France;
The insatiate greediness of his desires,
And his enforcement of the city wives;
His tyranny for trifles; his own bastardy,
As being got, your father then in France,           10
And his resemblance, being not like the duke:
Withal I did infer your lineaments,
Being the right idea of your father,
Both in your form and nobleness of mind;
Laid open all your victories in Scotland,         15
Your discipline in war, wisdom in peace,
Your bounty, virtue, fair humility;
Indeed, left nothing fitting for your purpose
Untouch'd or slightly handled in discourse;
And when my oratory drew toward end,         20
I bade them that did love their country's good
Cry 'God save Richard, England's royal king!'

    *Gloucester*. And did they so?

    *Buckingham*. No, so God help me, they spake not a
    word;

But, like dumb statuas or breathing stones,     25

**3 mum:** silent (usually an interjection).     **5 contráct:** see III.
v. 74.     **8 enforcement:** violation, ravishing.     **9 tyranny for
trifles:** making a lot of a little (i.e. increasing fines).     **10 got:**
begotten.     **your father then:** when your father was.     **11 And
. . . duke:** I also touched on the fact that he was not like the Duke
(of York) (loose syntax, cf. III. v. 91).     **12 Withal:** and at the
same time.     **infer:** bring forward.     **13 Being:** you being (as
'he' could be supplied in 11).     **right idea:** very image.     **16
discipline:** experience.     **17 humility:** (perhaps) humanity;
cf. II. i. 73.     **18 fitting . . . purpose:** that would promote your
interests.     **25 statuas:** statues.     **breathing:** i.e. endowed
with life but not speech.

Star'd each on other, and look'd deadly pale.
Which when I saw, I reprehended them;
And ask'd the mayor what meant this wilful silence:
His answer was, the people were not wont
To be spoke to but by the recorder.                      30
Then he was urg'd to tell my tale again:
'Thus saith the duke, thus hath the duke inferr'd;'
But nothing spoke in warrant from himself.
When he had done, some followers of mine own,
At lower end of the hall, hurl'd up their caps,          35
And some ten voices cried, 'God save King Richard!'
And thus I took the vantage of those few,
'Thanks, gentle citizens and friends,' quoth I;
'This general applause and cheerful shout
Argues your wisdom and your love to Richard:'            40
And even here brake off, and came away.
    *Gloucester.* What tongueless blocks were they! would
        they not speak?
Will not the mayor then and his brethren come?
    *Buckingham.* The mayor is here at hand. Intend some
        fear;
Be not you spoke with but by mighty suit:                45
And look you get a prayer-book in your hand,
And stand between two churchmen, good my lord:
For on that ground I'll make a holy descant:
And be not easily won to our requests;
Play the maid's part, still answer nay, and take it.     50
    *Gloucester.* I go; and if you plead as well for them

30 **récordér**: originally an official appointed by a mayor and aldermen to record their decisions.    33 **in warrant . . . himself**: on his own responsibility.    37 **vantage of**: opportunity furnished by.    40 **Argues**: proves.    44 **Intend**: pretend (as III. v. 8).    45 **mighty suit**: strong entreaty.    47 **churchmen**: clergymen.    48 i.e. I'll elaborate on, make the most of that point (for 'descant' see I. i. 27).    50 **take it**: accept a proposal [*N*].

As I can say nay to thee for myself,
No doubt we bring it to a happy issue.
   *Buckingham.*  Go, go, up to the leads!  the Lord Mayor
    knocks.                              [*Exit* GLOUCESTER.

   *Enter the* Lord Mayor, Aldermen, *and* Citizens.
Welcome, my lord: I dance attendance here;             55
I think the duke will not be spoke withal.

      *Enter, from the Castle*, CATESBY.
Now, Catesby! what says your lord to my request?
   *Catesby.*  He doth entreat your Grace, my noble lord,
To visit him to-morrow or next day.
He is within, with two right reverend fathers,          60
Divinely bent to meditation;
And in no wordly suit would he be mov'd,
To draw him from his holy exercise.
   *Buckingham.*  Return, good Catesby, to the gracious duke:
Tell him, myself, the mayor and aldermen,               65
In deep designs in matter of great moment,
No less importing than our general good,
Are come to have some conference with his Grace.
   *Catesby.*  I'll signify so much unto him straight.    [*Exit.*
   *Buckingham.*  Ah, ha, my lord, this prince is not an
    Edward!                                              70
He is not lolling on a lewd day-bed,
But on his knees at meditation;
Not dallying with a brace of courtezans,
But meditating with two deep divines;

   52 **say nay:** (pretend to) refuse.    **thee:** Buckingham as spokes-
man for the citizens.         53 **we bring:** we'll bring (as Q reads).
54 **leads !:** (flat) roof (covered with lead).       55 **dance attendance:**
await admission (*now* proverbial).         56 **withal:** with.     61 **Divinely:** devoutly.        62 **suit:** request.      **mov'd:** approached, applied to.
66 **deep:** important.               67 **No less importing:** concerned with
nothing less.        71 **day-bed:** couch (the epithet is explained by F's
'love-bed').

Not sleeping, to engross his idle body,                    75
But praying, to enrich his watchful soul.
Happy were England, would this virtuous prince
Take on his Grace the sovereignty thereof:
But sore I fear, we shall not win him to it.              79
  *Mayor.* Marry, God defend his Grace should say us nay!
  *Buckingham.* I fear he will. Here Catesby comes again.

          *Re-enter* CATESBY.

Now, Catesby, what says his Grace?
  *Catesby.* He wonders to what end you have assembled
Such troops of citizens to come to him,
His Grace not being warn'd thereof before:                85
My lord, he fears you mean no good to him.
  *Buckingham.* Sorry I am my noble cousin should
Suspect me that I mean no good to him.
By heaven, we come to him in perfect love;
And so once more return, and tell his Grace.              90
                              [*Exit* CATESBY.

When holy and devout religious men
Are at their beads, 'tis much to draw them thence;
So sweat is zealous contemplation.

*Enter* GLOUCESTER, *in a gallery above, between two Bishops.*
          CATESBY *returns.*

  *Mayor.* See, where his Grace stands 'tween two clergy-
    men!
  *Buckingham.* Two props of virtue for a Christian
    prince,                                                95
To stay him from the fall of vanity;
And, see, a book of prayer in his hand;

75 **engross**: fatten.        76 **watchful**: wakeful.        79 **win**:
his consent.        80 **defend**: forbid [*N*].        92 **beads**: prayers.
**much**: a serious matter.        93 **zealous**: fervent, whole-hearted.
**contemplation**: religious meditation.        96 **stay**: hold up.
**the fall of vanity**: the fall that awaits vanity (cf. 'pride goes before
a fall').

True ornament to know a holy man.
Famous Plantagenet, most gracious prince,
Lend favourable ear to our requests,                    100
And pardon us the interruption
Of thy devotion and right Christian zeal.

  *Gloucester.*  My lord, there needs no such apology;
I do beseech your Grace to pardon me,
Who, earnest in the service of my God,                    105
Deferr'd the visitation of my friends.
But, leaving this, what is your Grace's pleasure?

  *Buckingham.*  Even that, I hope, which pleaseth God
    above,
And all good men of this ungovern'd isle.

  *Gloucester.*  I do suspect I have done some offence    110
That seems disgracious in the city's eye;
And that you come to reprehend my ignorance.

  *Buckingham.*  You have, my lord: would it might please
    your Grace,
On our entreaties to amend your fault!

  *Gloucester.*  Else wherefore breathe I in a Christian
    land?                                                115

  *Buckingham.*  Know then, it is your fault that you resign
The supreme seat, the throne majestical,
The sceptred office of your ancestors,
Your state of fortune and your due of birth,
The lineal glory of your royal house,                    120
To the corruption of a blemish'd stock;
Whiles, in the mildness of your sleepy thoughts,—
Which here we waken to our country's good,—
This noble isle doth want her proper limbs;

---

  98 **to know**: by which to know.        106 **Deferr'd**: put off;
see 58–59.              107 **leaving this**: to say no more about that.
109 **ungovern'd**: left without a ruler.        111 **disgracious**:
ungracious.        119 **state of fortune**: the position to which fortune
has called you.

Her face defac'd with scars of infamy,                125
Her royal stock graft with ignoble plants,
And almost shoulder'd in the swallowing gulf
Of dark forgetfulness and deep oblivion.
Which to recure we heartily solicit
Your gracious self to take on you the charge                130
And kingly government of this your land;
Not as protector, steward, substitute,
Or lowly factor for another's gain;
But as successively from blood to blood,
Your right of birth, your empery, your own.                135
For this, consorted with the citizens,
Your very worshipful and loving friends,
And by their vehement instigation,
In this just cause come I to move your Grace.
*Gloucester.* I cannot tell if to depart in silence,                140
Or bitterly to speak in your reproof,
Best fitteth my degree or your condition:
If not to answer, you might haply think
Tongue-tied ambition, not replying, yielded
To bear the golden yoke of sovereignty,                145
Which fondly you would here impose on me;
If to reprove you for this suit of yours,
So season'd with your faithful love to me,
Then, on the other side, I check'd my friends.
Therefore, to speak, and to avoid the first,                150
And then, in speaking, not to incur the last,

---

126 **graft**: grafted (but 'graft' is the true p.p. of the original verb 'graft').        127 **shoulder'd in**: jostled into.        129 **recure**: cure, heal again.        133 **factor**: agent.        134 **successively**: in due order of succession.        135 **empery**: empire [*N*].        137 **worshipful**: honouring you (cf. III. iv. 39).        143 **If not to answer**: sc. best suited the occasion.        144 **yielded**: consented [*N*].        146 **fondly**: foolishly.        147 **If**: i.e. if it seemed more appropriate.        148 **season'd with**: recommended by.        149 **check'd**: should be checking.

Definitively thus I answer you.
Your love deserves my thanks; but my desert
Unmeritable shuns your high request.
First, if all obstacles were cut away,                              155
And that my path were even to the crown,
As the ripe revenue and due of birth,
Yet so much is my poverty of spirit,
So mighty and so many my defects,
That I would rather hide me from my greatness,    160
Being a bark to brook no mighty sea,
Than in my greatness covet to be hid,
And in the vapour of my glory smother'd.
But, God be thank'd, there is no need of me;
And much I need to help you, were there need;    165
The royal tree hath left us royal fruit,
Which, mellow'd by the stealing hours of time,
Will well become the seat of majesty,
And make, no doubt, us happy by his reign.
On him I lay that you would lay on me,              170
The right and fortune of his happy stars;
Which God defend that I should wring from him!
   *Buckingham.* My lord, this argues conscience in your
    Grace;
But the respects thereof are nice and trivial,
All circumstances well considered.                   175
You say that Edward is your brother's son:
So say we too, but not by Edward's wife;

---

154 **unmeritable**: undeserving.    156 **that**: if.    **even**:
smooth, easy.    157 **ripe revenue**: possession ready to be en-
joyed.    158 **much**: great [*N*].    161 i.e. like a ship unfit for
the high seas.    165 i.e. I am very deficient in the qualities I
should need to help you.    167 **stealing**: passing almost un-
observed (see v. iii. 86).    170 **that**: that which.    172 **defend**:
forbid.    173 **argues**: proves.    174 **respects thereof**: considerations which trouble your conscience.    **nice**: over scrupulous.

For first was he contract to Lady Lucy,
Your mother lives a witness to his vow,
And afterward by substitute betroth'd                    180
To Bona, sister to the King of France.
These both put by, a poor petitioner,
A care-craz'd mother to a many sons,
A beauty-waning and distressed widow,
Even in the afternoon of her best days,                  185
Made prize and purchase of his wanton eye,
Seduc'd the pitch and height of his degree
To base declension and loath'd bigamy:
By her, in his unlawful bed, he got
This Edward, whom our manners call the prince.           190
More bitterly could I expostulate,
Save that, for reverence to some alive,
I give a sparing limit to my tongue.
Then, good my lord, take to your royal self
This proffer'd benefit of dignity;                       195
If not to bless us and the land withal,
Yet to draw forth your noble ancestry
From the corruption of abusing times,
Unto a lineal true-derived course.

178 **contract**: contracted, engaged.    180 **substitute**: proxy,
deputy.         181 **sister**: in-law.    182 **These . . . by**: if we
ignore both these (near-marriages) [N].         183 **care-craz'd**:
broken, exhausted (by rearing children).    **a many**: cf. 'a few'.
186 **purchase**: booty.    **wanton**: cf. III. vii. 7.         187–8 i.e.
induced a proud king to marry a humble widow (**pitch** is the
highest point of a falcon's flight).    **declension**: debasement.
**loath'd**: loathsome [N].         190 **our manners call**: we call out
of politeness (and not by his right).         191 **expostulate**: discourse.    192 see III. v. 85–93.    193 **give . . . limit to**:
check.    195 **benefit of dignity**: the due bestowal of this high
honour.    196 **withal**: with it.    197 **draw forth**: rescue.
198 **abusing times**: times that have brought disgrace on your
house (in Edward's marriage).         199 i.e. to a position which is
rightfully yours by descent.

*Mayor.* Do, good my lord; your citizens entreat you.    200
*Buckingham.* Refuse not, mighty lord, this proffer'd love.
*Catesby.* O! make them joyful: grant their lawful suit:
*Gloucester.* Alas! why would you heap those cares on me?
I am unfit for state and majesty:
I do beseech you, take it not amiss,      205
I cannot nor I will not yield to you.
  *Buckingham.* If you refuse it, as, in love and zeal,
Loath to depose the child, your brother's son;
As well we know your tenderness of heart
And gentle, kind, effeminate remorse,      210
Which we have noted in you to your kindred,
And egally, indeed, to all estates,
Yet whether you accept our suit or no,
Your brother's son shall never reign our king;
But we will plant some other in the throne,      215
To the disgrace and downfall of your house:
And in this resolution here we leave you.
Come, citizens, we will entreat no more.
                   [*Exit* BUCKINGHAM *and* Citizens.
  *Catesby.* Call them again, sweet prince; accept their suit:
If you deny them, all the land will rue it.      220
  *Gloucester.* Will you enforce me to a world of cares?
Call them again: I am not made of stone,
But penetrable to your kind entreats,     [*Exit* CATESBY.
Albeit against my conscience and my soul.

          *Re-enter* BUCKINGHAM *and the rest.*
Cousin of Buckingham, and sage, grave men,      225
Since you will buckle fortune on my back,

---

    206 **nor . . . not:** (emphatic) No, and I will not.      209 **As
. . . we:** as we might expect, since.     210 **effeminate remorse:**
womanly pity.     212 **egally:** equally.    **estates:** of the realm,
classes.     221 **enforce me to:** compel me to undertake.     223
**penetrable to:** able to be pierced by.

To bear her burden, whe'r I will or no,
I must have patience to endure the load:
But if black scandal or foul-fac'd reproach
Attend the sequel of your imposition,                230
Your mere enforcement shall acquittance me
From all the impure blots and stains thereof;
For God doth know, and you may partly see,
How far I am from the desire of this.                234
  *Mayor.* God bless your Grace! we see it, and will say it.
  *Gloucester.* In saying so, you shall but say the truth.
  *Buckingham.* Then I salute you with this royal title:
Long live King Richard, England's worthy king!
  *All.* Amen.
  *Buckingham.* To-morrow may it please you to be
    crown'd?                                          240
  *Gloucester.* Even when you please, for you will have it so.
  *Buckingham.* To-morrow then we will attend your Grace:
And so most joyfully we take our leave.
  *Gloucester.* [*To the* BISHOPS.] Come, let us to our holy
    work again.                                       244
Farewell, my cousin;—farewell, gentle friends.    [*Exeunt.*

227 **whe'r**: whether.        230 **your imposition**: what you impose on me.        231 **Your mere enforcement**: the mere fact
that you have forced it on me.    **acquittance**: acquit.    232 **thereof**: in taking the crown.

# ACT IV

## *Scene I.* LONDON. BEFORE THE TOWER

*Enter on one side,* QUEEN ELIZABETH, DUCHESS OF YORK, *and* MARQUESS OF DORSET; *on the other,* ANNE, DUCHESS OF GLOUCESTER, *leading* LADY MARGARET PLANTAGENET, CLARENCE'S *young daughter.*

*Duchess.* Who meets us here? my niece Plantagenet,
Led in the hand of her kind aunt of Gloucester?
Now, for my life, she's wandering to the Tower,
On pure heart's love, to greet the tender princes.
Daughter, well met.

*Anne.*            God give your Graces both     5
A happy and a joyful time of day!

*Queen Elizabeth.* As much to you, good sister! whither
     away?

*Anne.* No farther than the Tower; and, as I guess,
Upon the like devotion as yourselves,
To gratulate the gentle princes there.           10

*Queen Elizabeth.* Kind sister, thanks: we'll enter all
     together:—

*Enter* BRAKENBURY.

And, in good time, here the lieutenant comes.
Master lieutenant, pray you, by your leave,
How doth the prince, and my young son of York?    14

*Brakenbury.* Right well, dear madam. By your patience,

1 **niece**: granddaughter (so 'nephew' was used for 'grandson').
The Duchess of York was mother of Clarence.      2 **in**: by.    3
**for**: upon.      **she's**: i.e. Anne.      4 **On**: in, out of.     7
**sister**: strictly, of course, she was her brother-in-law's wife [N].
9 **Upon . . . devotion**: with the same devout (worthy) object.
10 **gratulate**: congratulate.      12 **lieutenant**: governor of the
Tower (see I. i).      15 **By your patience**: Excuse me, but

I may not suffer you to visit them:
The king hath strictly charg'd the contrary.
 *Queen Elizabeth.* The king! who's that?
 *Brakenbury.*      I mean the Lord Protector.
 *Queen Elizabeth.* The Lord protect him from that kingly
  title!
Hath he set bounds between their love and me?    20
I am their mother; who shall bar me from them?
 *Duchess.* I am their father's mother; I will see them.
 *Anne.* Their aunt I am in law, in love their mother:
Then bring me to their sights; I'll bear thy blame,
And take thy office from thee, on my peril.    25
 *Brakenbury.* No, madam, no, I may not leave it so:
I am bound by oath, and therefore pardon me.    [*Exit.*

     *Enter* STANLEY.
 *Stanley.* Let me but meet you, ladies, one hour hence,
And I'll salute your Grace of York as mother,
And reverend looker-on, of two fair queens.    30
[*To the* DUCHESS OF GLOUCESTER.] Come, madam, you
  must straight to Westminster,
There to be crowned Richard's royal queen.
 *Queen Elizabeth.* Ah! cut my lace asunder.
That my pent heart may have some scope to beat,
Or else I swoon with this dead-killing news.    35
 *Anne.* Despiteful tidings! O! unpleasing news!
 *Dorset.* Be of good cheer: mother, how fares your Grace?
 *Queen Elizabeth.* O, Dorset! speak not to me, get thee
  gone;

23 **in law**: legally.   24 **their sights**: sight of them (hence
plural 'sight*s*').   25 **take ... thee**: take on the responsibility of
your office.   26 **leave it so**: abandon my office to you.   29
**mother**: -in-law.   30 **reverend**: honoured.   **looker-on**:
beholder.   **two fair queens**: i.e. Elizabeth and Anne.   33
**lace**: the cord holding stays or bodice [*N*].   35 **dead-killing**:
fatal (the first word only strengthens the second).   36 **Despiteful**:
cruel.

Death and destruction dog thee at the heels:
Thy mother's name is ominous to children.
If thou wilt outstrip death, go cross the seas,
And live with Richmond, from the reach of hell:
Go, hie thee, hie thee, from this slaughter-house,
Lest thou increase the number of the dead,
And make me die the thrall of Margaret's curse,    45
Nor mother, wife, nor England's counted queen.
    *Stanley.* Full of wise care is this your counsel, madam.
[*To* DORSET.] Take all the swift advantage of the hours;
You shall have letters from me to my son
In your behalf, to meet you on the way:    50
Be not ta'en tardy by unwise delay.
    *Duchess.* O ill-dispersing wind of misery!
O! my accursed womb, the bed of death,
A cockatrice hast thou hatch'd to the world,
Whose unavoided eye is murderous!    55
    *Stanley.* Come, madam, come; I in all haste was sent.
    *Anne.* And I with all unwillingness will go.
O! would to God that the inclusive verge
Of golden metal that must round my brow
Were red-hot steel to sear me to the brain.    60
Anointed let me be with deadly venom;
And die, ere men can say 'God save the queen!'
    *Queen Elizabeth.* Go, go, poor soul, I envy not thy glory;
To feed my humour, wish thyself no harm.

---

**41 cross:** (probably adverb) across.        **42 from:** away from,
out of [*N*].        **45 thrall:** victim; see I. iii. 209.        **46 counted:**
acknowledged.        48 i.e. Take advantage swiftly of the time left
you (cf. Commentary at I. i. 15).        **49 son:** step-son.        **51**
**ta'en tardy:** found lagging.        **52 ill-dispersing:** spreading
evil [*N*].        **53 bed:** breeding-place.        **54 cockatrice:** like a
basilisk (I. ii. 151).        **55 unavoided:** if you don't avoid it.
**56** to Anne (see 31).        **58 inclusive verge:** encircling edge.
**59 round:** surround.        **60 sear:** burn [*N*].        **64 feed my**
**humour:** please me in my unhappy state (humour = mood) [*N*].

*Anne.* No! why? When he, that is my husband now     65
Came to me, as I follow'd Henry's corse;
When scarce the blood was well wash'd from his hands,
Which issu'd from my other angel husband,
And that dead saint which then I weeping follow'd;
O! when I say, I look'd on Richard's face,                70
This was my wish, 'Be thou,' quoth I, 'accurs'd,
For making me so young, so old a widow!
And, when thou wedd'st, let sorrow haunt thy bed;
And be thy wife—if any be so mad—
More miserable by the life of thee                        75
Than thou hast made me by my dear lord's death!'
Lo! ere I can repeat this curse again,
Within so small a time, my woman's heart
Grossly grew captive to his honey words,
And prov'd the subject of mine own soul's curse:         80
Which hitherto hath held mine eyes from rest;
For never yet one hour in his bed
Did I enjoy the golden dew of sleep,
But with his timorous dreams was still awak'd.
Besides, he hates me for my father Warwick,              85
And will, no doubt, shortly be rid of me.
   *Queen Elizabeth.* Poor heart, adieu! I pity thy com-
      plaining.
   *Anne.* No more than with my soul I mourn for yours.
   *Queen Elizabeth.* Farewell! thou woeful welcomer of
      glory!
   *Anne.* Adieu, poor soul, that takest thy leave of it!    90
   *Duchess.* [*To* DORSET.] Go thou to Richmond, and good
      fortune guide thee!

65 **why?**: what is my position? [*N*].     69 **dead saint**: Henry VI
(cf. I. ii. 5).          72 **so old a widow**: feel as if I had long been a
widow.     74–76 see I. ii. 26–27.     74 **mad**: as to marry thee.
79 **Grossly**: foolishly.     **honey**: sweet.     80 **the subject of**:
subject to, victim of.     82 **hour**: a disyllable.     84 **still**:
constantly.     85 **for**: because of [*N*].

[*To* ANNE.] Go thou to Richard, and good angels tend
   thee!
[*To* QUEEN ELIZABETH.]   Go thou to sanctuary, and
   good thoughts possess thee!
I to my grave, where peace and rest lie with me!
Eighty odd years of sorrow have I seen,          95
And each hour's joy wrack'd with a week of teen.
  *Queen Elizabeth.* Stay yet, look back with me unto the
   Tower.
Pity, you ancient stones, those tender babes
Whom envy hath immur'd within your walls,
Rough cradle for such little pretty ones!        100
Rude ragged nurse, old sullen playfellow
For tender princes, use my babies well.
So foolish sorrow bids your stones farewell.    [*Exeunt.*

*Scene II.* THE SAME. A ROOM OF STATE IN THE
PALACE

*Sennet.* RICHARD, *in pomp, crowned*: BUCKINGHAM,
CATESBY, *a* Page, *and Others.*

*King Richard.* Stand all apart. Cousin of Buckingham.
*Buckingham.* My gracious sovereign!
*King Richard.* Give me thy hand. [*He ascends the throne.*]
   Thus high, by thy advice,
And thy assistance, is King Richard seated:
But shall we wear these glories for a day?        5
Or shall they last, and we rejoice in them?
  *Buckingham.* Still live they, and for ever let them last!
  *King Richard.* Ah! Buckingham, now do I play the
   touch,

  **94 lie:** may they lie.    **96 wrack'd:** ruined.   **teen:** sorrow.
**101 ragged:** rugged, rough.   **5 a day:** only one day (cf. IV. iii. 12).
**8 play the touch:** act like a touchstone [*N*].

To try if thou be current gold indeed:

Young Edward lives: think now what I would speak.    10

  *Buckingham.*  Say on, my loving lord.

  *King Richard.*  Why, Buckingham, I say, I would be king.

  *Buckingham.*  Why, so you are, my thrice-renowned liege.

  *King Richard.*  Ha! am I king? 'Tis so: but Edward lives.

  *Buckingham.*  True, noble prince.

  *King Richard.*                         O bitter consequence,    15

That Edward still should live! 'True, noble prince!'

Cousin, thou wast not wont to be so dull:

Shall I be plain? I wish the bastards dead;

And I would have it suddenly perform'd.

What sayest thou now? speak suddenly, be brief.    20

  *Buckingham.*  Your Grace may do your pleasure.

  *King Richard.*  Tut, tut! thou art all ice, thy kindness
    freezes:

Say, have I thy consent that they shall die?

  *Buckingham.*  Give me some little breath, some pause,
    dear lord,

Before I positively speak in this:    25

I will resolve you herein presently.                    [*Exit.*

  *Catesby.*  [*Aside to another.*]  The king is angry: see, he
    gnaws his lip.

  *King Richard.*  [*Descends from his throne.*]  I will converse
    with iron-witted fools

And unrespective boys: none are for me

That look into me with considerate eyes.    30

High-reaching Buckingham grows circumspect.

Boy!

---

9 **current**: genuine, good coin (cf. i. ii. 84).    15 **consequence**:
sequel, conclusion (to my thought).    19 **suddenly**: immediately.
26 **resolve**: answer.    **presently**: in a moment.    28 **iron-
witted**: thick, dense.    29 **unrespective**: unobservant, heedless.
30 **considerate**: thoughtful, calculating.    31 **High-reaching**:
ambitious.    **circumspect**: cautious [*N*].

*Page.* My lord!

*King Richard.* Know'st thou not any whom corrupting
    gold

Will tempt unto a close exploit of death?        35

*Page.* I know a discontented gentleman,

Whose humble means match not his haughty spirit:

Gold were as good as twenty orators,

And will, no doubt, tempt him to any thing.

*King Richard.* What is his name?

*Page.*               His name, my lord, is Tyrrell.   40

*King Richard.* I partly know the man: go, call him
    hither.                                   [*Exit* Page.

The deep-revolving witty Buckingham

No more shall be the neighbour to my counsel.

Hath he so long held out with me untir'd,

And stops he now for breath? well, be it so.     45

*Enter* STANLEY.

How now, Lord Stanley! what's the news?

*Stanley.* Know, my loving lord,

The Marquess Dorset, as I hear, is fled

To Richmond, in the parts where he abides.     49

*King Richard.* Come hither, Catesby: rumour it abroad,

That Anne my wife is very grievous sick;

I will take order for her keeping close.

Inquire me out some mean poor gentleman,

Whom I will marry straight to Clarence' daughter:

The boy is foolish, and I fear not him.     55

Look, how thou dream'st! I say again, give out

That Anne my queen is sick, and like to die:

---

35 **close ... death:** secret deed of killing.    41 **partly:** slightly.
42 **deep-revolving:** deeply reflective.    **witty:** cunning.    44–45
metaphor from hunting.    49 **parts:** place(s).    52 **keeping**
**close:** keeping to her room, or house.    54 **Clarence' daughter:**
Margaret Plantagenet; cf. II. ii and IV. i [*N*].    55 **foolish:**
soft, an idiot.    56 **Look ... dream'st!:** Wake up! [*N*]

About it; for it stands me much upon,
To stop all hopes whose growth may damage me.

[*Exit* CATESBY.

I must be married to my brother's daughter,          60
Or else my kingdom stands on brittle glass.
Murder her brothers, and then marry her!
Uncertain way of gain! But I am in
So far in blood, that sin will pluck on sin:
Tear-falling pity dwells not in this eye.             65


*Re-enter* Page, *with* TYRRELL.

Is thy name Tyrrell?
 *Tyrrell.* James Tyrrell, and your most obedient subject.
 *King Richard.* Art thou, indeed?
 *Tyrrell.*      Prove me, my gracious lord.
 *King Richard.* Darest thou resolve to kill a friend of
  mine?
 *Tyrrell.* Please you; but I had rather kill two enemies.  70
 *King Richard.* Why, then thou hast it: two deep enemies,
Foes to my rest and my sweet sleep's disturbers,
Are they that I would have thee deal upon.
Tyrrell, I mean those bastards in the Tower.
 *Tyrrell.* Let me have open means to come to them,    75
And soon I'll rid you from the fear of them.
 *King Richard.* Thou sing'st sweet music. Hark, come
  hither, Tyrrell:
Go, by this token: rise, and lend thine ear.   [*Whispers.*
There is no more but so: say it is done,
And I will love thee, and prefer thee for it.        80

---

58 **About it:** Quick! (cf. I. iii. 354).   **it stands . . . upon:**
it is of great importance to me.  60 **my brother's daughter:**
viz. Elizabeth, d. of Edward IV and Q. Elizabeth.  **64 pluck
on:** draw after it, involve.  65 **Tear-falling:** which drops tears.
70 **Please you:** as it pleases you.  71 **thou hast it:** that *is* what
I want.  73 **upon:** with.  75 **open . . . come:** free access.
79 **There . . . so:** that is all.  80 **prefer:** promote.

*Tyrrell.* I will dispatch it straight.            [*Exit.*

*Re-enter* BUCKINGHAM.

*Buckingham.* My lord, I have consider'd in my mind
The late demand that you did sound me in.

*King Richard.* Well, let that rest. Dorset is fled to
    Richmond.

*Buckingham.* I hear the news, my lord.            85

*King Richard.* Stanley, he is your wife's son: well, look
    to it.

*Buckingham.* My lord, I claim the gift, my due by
    promise,
For which your honour and your faith is pawn'd;
The earldom of Hereford and the moveables
Which you have promised I shall possess.            90

*King Richard.* Stanley, look to your wife: if she convey
Letters to Richmond, you shall answer it.

*Buckingham.* What says your highness to my just
    request?

*King Richard.* I do remember me, Henry the Sixth
Did prophesy that Richmond should be king,            95
When Richmond was a little peevish boy.
A king! perhaps—

*Buckingham.* My lord!

*King Richard.* How chance the prophet could not at that
    time
Have told me, I being by, that I should kill him?            100

*Buckingham.* My lord, your promise for the earldom,—

*King Richard.* Richmond! When last I was at Exeter,
The mayor in courtesy show'd me the castle,
And call'd it Rougemont: at which name I started,

84 see IV. i. 41–42.        86 **he:** Richmond.        89 see III. i. 194–
6 and Commentary there.                92 **answer it:** answer for it [*N*].
96 **peevish:** silly (cf. I. iii. 194).        99 **chance:** did it chance that.
100 **him:** the prophet, i.e. Henry VI (see *3 Henry VI*, v. vi. 57).

Because a bard of Ireland told me once                    105
I should not live long after I saw Richmond.
    *Buckingham.* My lord!
    *King Richard.* Ay, what's o'clock?
    *Buckingham.* I am thus bold to put your Grace in mind
Of what you promis'd me.                                  110
    *King Richard.* Well, but what is 't o'clock?
    *Buckingham.*                    Upon the stroke of ten.
    *King Richard.* Well, let it strike.
    *Buckingham.*                    Why let it strike?
    *King Richard.* Because that, like a Jack, thou keep'st
        the stroke
Betwixt thy begging and my meditation.
I am not in the giving vein to-day.                       115
    *Buckingham.* Why, then resolve me whether you will
        or no.
    *King Richard.* Thou troublest me: I am not in the vein.
                        [*Exeunt* KING RICHARD *and train.*
    *Buckingham.* And is it thus? repays he my deep service
With such contempt? made I him king for this?
O, let me think on Hastings, and be gone                  120
To Brecknock, while my fearful head is on.        [*Exit.*


## Scene III. THE SAME

### Enter TYRRELL.

    *Tyrrell.* The tyrannous and bloody act is done;
The most arch deed of piteous massacre
That ever yet this land was guilty of.
Dighton and Forrest, whom I did suborn

---

112 **Why ... strike?**: Why do you say 'let it strike'?    113–14
i.e. your repeated requests are like the stroke of a clock [N].   116
**resolve me**: give me a definite answer.    **2 arch**: chief (cf.
'archbishop'), pre-eminent.

To do this piece of ruthless butchery,                              5
Albeit they were flesh'd villains, bloody dogs,
Melting with tenderness and mild compassion,
Wept like to children in their death's sad story.
'Oh! thus,' quoth Dighton, 'lay the gentle babes:'
'Thus, thus,' quoth Forrest, 'girdling one another        10
Within their alabaster innocent arms:
Their lips were four red roses on a stalk,
Which in their summer beauty kiss'd each other.
A book of prayers on their pillow lay;
Which once,' quoth Forrest, 'almost chang'd my mind;   15
But, O, the devil'—there the villain stopp'd;
When Dighton thus told on: 'We smothered
The most replenished sweet work of nature,
That from the prime creation e'er she fram'd.'
Hence both are gone with conscience and remorse;        20
They could not speak; and so I left them both,
To bear this tidings to the bloody king:
And here he comes.

*Enter* KING RICHARD.
                    All health, my sovereign lord!
*King Richard.*  Kind Tyrrell, am I happy in thy news?
*Tyrrell.*  If to have done the thing you gave in charge    25
Beget your happiness, be happy then,
For it is done.
*King Richard.*  But didst thou see them dead?
*Tyrrell.*  I did, my lord.
*King Richard.*          And, buried, gentle Tyrrell?
*Tyrrell.*  The chaplain of the Tower hath buried them;

5 **piece**: example (almost = 'masterpiece').          6 **flesh'd**:
experienced [*N*].          8 **their . . . story**: in relating how they died.
11 **alabaster**: like marble [*N*].          12 **a stalk**: one stalk.
18 **replenishéd**: complete(ly sweet).          19 **prime**: first.
20 **gone**: overcome, done for.          22 **tidings**: can be singular in Sh.
25 **gave in charge**: entrusted to me, commanded.

But how or in what place I do not know.                    30

*King Richard.* Come to me, Tyrrell, soon at after-supper,
When thou shalt tell the process of their death.
Meantime, but think how I may do thee good,
And be inheritor of thy desire.                            34
Farewell till then.

    *Tyrrell.*       I humbly take my leave.          [*Exit.*

    *King Richard.* The son of Clarence have I pent up close;
His daughter meanly have I match'd in marriage;
The sons of Edward sleep in Abraham's bosom,
And Anne my wife hath bid the world good night.
Now, for I know the Breton Richmond aims                   40
At young Elizabeth, my brother's daughter,
And, by that knot, looks proudly on the crown,
To her go I, a jolly thriving wooer.

*Enter* CATESBY.

*Catesby.* My lord!

    *King Richard.* Good or bad news, that thou comest in so
      bluntly?                                           45

    *Catesby.* Bad news, my lord: Morton is fled to Richmond;
And Buckingham, back'd with the hardy Welshmen,
Is in the field, and still his power increaseth.

    *King Richard.* Ely with Richmond troubles me more near
Than Buckingham and his rash-levied strength.             50
Come; I have learn'd that fearful commenting
Is leaden servitor to dull delay:

31 **after-supper:** dessert, or late supper [*N*].          32 **process:**
story.          33 **but:** merely.          **do thee good:** benefit, reward thee.
34 i.e. And you shall at once have your wish granted (inheritor = pos-
sessor) [*N*].          38 **sleep . . . bosom:** are dead (from Luke xvi. 22).
40 **Breton:** not by birth, but by present residence [*N*].          42
**looks proudly on:** i.e. counts it as his already.          46 **Morton:**
the Bishop of Ely; see III. iv.          48 **power:** forces.          50 **rash-
levied:** hastily conscripted.          51 **commenting:** pondering and
talking about a matter [*N*].          52 i.e. only serves to postpone
the necessary action.

Delay leads impotent and snail-pac'd beggary:
Then fiery expedition be my wing,
Jove's Mercury, and herald for a king!                    55
Go, muster men: my counsel is my shield;
We must be brief when traitors brave the field.    [*Exeunt.*

*Scene IV.* The Same. Before the Palace

*Enter* QUEEN MARGARET.

*Queen Margaret.* So, now prosperity begins to mellow
And drop into the rotten mouth of death.
Here in these confines slily have I lurk'd
To watch the waning of mine enemies.
A dire induction am I witness to,                        5
And will to France, hoping the consequence
Will prove as bitter, black, and tragical.
Withdraw thee, wretched Margaret: who comes here?

*Enter* QUEEN ELIZABETH *and the* DUCHESS OF YORK.

*Queen Elizabeth.* Ah! my poor princes! ah, my tender
    babes,
My unblown flowers, new-appearing sweets,               10
If yet your gentle souls fly in the air
And be not fix'd in doom perpetual,
Hover about me with your airy wings,
And hear your mother's lamentation.

---

53 **leads**: leads on, produces.    **snail-pac'd**: sluggish.    **beggary**: ruin [*N*].    54 **expedition**: speed.    **be my wing**: carry
me forward.    55 **Jove's Mercury**: i.e. speed must be for me
what Mercury was for Jove [*N*].    56 **my counsel . . . shield**: the
only good advice for me is fighting.    57 **brave the field**: take
up arms.    1 **mellow**: ripen (and suggesting here over-ripeness).
2 **rotten**: adjective transferred from the fruit.    5 **induction**:
beginning [*N*].    6 **will** (go) **to.**    **consequence**: what follows.
10 **unblown**: unopened.    12 **doom**: death.

*Queen Margaret.* Hover about her; say, that right for
   right                                                15
Hath dimm'd your infant morn to aged night.
   *Duchess.* So many miseries have craz'd my voice,
That my woe-wearied tongue is still and mute.
Edward Plantagenet, why art thou dead?
   *Queen Margaret.* Plantagenet doth quit Plantagenet;   20
Edward for Edward pays a dying debt.
   *Queen Elizabeth.* Wilt thou, O God! fly from such gentle
   lambs,
And throw them in the entrails of the wolf?
When didst thou sleep when such a deed was done?
   *Queen Margaret.* When holy Harry died, and my sweet
   son.                                                25
   *Duchess.* Dead life, blind sight, poor mortal living ghost,
Woe's scene, world's shame, grave's due by life usurp'd,
Brief abstract and record of tedious days,
Rest thy unrest on England's lawful earth,   [*Sitting down.*
Unlawfully made drunk with innocent blood!              30
   *Queen Elizabeth.* Ah! that thou wouldst as soon afford
   a grave
As thou canst yield a melancholy seat;
Then would I hide my bones, not rest them here.
Ah! who hath any cause to mourn but I?
                        [*Sitting down by her.*

---

15 **right for right**: justice answering to the claim for justice
[*N*].      16 **infant morn**: bright young lives.      **aged night:**
the night that belongs to the aged.      17 **craz'd**: cracked.
18 **still**: silenced.      19 **Edward P.**: Edward IV.      20 **quit:**
pay for.      21 **Edward for Edward**: Edward IV for Prince
Edward, Margaret's son.      **dying debt**: debt of death.      22 **fly
from**: abandon.      23 i.e. let the wolf make them his prey
(phraseology from John x. 12).      24 i.e. when previously hast
Thou permitted such a deed?      26 The Duchess addresses herself.
**mortal**: alive [*N*].      28 **abstract**: epitome.      accent *rec'ord*,
as III. i. 72.

*Queen Margaret.*  If ancient sorrow be most reverend,    35
Give mine the benefit of seniory,
And let my griefs frown on the upper hand,
If sorrow can admit society.          [*Sitting down with them.*
Tell o'er your woes again by viewing mine:
I had an Edward, till a Richard kill'd him;          40
I had a Harry, till a Richard kill'd him;
Thou hadst an Edward, till a Richard kill'd him;
Thou hadst a Richard, till a Richard kill'd him.
  *Duchess.*  I had a Richard too, and thou didst kill him;
I had a Rutland too, thou holp'st to kill him.          45
  *Queen Margaret.*  Thou hadst a Clarence too, and Richard
    kill'd him.
From forth the kennel of thy womb hath crept
A hell-hound that doth hunt us all to death:
That dog, that had his teeth before his eyes,
To worry lambs, and lap their gentle blood,          50
That foul defacer of God's handiwork,
That excellent grand tyrant of the earth,
That reigns in galled eyes of weeping souls,
Thy womb let loose, to chase us to our graves.
O! upright, just, and true-disposing God,          55
How do I thank thee that this carnal cur
Preys on the issue of his mother's body,
And makes her pew-fellow with others' moan.
  *Duchess.*  O! Harry's wife, triumph not in my woes:

---

36 **seniory:** seniority (but probably derived from 'seigneur').
37 **frown ... hand:** take first place.          40 **Edward:** Prince
Edward, killed at Tewkesbury (cf. i. ii. 182).          42 **Thou:** to Elizabeth.      **Edward:** Edward V.          43 **Richard:** of York, younger
brother of Edward V.      44 **Richard:** of York, father of Edward IV.
45 **Rutland:** see i. iii. 182, &c.      **holp'st:** didst help.          51 **handi-**
**work:** workmanship.                    52 **excellent grand:** supreme.
53 **galled:** sore with weeping.          56 **carnal:** carnivorous [*N*].
58 **pew-fellow:** companion.

God witness with me, I have wept for thine.                    60
  *Queen Margaret.*  Bear with me; I am hungry for revenge,
And now I cloy me with beholding it.
Thy Edward he is dead, that kill'd my Edward;
Thy other Edward dead, to quit my Edward;
Young York he is but boot, because both they                    65
Match not the high perfection of my loss:
Thy Clarence he is dead that stabb'd my Edward;
And the beholders of this tragic play,
The adulterate Hastings, Rivers, Vaughan, Grey,
Untimely smother'd in their dusky graves,                    70
Richard yet lives, hell's black intelligencer,
Only reserv'd their factor, to buy souls
And send them thither; but at hand, at hand,
Ensues his piteous and unpitied end:
Earth gapes, hell burns, fiends roar, saints pray,                    75
To have him suddenly convey'd from hence.
Cancel his bond of life, dear God! I pray,
That I may live to say, The dog is dead.
  *Queen Elizabeth.*  O! thou didst prophesy the time would
    come
That I should wish for thee to help me curse                    80
That bottled spider, that foul bunch-back'd toad.
  *Queen Margaret.*  I call'd thee then vain flourish of my
    fortune;
I call'd thee then poor shadow, painted queen;

**60 with me:** i.e. to the truth of my words.        **62 me:** myself.
**63 Thy Edward:** Edward IV.        **my Edward:** see 40.        **64**
**Thy other Edward:** Edward V.        **quit:** pay for.        **65 but**
**boot:** merely an additional item, a make-weight.        **both they:**
both together [N].        **68** i.e. those who stood by when that deed
was done [N].        **69 adulterate:** adulterous (with Mistress Shore).
**71 intelligencer:** go-between.        **72 reserv'd ... buy:** kept alive
to act as Hell's agent in buying [N].        **77 his bond of life:** the
span of life allotted him in Thy books.        **79** see I. iii. 245–6.
**81** see I. iii. 242 and 246.        **82–83** see I. iii. 241.

The presentation of but what I was;
The flattering index of a direful pageant;                    85
One heav'd a-high to be hurl'd down below;
A mother only mock'd with two fair babes;
A dream of what thou wert, a breath, a bubble,
A sign of dignity, a garish flag,
To be the aim of every dangerous shot;                    90
A queen in jest, only to fill the scene.
Where is thy husband now? where be thy brothers?
Where are thy children? wherein dost thou joy?
Who sues and kneels and cries God save the queen?
Where be the bending peers that flatter'd thee?                    95
Where be the thronging troops that follow'd thee?
Decline all this, and see what now thou art:
For happy wife, a most distressed widow:
For joyful mother, one that wails the name;
For one being sued to, one that humbly sues;                    100
For queen, a very caitiff crown'd with care;
For one that scorn'd at me, now scorn'd of me;
For one being fear'd of all, now fearing one;
For one commanding all, obey'd of none.
Thus hath the course of justice whirl'd about,                    105
And left thee but a very prey to time;
Having no more but thought of what thou wert,
To torture thee the more, being what thou art.

---

84 **presentation . . . what:** only the semblance.        85 **flattering index of:** fine-seeming prologue to (see II. ii. 148).        86
**a-high:** on high.        87 **only mock'd:** i.e. not really blest.
89 **sign:** i.e. a mere sign (not the reality).        **garish flag:** gaudy,
sham standard-bearer.        90 i.e. which (who) would attract the
enemy's fire.        97 **Decline:** go through (like a learner 'declining'
his Latin nouns).        98 **For:** instead of [N].        101 **caitiff:**
miserable wretch (*captivus* = prisoner).        103 **one:** i.e. Richard
(only).        105 i.e. justice has reversed things [N].        106 **very:**
absolute, veritable.        107 **no . . . thought:** nothing but the
thought.

Thou didst usurp my place, and dost thou not
Usurp the just proportion of my sorrow?                    110
Now thy proud neck bears half my burden'd yoke;
From which even here, I slip my wearied head,
And leave the burden of it all on thee.
Farewell, York's wife, and queen of sad mischance:
These English woes shall make me smile in France.        115
   *Queen Elizabeth.* O thou, well skill'd in curses, stay awhile,
And teach me how to curse mine enemies.
   *Queen Margaret.* Forbear to sleep the night, and fast the
     day;
Compare dead happiness with living woe;
Think that thy babes were fairer than they were,        120
And he that slew them fouler than he is:
Bettering thy loss makes the bad causer worse:
Revolving this will teach thee how to curse.
   *Queen Elizabeth.* My words are dull; O! quicken them
     with thine!                    124
   *Queen Margaret.* Thy woes will make them sharp, and
     pierce like mine.                    [*Exit.*
   *Duchess.* Why should calamity be full of words?
   *Queen Elizabeth.* Windy attorneys to their client woes,
Airy succeeders of intestate joys,
Poor breathing orators of miseries!
Let them have scope: though what they do impart        130
Help nothing else, yet do they ease the heart.
   *Duchess.* If so, then be not tongue-tied: go with me,
And in the breath of bitter words let's smother
My damned son, that thy two sweet sons smother'd.
                     [*A trumpet heard.*

---

   111 **burden'd**: burdensome.    118 **fast the day**: fast (impera-
tive) by day.    122 **Bettering**: exaggerating.    **causer**: i.e.
Richard.    127 i.e. they are wordy pleaders, acting for the sorrows
that inspire (brief) them.    128 **intestate**: dying without heirs [*N*].
131 **Help ... else**: does no other good.

The trumpet sounds: be copious in exclaims.　　　135

*Enter* KING RICHARD, *and his Train, marching.*
*King Richard.* Who intercepts me in my expedition?
*Duchess.* O! she that might have intercepted thee,
By strangling thee in her accursed womb,
From all the slaughters, wretch, that thou hast done!
　*Queen Elizabeth.* Hid'st thou that forehead with a golden
　　crown,　　　140
Where should be branded, if that right were right,
The slaughter of the prince that ow'd that crown,
And the dire death of my poor sons and brothers?
Tell me, thou villain slave, where are my children?
　*Duchess.* Thou toad, thou toad, where is thy brother
　　Clarence　　　145
And little Ned Plantagenet, his son?
　*Queen Elizabeth.* Where is the gentle Rivers, Vaughan,
　　Grey?
　*Duchess.* Where is kind Hastings?
　*King Richard.* A flourish, trumpets! strike alarum,
　　drums!
Let not the heavens hear these tell-tale women　　　150
Rail on the Lord's anointed. Strike, I say!
　　　　　　　　　　[*Flourish. Alarums.*
Either be patient, and entreat me fair,
Or with the clamorous report of war
Thus will I drown your exclamations.
　*Duchess.* Art thou my son?　　　155

---

135 **exclaims**: exclamation (as in I. ii. 52).　　　136 **expedition**:
march [*N*].　　　141 **Where**: on which.　　**right were right**: everything were as it should be.　　　142 **ow'd**: owned (common in Sh.).
148 **kind**: i.e. loyal (to Edward IV).　　　149 **alarum**: see I. i. 7.
150 **tell-tale**: mischief-making.　　　151 **the Lord's anointed**: the
King (O.T. phrase).　　　152 **entreat**: treat.　　　153 **clamorous
report**: noisy sound.

*King Richard.*  Ay; I thank God, my father, and yourself.

*Duchess.*  Then patiently hear my impatience.

*King Richard.*  Madam, I have a touch of your condition.
That cannot brook the accent of reproof.

*Duchess.*  O, let me speak!

*King Richard.*                 Do, then; but I'll not hear.    160

*Duchess.*  I will be mild and gentle in my words.

*King Richard.*  And brief, good mother; for I am in haste.

*Duchess.*  Art thou so hasty?  I have stay'd for thee,
God knows, in torment and in agony.

*King Richard.*  And came I not at last to comfort you? 165

*Duchess.*  No, by the holy rood, thou know'st it well,
Thou cam'st on earth to make the earth my hell.
A grievous burden was thy birth to me;
Tetchy and wayward was thy infancy;
Thy school-days frightful, desperate, wild and furious; 170
Thy prime of manhood daring, bold, and venturous;
Thy age confirm'd, proud, subtle, sly, and bloody,
More mild, but yet more harmful, kind in hatred:
What comfortable hour canst thou name
That ever grac'd me in thy company?                    175

*King Richard.*  Faith, none, but Humphrey Hour, that
    call'd your Grace
To breakfast once forth of my company.
If I be so disgracious in your eye,
Let me march on, and not offend you, madam.
Strike up the drum!

*Duchess.*                 I prithee, hear me speak.    180

*King Richard.*  You speak too bitterly.

---

158 **condition**: temperament.          166 **rood**: see III. ii. 75.
169 **Tetchy**: fretful, peevish.          170 **desperate**: utterly careless, reckless.          171 **prime of manhood**: early manhood.
172 **age confirm'd**: settled time of life, full age.          173 **mild**:
i.e. outwardly.          **kind in hatred**: veiling hatred under a show of
kindness [N].          176 **Humphrey Hour**: (perhaps) meal-time [N].
177 **forth**: out of.          178 **disgracious**: cf. III. vii. 111.

*Duchess.*                                    Hear me a word;
For I shall never speak to thee again.
*King Richard.* So!
*Duchess.* Either thou wilt die by God's just ordinance,
Ere from this war thou turn a conqueror;                    185
Or I with grief and extreme age shall perish
And never look upon thy face again.
Therefore take with thee my most grievous curse,
Which, in the day of battle, tire thee more
Than all the complete armour that thou wear'st!           190
My prayers on the adverse party fight;
And there the little souls of Edward's children
Whisper the spirits of thine enemies
And promise them success and victory.
Bloody thou art, bloody will be thy end;                   195
Shame serves thy life and doth thy death attend.    [*Exit.*
*Queen Elizabeth.* Though far more cause, yet much less
        spirit to curse
Abides in me: I say amen to her.                    [*Going.*
*King Richard.* Stay, madam; I must talk a word with
        you.
*Queen Elizabeth.* I have no moe sons of the royal blood 200
For thee to slaughter: for my daughters, Richard,
They shall be praying nuns, not weeping queens;
And therefore level not to hit their lives.
*King Richard.* You have a daughter call'd Elizabeth,
Virtuous and fair, royal and gracious.                     205
*Queen Elizabeth.* And must she die for this? O! let her
        live,

---

183 **So !**: Is that really so?          184 **Either**: scans as one
syllable.          186 **éxtreme**: accented as in *Hamlet* III. v. 43. Cf.
cómplete (190).          189 **tire**: may it tire (so 'fight' and 'whisper');
which meant 'prey upon' as well as 'exhaust'.          192 **Whisper**:
whisper to.          196 **serves**: accompanies.    **attend**: wait for (but
with a pun on the other meaning of 'wait upon').          200 **moe**:
more.          203 **level not**: do not aim.

And I'll corrupt her manners, stain her beauty;
Slander myself as false to Edward's bed;
Throw over her the veil of infamy:
So she may live unscarr'd of bleeding slaughter,      210
I will confess she was not Edward's daughter.

  *King Richard.* Wrong not her birth; she is of royal blood.

  *Queen Elizabeth.* To save her life, I'll say she is not so.

  *King Richard.* Her life is safest only in her birth.

  *Queen Elizabeth.* And only in that safety died her
    brothers.      215

  *King Richard.* Lo! at their births good stars were
    opposite!

  *Queen Elizabeth.* No, to their lives ill friends were con-
    trary.

  *King Richard.* All unavoided is the doom of destiny.

  *Queen Elizabeth.* True, when avoided grace makes
    destiny.

My babes were destin'd to a fairer death,      220
If grace had bless'd thee with a fairer life.

  *King Richard.* You speak as if that I had slain my
    cousins.

  *Queen Elizabeth.* Cousins, indeed; and by their uncle
    cozen'd

Of comfort, kingdom, kindred, freedom, life.
Whose hand soever lanc'd their tender hearts,      225
Thy head, all indirectly, gave direction:
No doubt the murderous knife was dull and blunt
Till it was whetted on thy stone-hard heart,

207 **manners**: morals (cf. L. *mores*).      210 **So**: provided that.
**of**: by.      215 **only ... safety**: just because of the safety of their
high birth.      216 **opposite**: adverse [*N*].      218 **unavoided**:
unavoidable.      219 **avoided grace**: i.e. a man who has deliberately rejected goodness (God's grace).      222 **cousins**: de-
nephews.      223 **cozen'd**: cheated [*N*].      225 **Whose hand
soever**: whosoever's hand.      226 **indirectly**: not in explicit
terms, *or* unjustly (cf. III. i. 31).

To revel in the entrails of my lambs.
But that still use of grief makes wild grief tame,          230
My tongue should to thy ears not name my boys
Till that my nails were anchor'd in thin eyes;
And I, in such a desperate bay of death,
Like a poor bark, of sails and tackling reft,
Rush all to pieces on thy rocky bosom.                     235
   *King Richard.* Madam, so thrive I in my enterprise
And dangerous success of bloody wars,
As I intend more good to you and yours
Than ever you or yours by me were harm'd.
   *Queen Elizabeth.* What good is cover'd with the face of
    heaven,                                               240
To be discover'd, that can do me good?
   *King Richard.* The advancement of your children, gentle
    lady.
   *Queen Elizabeth.* Up to some scaffold, there to lose their
    heads?
   *King Richard.* No, to the dignity and height of fortune,
The high imperial type of this earth's glory.              245
   *Queen Elizabeth.* Flatter my sorrow with report of it:
Tell me what state, what dignity, what honour,
Canst thou demise to any child of mine?
   *King Richard.* Even all I have; ay, and myself and all,
Will I withal endow a child of thine;                      250
So in the Lethe of thy angry soul
Thou drown the sad remembrance of those wrongs

---

229 **revel**: glut itself, enjoy itself.    230 **But that**: were it
not that.    **still**: constant.    234 **tackling**: rigging.
**reft**: bereaved.    235 **Rush**: were rushing [*N*].    236 **thrive
I**: may I thrive.    237 **dangerous success**: result won at the
cost of danger.    241 **To be discovered**: yet to be uncovered.
245 **high imperial type**: i.e. the throne ('type' may here mean
'badge' or 'title').    248 **demise**: hand on.    250 **withal**:
with (take before 'myself').    251 **So**: cf. 210.    **Lethe**: (river
of) forgetfulness (in Hell) [*N*].

Which thou supposest I have done to thee.

  *Queen Elizabeth.* Be brief, lest that the process of thy
    kindness

Last longer telling than thy kindness' date.      255

  *King Richard.* Then know, that from my soul I love thy
    daughter.

  *Queen Elizabeth.* My daughter's mother thinks it with
    her soul.

  *King Richard.* What do you think?

  *Queen Elizabeth.* That thou dost love my daughter from
    thy soul:

So from thy soul's love didst thou love her brothers;   260

And from my heart's love I do thank thee for it.

  *King Richard.* Be not too hasty to confound my mean-
    ing:

I mean, that with my soul I love thy daughter,

And do intend to make her Queen of England.

  *Queen Elizabeth.* Well then, who dost thou mean shall
    be her king?      265

  *King Richard.* Even he that makes her queen: who else
    should be?

  *Queen Elizabeth.* What! thou?

  *King Richard.* Even so: what think you of it?

  *Queen Elizabeth.* How canst thou woo her?

  *King Richard.*           That I would learn of you,

As one being best acquainted with her humour.   270

  *Queen Elizabeth.* And wilt thou learn of me?

  *King Richard.*          Madam, with all my heart.

  *Queen Elizabeth.* Send to her, by the man that slew her
    brothers,

A pair of bleeding hearts; thereon engrave

---

254 **process:** story (as in IV. iii. 32).      255 **telling:** being
told.    **date:** duration.    256 **from:** out of, with (but Elizabeth
takes it as 'away from').    262 **confound:** misunderstand.
270 **humour:** disposition.

Edward and York; then haply will she weep:
Therefore present to her, as sometime Margaret          275
Did to thy father, steep'd in Rutland's blood,
A handkerchief, which, say to her, did drain
The purple sap from her sweet brother's body,
And bid her wipe her weeping eyes withal.
If this inducement move her not to love,                280
Send her a letter of thy noble deeds;
Tell her thou madest away her uncle Clarence,
Her uncle Rivers; ay, and for her sake,
Madest quick conveyance with her good aunt Anne.

   *King Richard.* You mock me, madam; this is not the
    way                                            285
To win your daughter.

   *Queen Elizabeth.*      There is no other way
Unless thou couldst put on some other shape,
And not be Richard that hath done all this.

   *King Richard.* Say, that I did all this for love of her.

   *Queen Elizabeth.* Nay, then indeed she cannot choose but
    hate thee,                                       290
Having bought love with such a bloody spoil.

   *King Richard.* Look, what is done cannot be now
    amended:
Men shall deal unadvisedly sometimes,
Which after-hours give leisure to repent.
If I did take the kingdom from your sons,                295
To make amends I'll give it to your daughter.
If I have kill'd the issue of your womb,
To quicken your increase, I will beget
Mine issue of your blood upon your daughter:

276 see I. iii. 177–8.          279 **withal:** with it.          284 **Madest
quick conveyance:** quickly removed.          290 **cannot choose
but:** is bound to.          291 **spoil:** destruction, waste.          292
**amended:** cured [*N*].          293 **shall deal unadvisedly:** must
sometimes act unwisely (a masterpiece of understatement!).
294 **Which:** for which deeds.

A grandam's name is little less in love                    300
Than is the doting title of a mother;
They are as children but one step below,
Even of your mettle, of your very blood;
Of all one pain, save for a night of groans
Endur'd of her for whom you bid like sorrow.              305
Your children were vexation to your youth,
But mine shall be a comfort to your age.
The loss you have is but a son being king,
And by that loss your daughter is made queen.
I cannot make you what amends I would,                    310
Therefore accept such kindness as I can.
Dorset your son, that with a fearful soul
Leads discontented steps in foreign soil,
This fair alliance quickly shall call home
To high promotions and great dignity:                     315
The king that calls your beauteous daughter wife,
Familiarly shall call thy Dorset brother;
Again shall you be mother to a king,
And all the ruins of distressful times
Repair'd with double riches of content.                   320
What! we have many goodly days to see:
The liquid drops of tears that you have shed
Shall come again, transform'd to orient pearl,
Advantaging their loan with interest
Of ten times double gain of happiness.                    325

---

301 **doting**: fond, loving.        302 **one step below**: one genera-
tion further on, grandchildren.        303 **mettle**: substance [*N*].
304 **Of all one pain . . . groans**: i.e. giving the grandmother the
same trouble as the mother, except for the actual time of birth.
305 **of**: by.        **bid**: endured (past tense of 'bide' = 'abide') [*N*].
308 **a son . . . king**: i.e that of a son (not) being king.        313
**Leads**: drags along.        320 **of content**: bringing you contentment.        322–5 i.e. the tears you have shed shall be turned into
gems, so as to give you tenfold happiness in repayment for your sorrow.
**orient**: bright [*N*].        **Advantaging**: paying back with interest.

Go then, my mother; to thy daughter go:
Make bold her bashful years with your experience;
Prepare her ears to hear a wooer's tale;
Put in her tender heart the aspiring flame
Of golden sovereignty; acquaint the princess          330
With the sweet silent hours of marriage joys:
And when this arm of mine hath chastised
The petty rebel, dull-brain'd Buckingham,
Bound with triumphant garlands will I come,
And lead thy daughter to a conqueror's bed;          335
To whom I will retail my conquest won,
And she shall be sole victress, Cæsar's Cæsar.

   *Queen Elizabeth.*  What were I best to say? her father's
brother
Would be her lord? Or shall I say, her uncle?
Or, he that slew her brothers and her uncles?          340
Under what title shall I woo for thee,
That God, the law, my honour, and her love
Can make seem pleasing to her tender years?

   *King Richard.*  Infer fair England's peace by this alliance.

   *Queen Elizabeth.*  Which she shall purchase with still-
lasting war.          345

   *King Richard.*  Tell her, the king, that may command,
entreats.

   *Queen Elizabeth.*  That at her hands which the king's
King forbids.

   *King Richard.*  Say, she shall be a high and mighty queen.

   *Queen Elizabeth.*  To vail the title, as her mother doth.

   *King Richard.*  Say, I will love her everlastingly.          350

   332 **chastised**: accent on first, as usually in Sh.          336 **retail**:
recount.                          338 **were I best**: would it be best for me.
341–3 i.e. How shall I describe you to her so as not to make the
marriage sound against the laws of God and man, dishonourable to
me, and hateful to her?          344 **Infer**: adduce (as an argument in
its favour) [*N*].          345 **still-lasting**: continuous.          347 **king's
King**: God.          349 **vail**: lower (a fairly common word in Sh.) [*N*].

*Queen Elizabeth.* But how long shall that title 'ever' last?

*King Richard.* Sweetly in force unto her fair life's end.

*Queen Elizabeth.* But how long fairly shall her sweet life last?

*King Richard.* As long as heaven and nature lengthens it.

*Queen Elizabeth.* As long as hell and Richard likes of it. 355

*King Richard.* Say, I, her sovereign, am her subject low.

*Queen Elizabeth.* But she, your subject, loathes such sovereignty.

*King Richard.* Be eloquent in my behalf to her.

*Queen Elizabeth.* An honest tale speeds best being plainly told.

*King Richard.* Then plainly to her tell my loving tale. 360

*Queen Elizabeth.* Plain and not honest is too harsh a style.

*King Richard.* Your reasons are too shallow and too quick.

*Queen Elizabeth.* O, no! my reasons are too deep and dead;

Too deep and dead, poor infants, in their graves.

*King Richard.* Harp not on that string, madam; that is past. 365

*Queen Elizabeth.* Harp on it still shall I till heart-strings break.

*King Richard.* Now, by my George, my garter, and my crown,—

*Queen Elizabeth.* Profan'd, dishonour'd, and the third usurp'd.

*King Richard.* I swear,—

---

353 **fairly**: in happiness. 360 **my loving tale**: the tale of my love. 361 **Plain and not honest**: i.e. a plain tale of a love that is not honourable (or, perhaps, sincere). 362 **reasons**: reasoning, logic. **quick**: hasty, glib; but the Queen plays on its other sense of 'alive'. 367 **my George, my garter**: i.e. my faith as a Knight of the Garter (K.G.) [N].

*Queen Elizabeth.*          By nothing; for this is no oath.
Thy George, profan'd, hath lost his holy honour;          370
Thy garter, blemish'd, pawn'd his knightly virtue;
Thy crown, usurp'd, disgrac'd his kingly glory.
If something thou wouldst swear to be believ'd,
Swear, then, by something that thou hast not wrong'd.
  *King Richard.* Now, by the world,—
  *Queen Elizabeth.*          'Tis full of thy foul wrongs. 375
  *King Richard.* My father's death,—
  *Queen Elizabeth.*          Thy life hath that dishonour'd.
  *King Richard.* Then, by myself,—
  *Queen Elizabeth.*               Thyself is self-misus'd.
  *King Richard.* Why, then, by God,—
  *Queen Elizabeth.*               God's wrong is most of all.
If thou hadst fear'd to break an oath by him,
The unity the king my husband made          380
Had not been broken, nor my brothers died:
If thou hadst fear'd to break an oath by him,
The imperial metal, circling now thy head,
Had grac'd the tender temples of my child,
And both the princes had been breathing here,          385
Which now, too tender bedfellows for dust,
Thy broken faith hath made a prey for worms.
What canst thou swear by now?
  *King Richard.*               The time to come.
  *Queen Elizabeth.* That thou hast wronged in the time
    o'erpast;
For I myself have many tears to wash          390
Hereafter time for time past wrong'd by thee.
The children live, whose parents thou hast slaughter'd,

---

370 **his**: its.     371 **pawn'd**: has forfeited its efficacy as a
symbol of knighthood.     378 **God's wrong**: the wrong done to
God.     380 **unity**: the reconciliation of II. i.     389 i.e. by
doing wrongs of which the results continue into the present and
future.     391 **Hereafter time**: the future.

Ungovern'd youth, to wail it in their age:
The parents live, whose children thou hast butcher'd,
Old barren plants, to wail it with their age.      395
Swear not by time to come; for that thou hast
Misus'd ere us'd, by times ill-us'd o'erpast.

  *King Richard.* As I intend to prosper, and repent,
So thrive I in my dangerous affairs
Of hostile arms! myself myself confound!      400
Heaven and fortune bar me happy hours!
Day, yield me not thy light; nor, night, thy rest!
Be opposite all planets of good luck
To my proceeding, if, with pure heart's love,
Immaculate devotion, holy thoughts,      405
I tender not thy beauteous princely daughter!
In her consists my happiness and thine;
Without her, follows to myself, and thee,
Herself, the land, and many a Christian soul,
Death, desolation, ruin, and decay:      410
It cannot be avoided but by this;
It will not be avoided but by this.
Therefore, dear mother,—I must call you so,—
Be the attorney of my love to her:
Plead what I will be, not what I have been;      415
Not my deserts, but what I will deserve:
Urge the necessity and state of times,
And be not peevish-fond in great designs.

---

393 **Ungovern'd youth**: children with no parents to guide them.
**in their age**: when they grow older.      395 **with**: along with
397 **ere us'd**: before the (proper) time came for using it. **by times . . .
o'er past**: by using ill the times that are past.      398–9 **As** (truly
as) . . . **So** (may I) . . .      400–6 i.e. May I bring destruction on
myself . . . if I am not sincere in my feelings for your daughter.
403 **opposite**: opposed.      405 **Immaculate**: unstained,
genuine.      406 **tender**: care for.      411 **this**: i.e. this marriage.
414 **attorney**: go-between, pleader (cf. 127).      418 **peevish-
fond**: childishly foolish.

*Queen Elizabeth.* Shall I be tempted of the devil thus?

*King Richard.* Ay, if the devil tempt thee to do good.   420

*Queen Elizabeth.* Shall I forget myself to be myself?

*King Richard.* Ay, if your self's remembrance wrong yourself.

*Queen Elizabeth.* Yet thou didst kill my children.

*King Richard.* But in your daughter's womb I bury them:

Where, in that nest of spicery, they shall breed   425

Selves of themselves, to your recomforture.

*Queen Elizabeth.* Shall I go win my daughter to thy will?

*King Richard.* And be a happy mother by the deed.

*Queen Elizabeth.* I go. Write to me very shortly,

And you shall understand from me her mind.   430

*King Richard.* Bear her my true love's kiss; and so, farewell.       [*Kissing her. Exit* QUEEN ELIZABETH.

Relenting fool, and shallow changing woman!

        *Enter* RATCLIFF; CATESBY *following.*

How now! what news?

*Ratcliff.* Most mighty sovereign, on the western coast

Rideth a puissant navy; to the shores   435

Throng many doubtful hollow-hearted friends,

Unarm'd, and unresolv'd to beat them back.

'Tis thought that Richmond is their admiral;

And there they hull, expecting but the aid

Of Buckingham to welcome them ashore.   440

*King Richard.* Some light-foot friend post to the Duke of Norfolk:

Ratcliff, thyself, or Catesby; where is he?

*Catesby.* Here, my good lord.

421 i.e. shall I forget my wrongs as a mother in order to be (again)
a queen-mother?       422 i.e. Yes, if you only hurt yourself by
remembering your wrongs.       425 **spicery:** sweetness [*N*].
426 **Selves of themselves:** new selves out of ashes (like the phoenix).
**recomforture:** consolation.       428 **And:** Yes, and.       435
**puissant:** powerful.       439 **hull:** drift (without sails).   **expecting but:** only waiting for.       441 **light-foot**(ed): swift.

*King Richard.*                    Catesby, fly to the duke.

*Catesby.* I will, my lord, with all convenient haste.

*King Richard.* Ratcliff, come hither. Post to Salisbury:                                                         445

When thou com'st thither,—[*To* CATESBY.] Dull, unmind-
ful villain,

Why stay'st thou here, and go'st not to the duke?

*Catesby.* First, mighty liege, tell me your highness'
pleasure,

What from your Grace I shall deliver to him.

*King Richard.* O! true, good Catesby: bid him levy
straight                                                     450

The greatest strength and power he can make,

And meet me suddenly at Salisbury.

*Catesby.* I go.                                    [*Exit.*

*Ratcliff.* What, may it please you, shall I do at Salisbury?

*King Richard.* Why, what wouldst thou do there before
I go?                                                         455

*Ratcliff.* Your highness told me I should post before.

*Enter* STANLEY.

*King Richard.* My mind is chang'd. Stanley, what news
with you?

*Stanley.* None good, my liege, to please you with the
hearing;

Nor none so bad but well may be reported.                    459

*King Richard.* Hoyday, a riddle! neither good nor bad!

What need'st thou run so many miles about,

When thou mayst tell thy tale the nearest way?

Once more, what news?

*Stanley.*                        Richmond is on the seas.

*King Richard.* There let him sink, and be the seas on him!

White-liver'd runagate! what doth he there?                  465

*Stanley.* I know not, mighty sovereign, but by guess.

451 **power:** forces.   452 **suddenly:** quickly.      465 **White-
liver'd runagate:** cowardly fugitive [*N*].

*King Richard.* Well, as you guess?

*Stanley.* Stirr'd up by Dorset, Buckingham, and Morton,
He makes for England, here to claim the crown.

*King Richard.* Is the chair empty? is the sword un-
sway'd?                                                   470
Is the king dead? the empire unpossess'd?
What heir of York is there alive but we?
And who is England's king but great York's heir?
Then, tell me, what makes he upon the seas?

*Stanley.* Unless for that, my liege, I cannot guess.     475

*King Richard.* Unless for that he comes to be your liege,
You cannot guess wherefore the Welshman comes.
Thou wilt revolt and fly to him, I fear.

*Stanley.* No, my good lord; therefore mistrust me not.

*King Richard.* Where is thy power then to beat him
back?                                                     480
Where be thy tenants and thy followers?
Are they not now upon the western shore,
Safe-conducting the rebels from their ships?

*Stanley.* No, my good lord, my friends are in the north.

*King Richard.* Cold friends to me: what do they in the
north,                                                    485
When they should serve their sovereign in the west?

*Stanley.* They have not been commanded, mighty king:
Pleaseth your majesty to give me leave,
I'll muster up my friends, and meet your Grace,
Where and what time your majesty shall please.           490

*King Richard.* Ay, ay, thou wouldst be gone to join with
Richmond:

468 **Morton:** the bishop of Ely (see IV. iii. 46) [*N*].          470
**chair:** throne.    **the sword:** of state.        471 **empire:** kingdom.
474 **makes he:** is he doing.        475 **for that:** to claim the throne.
476 **for that:** because (Richard gives the words a different turn).
480 **power:** forces.        483 **safe-conducting:** giving them an
unopposed landing.        487 **been commanded:** received any
orders.        488 **Pleaseth:** if it please.

But I'll not trust thee.

*Stanley.*                    Most mighty sovereign,
You have no cause to hold my friendship doubtful.
I never was nor never will be false.

*King Richard.*  Go then and muster men: but leave
behind                                            495
Your son, George Stanley: but look your heart be firm,
Or else his head's assurance is but frail.

*Stanley.*  So deal with him as I prove true to you.  [*Exit.*

*Enter a* Messenger.

*Messenger.*  My gracious sovereign, now in Devonshire,
As I by friends am well advertised,               500
Sir Edward Courtney, and the haughty prelate,
Bishop of Exeter, his brother there,
With many moe confederates are in arms.

*Enter a second* Messenger.

*Second Messenger.*  In Kent, my liege, the Guildfords
are in arms:
And every hour more competitors                   505
Flock to the rebels, and their power grows strong.

*Enter a third* Messenger.

*Third Messenger.*  My lord, the army of great Buckingham—

*King Richard.*  Out on ye, owls! nothing but songs of
death?                              [*He strikes him.*
There, take thou that, till thou bring better news.   509

*Third Messenger.*  The news I have to tell your majesty
Is, that by sudden floods and fall of waters,

497 **his head's assurance**: the security of his head.    500 **advertised**: (pronounce advértiséd) warned.    503 **moe**: more.
505 **hour**: two syllables.      **competitors**: associates (on the *same*
side).      508 **owls**: birds of bad omen [*N*].    511 **fall of waters**:
rain.

Buckingham's army is dispers'd and scatter'd;
And he himself wander'd away alone,
No man knows whither.

*King Richard.*            I cry thee mercy:
There is my purse, to cure that blow of thine.          515
Hath any well-advised friend proclaim'd
Reward to him that brings the traitor in?

*Third Messenger.* Such proclamation hath been made,
   my liege.

*Enter a fourth* Messenger.

*Fourth Messenger.* Sir Thomas Lovel, and Lord Marquess
   Dorset,
'Tis said, my liege, in Yorkshire are in arms:          520
But this good comfort bring I to your highness,
The Breton navy is dispers'd by tempest.
Richmond, in Dorsetshire, sent out a boat
Unto the shore to ask those on the banks
If they were his assistants, yea or no;                  525
Who answer'd him, they came from Buckingham
Upon his party: he, mistrusting them,
Hois'd sail, and made away for Brittany.

*King Richard.* March on, march on, since we are up in
   arms;
If not to fight with foreign enemies,                    530
Yet to beat down these rebels here at home.

*Re-enter* CATESBY.

*Catesby.* My liege, the Duke of Buckingham is taken,
That is the best news: that the Earl of Richmond
Is with a mighty power landed at Milford

514 **cry thee mercy**: beg your pardon.        516 **well-advised**:
prudent, far-seeing (cf. i. iii. 318).          522 **Breton**: from
Brittany (528).        524 **banks**: sea-shore (not so used after Sh.).
527 **party**: side (cf. i. iii. 128) [*N*].        528 **Hois'd**: hoisted (from
a form 'hoise').      534 **Milford** Haven, in Pembrokeshire.

Is colder tidings, yet they must be told.                535
  *King Richard.* Away towards Salisbury! while we reason
    here,
A royal battle might be won and lost.
Some one take order Buckingham be brought
To Salisbury; the rest march on with me.          [*Exeunt.*


*Scene V.* THE SAME. A ROOM IN LORD STANLEY'S
HOUSE

    *Enter* STANLEY *and* SIR CHRISTOPHER URSWICK.

  *Stanley.* Sir Christopher, tell Richmond this from me:
That in the sty of this most bloody boar
My son George Stanley is frank'd up in hold:
If I revolt, off goes young George's head;
The fear of that holds off my present aid.                5
So, get thee gone: commend me to thy lord.
Withal, say that the queen hath heartily consented
He should espouse Elizabeth her daughter.
But, tell me, where is princely Richmond now?
  *Christopher.* At Pembroke, or at Ha'rford-west, in
    Wales.                                                10
  *Stanley.* What men of name resort to him?
  *Christopher.* Sir Walter Herbert, a renowned soldier,
Sir Gilbert Talbot, Sir William Stanley,
Oxford, redoubted Pembroke, Sir James Blunt,
And Rice ap Thomas, with a valiant crew;                15
And many other of great name and worth:

---

    536 **reason:** argue.    537 **royal battle:** battle for the crown.
538 **take order:** arrange for (cf. III. v. 105).    1 **Sir:** cf. III. ii.
108 [*N*].    2 cf. I. iii. 228.    3 **frank'd up:** see I. iii. 314.
**hold:** prison.    7 **Withal:** at the same time [*N*].    11 **name:**
repute.    14 **redoubted:** redoubtable, doughty [*N*].    15 **crew:**
company.    16 **other:** a frequent plural in Sh.

And towards London do they bend their power,
If by the way they be not fought withal.

   *Stanley.*  Well, hie thee to thy lord; I kiss his hand:
My letter will resolve him of my mind.         20
Farewell.                                *[Exeunt.*

    18 **withal**: with.     20 **resolve . . . mind**: tell him my purpose [*N*].

# ACT V

*Scene I.* SALISBURY. AN OPEN PLACE

*Enter the* Sheriff *and* Guard, *with* BUCKINGHAM,
*led to execution.*

*Buckingham.* Will not King Richard let me speak with
him?

*Sheriff.* No, my good lord; therefore be patient.

*Buckingham.* Hastings, and Edward's children, Grey and
Rivers,
Holy King Henry, and thy fair son Edward,
Vaughan, and all that have miscarried                    5
By underhand corrupted foul injustice,
If that your moody discontented souls
Do through the clouds behold this present hour,
Even for revenge mock my destruction!
This is All-Souls' day, fellows, is it not?              10

*Sheriff.* It is, my lord.

*Buckingham.* Why, then All-Souls' day is my body's
doomsday.
This is the day that, in King Edward's time,
I wish'd might fall on me, when I was found
False to his children or his wife's allies;              15
This is the day wherein I wish'd to fall
By the false faith of him whom most I trusted;
This, this All-Souls' day to my fearful soul
Is the determin'd respite of my wrongs.

3–5 **Hastings . . . Henry:** all in vocative case.      5 **Vaughan**
is, as usual, two, and **miscarried** four syllables; on 'miscarried' for
'died' cf. I. iii. 16.      7 **moody:** angry.      10 **All-Souls' day:**
2 November.      12 **doomsday:** day of death.      13 see II.
i. 29–40.      16 **wish'd to fall:** i.e. prayed that I might fall, if I
was untrue (II. i. 36–39).      19 **the determin'd . . . wrongs:**
the pre-determined day to which I put off paying for my wrong-doings.

That high All-Seer which I dallied with                    20
Hath turn'd my feigned prayer on my head,
And given in earnest what I begg'd in jest.
Thus doth he force the swords of wicked men
To turn their own points on their masters' bosoms:
Thus Margaret's curse falls heavy on my neck:            25
'When he,' quoth she, 'shall split thy heart with sorrow,
Remember Margaret was a prophetess.'
Come, lead me, officers, to the block of shame:
Wrong hath but wrong, and blame the due of blame.
                                        [*Exeunt.*

## Scene II. A Plain near Tamworth

*Enter with drum and colours,* RICHMOND, OXFORD, SIR
    JAMES BLUNT, SIR WALTER HERBERT, *and Others, with*
    *Forces, marching.*

  *Richmond.* Fellows in arms, and my most loving friends,
Bruis'd underneath the yoke of tyranny,
Thus far into the bowels of the land
Have we march'd on without impediment:
And here receive we from our father Stanley              5
Lines of fair comfort and encouragement.
The wretched, bloody, and usurping boar,
That spoil'd your summer fields and fruitful vines,
Swills your warm blood like wash, and makes his trough
In your embowell'd bosoms, this foul swine             10
Is now even in the centre of this isle,

20 i.e. God whom I deceived.                    21 **feigned**: insincere.
24 **their masters'**: the owners of the swords.            25–27 see I. iii.
299–301.            29 **Wrong . . . wrong**: my wrong-doing has brought
on me an unjust death.            **the due of blame**: what it deserves.
3 **bowels**: heart (a similar metaphor).            5 **father**: father-in-
law [*N*].            7 **boar**: see I. iii. 228 and III. ii. 11.            9 **Swills**:
gulps down.            **wash**: hog's wash, refuse and water from pans, &c.
10 **embowell'd**: disembowelled.

Near to the town of Leicester, as we learn:
From Tamworth thither is but one day's march.
In God's name, cheerly on, courageous friends,
To reap the harvest of perpetual peace                    15
By this one bloody trial of sharp war.

*Oxford.* Every man's conscience is a thousand men,
To fight against this guilty homicide.

*Herbert.* I doubt not but his friends will turn to us.

*Blunt.* He hath no friends but what are friends for
    fear,                                                 20
Which in his dearest need will fly from him.

*Richmond.* All for our vantage: then, in God's name,
    march:
True hope is swift, and flies with swallow's wings;
Kings it makes gods, and meaner creatures kings.
                                            [*Exeunt.*

## *Scene III.* BOSWORTH FIELD

*Enter* KING RICHARD *and Forces;* *the* DUKE OF NORFOLK,
    EARL OF SURREY, *and Others.*

*King Richard.* Here pitch our tent, even here in Bos-
    worth field.
My Lord of Surrey, why look you so sad?

*Surrey.* My heart is ten times lighter than my looks.

*King Richard.* My Lord of Norfolk,—

*Norfolk.*                          Here, most gracious liege.

*King Richard.* Norfolk, we must have knocks; ha! must
    we not?                                               5

*Norfolk.* We must both give and take, my loving lord.

*King Richard.* Up with my tent! here will I lie to-night;
                [*Soldiers begin to set up the* KING'S *tent.*

14 **cheerly on:** march on cheerfully.       17 i.e. a good conscience is as good as many more soldiers.    21 **dearest need:**
greatest extremity (cf. I. iv. 215).          23 **True hope:** i.e. hope
based on good grounds as ours is.            5 **ha!** eh!

But where to-morrow? Well, all's one for that.
Who hath descried the number of the traitors?
  *Norfolk.* Six or seven thousand is their utmost power.   10
  *King Richard.* Why, our battalia trebles that account;
Besides, the king's name is a tower of strength,
Which they upon the adverse faction want.
Up with the tent! Come, noble gentlemen,
Let us survey the vantage of the ground;   15
Call for some men of sound direction:
Let's lack no discipline, make no delay;
For, lords, to-morrow is a busy day.      [*Exeunt.*

*Enter on the other side of the field*, RICHMOND, SIR WILLIAM
   BRANDON, OXFORD, *and other Officers. Some of the
   Soldiers pitch* RICHMOND'S *tent.*

  *Richmond.* The weary sun hath made a golden set,
And, by the bright track of his fiery car,   20
Gives token of a goodly day to-morrow.
Sir William Brandon, you shall bear my standard.
Give me some ink and paper in my tent:
I'll draw the form and model of our battle,
Limit each leader to his several charge,   25
And part in just proportion our small power.
My Lord of Oxford, you, Sir William Brandon,
And you, Sir Walter Herbert, stay with me.
The Earl of Pembroke keeps his regiment:
Good Captain Blunt, bear my good-night to him,   30
And by the second hour in the morning
Desire the earl to see me in my tent.

   8 **all's one for that**: that doesn't matter.    9 **descried**:
made out.    11 **battalia**: armed force (Ital. *battaglia*).    **account**: number.    15 **the vantage of the ground**: i.e. how we
can use the ground to advantage.    16 **direction**: capacity in
directing the movement of soldiers.    17 **discipline**: (the fruit of)
experience (cf. III. vii. 16).    19 **set**: setting [*N*].    25 **Limit**:
appoint.    29 **keeps**: stays with.

Yet one thing more, good captain, do for me;
Where is Lord Stanley quarter'd, do you know?
  *Blunt.* Unless I have mista'en his colours much,—    35
Which, well I am assur'd, I have not done,—
His regiment lies half a mile at least
South from the mighty power of the king.
  *Richmond.* If without peril it be possible,
Good Captain Blunt, bear my good-night to him,    40
And give him from me this most needful note.
  *Blunt.* Upon my life, my lord, I'll undertake it;
And so, God give you quiet rest to-night!
  *Richmond.* Good night, good Captain Blunt. Come,
    gentlemen,
Let us consult upon to-morrow's business;    45
In to my tent, the air is raw and cold.
                          [*They withdraw into the tent.*

*Enter, to his tent,* KING RICHARD, NORFOLK, RATCLIFF,
                *and* CATESBY.
  *King Richard.* What is 't o'clock?
  *Catesby.*                   It's supper-time, my lord:
It's nine o'clock.
  *King Richard.* I will not sup to-night.
Give me some ink and paper.
What, is my beaver easier than it was,    50
And all my armour laid into my tent?
  *Catesby.* It is, my liege; and all things are in readiness.
  *King Richard.* Good Norfolk, hic thee to thy charge;
Use careful watch; choose trusty sentinels.
  *Norfolk.* I go, my lord.    55
  *King Richard.* Stir with the lark to-morrow, gentle
    Norfolk.
  *Norfolk.* I warrant you, my lord.        [*Exit.*

 38 **power:** forces.     46 **In:** let us go in.     50 **beaver:** helmet
(as occasionally elsewhere).

*King Richard.* Ratcliff!

*Ratcliff.* My lord!

*King Richard.*        Send out a pursuivant-at-arms

To Stanley's regiment; bid him bring his power        60

Before sunrising, lest his son George fall

Into the blind cave of eternal night.

Fill me a bowl of wine. Give me a watch.

Saddle white Surrey for the field to-morrow.

Look that my staves be sound, and not too heavy.        65

Ratcliff!

*Ratcliff.* My lord?

*King Richard.* Saw'st thou the melancholy Lord Northumberland?

*Ratcliff.* Thomas the Earl of Surrey, and himself,

Much about cock-shut time, from troop to troop        70

Went through the army, cheering up the soldiers.

*King Richard.* So, I am satisfied. Give me a bowl of
wine:

I have not that alacrity of spirit,

Nor cheer of mind, that I was wont to have.

Set it down. Is ink and paper ready?        75

*Ratcliff.* It is, my lord.

*King Richard.* Bid my guard watch; leave me.

Ratcliff, about the mid of night come to my tent

And help to arm me. Leave me, I say.

> [KING RICHARD *retires into his tent. Exeunt* RATCLIFF
> *and* CATESBY.

RICHMOND'S *tent opens, and discovers him and his Officers,*
*&c. Enter* STANLEY.

*Stanley.* Fortune and victory sit on thy helm!        80

**59 pursuivant-at-arms:** herald's attendant, messenger.
**62 blind:** dark.        **eternal night:** cf. I. iv. 47.        **63 watch:**
candle marked in hours [N].        **65 staves:** shafts of lances.
**70 cock-shut:** twilight [N].        **75 it:** the wine.        **78–79 s.d.**
*discovers:* reveals.

*Richmond.*  All comfort that the dark night can afford
Be to thy person, noble father-in-law!
Tell me, how fares our loving mother?
  *Stanley.*  I, by attorney, bless thee from thy mother,
Who prays continually for Richmond's good:                    85
So much for that.  The silent hours steal on,
And flaky darkness breaks within the east.
In brief, for so the season bids us be,
Prepare thy battle early in the morning,
And put thy fortune to the arbitrement                    90
Of bloody strokes and mortal-staring war.
I, as I may,—that which I would I cannot,—
With best advantage will deceive the time,
And aid thee in this doubtful shock of arms.
But on thy side I may not be too forward,                    95
Lest, being seen, thy brother, tender George,
Be executed in his father's sight.
Farewell: the leisure and the fearful time
Cuts off the ceremonious vows of love
And ample interchange of sweet discourse,                    100
Which so long sunder'd friends should dwell upon:
God give us leisure for these rites of love!
Once more, adieu: be valiant, and speed well!
  *Richmond.*  Good lords, conduct him to his regiment.
I'll strive, with troubled thoughts, to take a nap,                    105
Lest leaden slumber peise me down to-morrow,
When I should mount with wings of victory.

---

82 **father-in-law**: for stepfather, as often.      84 **by attorney**: in
her name, acting for her (cf. IV. iv. 414).      87 **flaky**: i.e. broken up
into flakes of cloud as the light streams through it.      88 **season**:
time (of night).      89 **battle**: order of battle.      91 **mortal-
staring**: that stares fatally on its victims.      93 i.e. will temporize,
not commit myself, as best I can.      96 **being seen**: if I am seen
(to be on thy side).      98 **leisure**: time available.      **time**:
occasion, circumstances.      105 **with**: i.e. in spite of.      106
**peise**: weigh.

Once more, good night, kinds lords and gentlemen.

[*Exeunt all but* RICHMOND.

O! thou, whose captain I account myself,
Look on my forces with a gracious eye;                    110
Put in their hands thy bruising irons of wrath,
That they may crush down with a heavy fall
The usurping helmets of our adversaries!
Make us thy ministers of chastisement,
That we may praise thee in thy victory!                   115
To thee I do commend my watchful soul,
Ere I let fall the windows of mine eyes:
Sleeping and waking, O! defend me still!          [*Sleeps.*

*The Ghost of* PRINCE EDWARD, *Son to* Henry the Sixth, *rises
between the two tents.*

Ghost. [*To* KING RICHARD.] Let me sit heavy on thy soul
to-morrow!
Think how thou stab'dst me in my prime of youth          120
At Tewksbury: despair, therefore, and die!
[*To* RICHMOND.] Be cheerful, Richmond; for the wronged
souls
Of butcher'd princes fight in thy behalf:
King Henry's issue, Richmond, comforts thee.

*The Ghost of* KING HENRY THE SIXTH *rises.*

Ghost. [*To* KING RICHARD.] When I was mortal, my
anointed body                                            125
By thee was punched full of deadly holes:
Think on the Tower and me; despair and die!
Henry the Sixth bids thee despair and die.
[*To* RICHMOND.] Virtuous and holy, be thou conqueror!

111 **bruising irons**: heavy maces, metal-headed clubs ('bruise' =
crush as in v. ii. 2).            113 **usurping**: really applies to 'adversaries'.            116 **watchful**: wakeful.            125 **mortal**: alive (as
in IV. iv. 26).        **anointed**: royal (and therefore sacred).        126
**punched**: pierced.        127 see *3 Henry VI*, v. vi.

Harry, that prophesied thou shouldst be king,                 130
Doth comfort thee in thy sleep: live thou and flourish!

*The Ghost of* CLARENCE *rises.*

*Ghost.* [*To* KING RICHARD.] Let me sit heavy on thy soul
    to-morrow!
I, that was wash'd to death with fulsome wine,
Poor Clarence, by thy guile betray'd to death!
To-morrow in the battle think on me,                          135
And fall thy edgeless sword: despair, and die!
  [*To* RICHMOND.] Thou offspring of the house of Lan-
    caster,
The wronged heirs of York do pray for thee:
Good angels guard thy battle! live, and flourish!

*The Ghosts of* RIVERS, GREY, *and* VAUGHAN *rise.*

*Ghost of Rivers.* [*To* KING RICHARD.] Let me sit heavy on
    thy soul to-morrow!                                    140
Rivers, that died at Pomfret! despair, and die!
  *Ghost of Grey.* [*To* KING RICHARD]. Think upon Grey,
    and let thy soul despair.
  *Ghost of Vaughan.* [*To* KING RICHARD.] Think upon
    Vaughan, and with guilty fear
Let fall thy pointless lance: despair, and die!—
  *All Three.* [*To* RICHMOND.] Awake! and think our
    wrongs in Richard's bosom                              145
Will conquer him: awake, and win the day!

*The Ghost of* HASTINGS *rises.*

*Ghost.* [*To* KING RICHARD.] Bloody and guilty, guiltily
    awake;
And in a bloody battle end thy days!

130 see IV. ii. 94–95.          133 **fulsome:** *either* cloying *or* excess of.
136 **fall:** let fall (cf. I. iii. 353).     **edgeless:** so that it becomes ineffec-
tive.          144 **pointless:** cf. 'edgeless' in 136 (but the word is here
supplied to fill a metrical gap).          145 **in:** working in.

Think on Lord Hastings, so despair, and die!—          149
  [*To* RICHMOND.] Quiet, untroubled soul, awake, awake!
Arm, fight, and conquer, for fair England's sake!

*The Ghosts of the two young* PRINCES *rise.*
  *Ghosts.* [*To* KING RICHARD.] Dream on thy cousins
    smother'd in the Tower:
Let us be lead within thy bosom, Richard,
And weigh thee down to ruin, shame, and death!
Thy nephews' souls bid thee despair and die!          155
  [*To* RICHMOND.] Sleep, Richmond, sleep in peace, and
    wake in joy;
Good angels guard thee from the boar's annoy!
Live, and beget a happy race of kings!
Edward's unhappy sons do bid thee flourish.

*The Ghost of* LADY ANNE *rises.*
  *Ghost.* [*To* KING RICHARD.] Richard, thy wife, that
    wretched Anne thy wife,                         160
That never slept a quiet hour with thee,
Now fills thy sleep with perturbations:
To-morrow in the battle think on me,
And fall thy edgeless sword: despair, and die!        164
  [*To* RICHMOND.] Thou quiet soul, sleep thou a quiet sleep,
Dream of success and happy victory!
Thy adversary's wife doth pray for thee.

*The Ghost of* BUCKINGHAM *rises.*
  *Ghost.* [*To* KING RICHARD.] The first was I that help'd
    thee to the crown:
The last was I that felt thy tyranny.
O! in the battle think on Buckingham,                 170

---

152 **cousins**: nephews (cf. III. i. 101).    153 **lead**: as heavy as
lead.    157 **annoy!**: annoyance (but probably used for the rhyme
with 'joy').    161 see IV. i. 82–84.

And die in terror of thy guiltiness!
Dream on, dream on, of bloody deeds and death:
Fainting, despair; despairing, yield thy breath!
  [*To* RICHMOND.] I died for hope ere I could lend thee aid:
But cheer thy heart, and be thou not dismay'd:    175
God and good angels fight on Richmond's side;
And Richard falls in height of all his pride.

           [KING RICHARD *starts out of his dream.*
  *King Richard.*  Give me another horse! bind up my
    wounds!
Have mercy, Jesu! Soft! I did but dream.
O coward conscience, how dost thou afflict me!    180
The lights burn blue. It is now dead midnight.
Cold fearful drops stand on my trembling flesh.
What! do I fear myself? there's none else by:
Richard loves Richard; that is, I am I.
Is there a murderer here? No. Yes, I am:    185
Then fly: what! from myself? Great reason why:
Lest I revenge myself upon myself.
Alack! I love myself. For any good
That I myself have done unto myself?
O! no: alas! I rather hate myself    190
For hateful deeds committed by myself.
I am a villain. Yet I lie; I am not.
Fool, of thyself speak well: fool, do not flatter.
My conscience hath a thousand several tongues,
And every tongue brings in a several tale,    195
And every tale condemns me for a villain.
Perjury, perjury, in the high'st degree:
Murder, stern murder, in the direst degree;
All several sins, all us'd in each degree,

---

   174 **for hope:** for hoping to aid thee [*N*].     186 **Great reason**
**why:** there is good reason why I should.    187 **revenge . . .**
**myself:** punish myself for my deeds [*N*].    194 **several:** separate (as in III. ii. 76) [*N*].    199 **us'd:** practised.

Throng to the bar, crying all, 'Guilty! guilty!'                200
I shall despair. There is no creature loves me;
And if I die, no soul will pity me:
Nay, wherefore should they, since that I myself
Find in myself no pity to myself?
Methought the souls of all that I had murder'd                205
Came to my tent; and every one did threat
To-morrow's vengeance on the head of Richard.

*Enter* RATCLIFF.

*Ratcliff.* My lord!
*King Richard.* 'Zounds! who's there?
*Ratcliff.* My lord; 'tis I. The early village cock          210
Hath twice done salutation to the morn;
Your friends are up, and buckle on their armour.
*King Richard.* O Ratcliff! I have dream'd a fearful
    dream.
What thinkest thou, will our friends prove all true?
*Ratcliff.* No doubt, my lord.
*King Richard.*          O Ratcliff! I fear, I fear,— 215
*Ratcliff.* Nay, good my lord, be not afraid of shadows.
*King Richard.* By the apostle Paul, shadows to-night
Have struck more terror to the soul of Richard
Than can the substance of ten thousand soldiers
Armed in proof, and led by shallow Richmond.                220
It is not yet near day. Come, go with me;
Under our tents I'll play the eaves-dropper,
To hear if any mean to shrink from me.          [*Exeunt.*

RICHMOND *wakes. Enter* OXFORD *and others.*
*Lords.* Good morrow, Richmond!
*Richmond.* Cry mercy, lords, and watchful gentlemen, 225

217 **shadows**: shades, ghosts (but with play on 'shade' *v.* 'substance'). 220 **proof**: armour of *proved* strength, proof against weapons. 225 **Cry mercy**: pardon me (cf. I. iii. 235).

That you have ta'en a tardy sluggard here.
*Lords.* How have you slept, my lord?
*Richmond.* The sweetest sleep, the fairest-boding dreams
That ever enter'd in a drowsy head,
Have I since your departure had, my lords.                    230
Methought their souls, whose bodies Richard murder'd,
Came to my tent and cried on victory:
I promise you, my heart is very jocund
In the remembrance of so fair a dream.
How far into the morning is it, lords?                    235
*Lords.* Upon the stroke of four.
*Richmond.* Why, then 'tis time to arm and give direction.

RICHMOND'S *oration to his Soldiers.*

More than I have said, loving countrymen,
The leisure and enforcement of the time
Forbids to dwell on: yet remember this,                    240
God and our good cause fight upon our side;
The prayers of holy saints and wronged souls,
Like high-rear'd bulwarks, stand before our faces;
Richard except, those whom we fight against
Had rather have us win than him they follow.                    245
For what is he they follow? truly, gentlemen,
A bloody tyrant and a homicide;
One rais'd in blood, and one in blood establish'd;
One that made means to come by what he hath,                    249
And slaughter'd those that were the means to help him;
A base foul stone, made precious by the foil

226 **ta'en**: come upon, caught.                    232 **cried on**: called out.
237 **direction**: orders [N].                    239 **leisure . . . time**: the limited
time at my disposal.                    244 **Richard except**: Richard being
excluded, apart from R.                    247 **homicide**: murderer.
248 **rais'd in**: reared up amid.                    **in blood establish'd**: holding his
throne by bloodshed.                    249 **made means**: contrived (unjustly).
251 **foul stone**: i.e. not really a precious stone.                    **foil**: setting
[N].

Of England's chair, where he is falsely set;
One that hath ever been God's enemy.
Then, if you fight against God's enemy,
God will in justice ward you as his soldiers;          255
If you do sweat to put a tyrant down,
You sleep in peace, the tyrant being slain;
If you do fight against your country's foes,
Your country's fat shall pay your pains the hire;
If you do fight in safeguard of your wives,          260
Your wives shall welcome home the conquerors;
If you do free your children from the sword,
Your children's children quit it in your age.
Then, in the name of God and all these rights,
Advance your standards, draw your willing swords.    265
For me, the ransom of my bold attempt
Shall be this cold corse on the earth's cold face;
But if I thrive, the gain of my attempt
The least of you shall share his part thereof.
Sound drums and trumpets, boldly and cheerfully;     270
God and Saint George! Richmond and victory!   [*Exeunt.*

*Re-enter* KING RICHARD, RATCLIFF, Attendants, *and Forces.*
  *King Richard.* What said Northumberland as touching
    Richmond?
  *Ratcliff.* That he was never trained up in arms.
  *King Richard.* He said the truth: and what said Surrey
    then?
  *Ratcliff.* He smil'd, and said, 'The better for our pur-
    pose.'                                              275

---

  252 **chair**: throne (cf. IV. iv. 470).          255 **ward**: guard.
259 **fat**: wealth (cf. 'the fat of the land', Genesis xlv. 18).
263 **quit**: will repay.     265 **Advance**: raise up.     266 **ransom**:
price.      266–7 i.e. I won't be taken prisoner ('on a carpet in a
lady's chamber', Holinshed).          268–9 **the gain ... thereof**: in
the gain.

*King Richard.* He was i' the right; and so, indeed, it is,
                                        [*Clock strikes.*
Tell the clock there. Give me a calendar.
Who saw the sun to-day?
  *Ratcliff.*                    Not I, my lord.
  *King Richard.* Then he disdains to shine; for by the book
He should have brav'd the east an hour ago:          280
A black day will it be to somebody.
Ratcliff!
  *Ratcliff.* My lord?
  *King Richard.*      The sun will not be seen to-day;
The sky doth frown and lower upon our army.
I would these dewy tears were from the ground.       285
Not shine to-day! Why, what is that to me
More than to Richmond? for the selfsame heaven
That frowns on me looks sadly upon him.


                    *Enter* NORFOLK.
  *Norfolk.* Arm, arm, my lord! the foe vaunts in the field.
  *King Richard.* Come, bustle, bustle; caparison my
    horse.                                           290
Call up Lord Stanley, bid him bring his power:
I will lead forth my soldiers to the plain,
And thus my battle shall be ordered:
My foreward shall be drawn out all in length
Consisting equally of horse and foot;                295
Our archers shall be placed in the midst:
John Duke of Norfolk, Thomas Earl of Surrey,
Shall have the leading of this foot and horse.
They thus directed, we will follow

---

  277 **Tell:** count.        278 **saw:** has seen.      279 **book:**
calendar.        280 **brav'd:** made brave, adorned.       285 **dewy**
**tears:** dew.      **from:** (melted) away from.      290 **caparison:**
put on his trappings (derived from Med. L. *capa* = cloak).       293
**battle:** array (cf. 89).          294 **foreward:** vanguard.

In the main battle, whose puissance on either side        300
Shall be well winged with our chiefest horse.
This, and Saint George to boot! What think'st thou,
    Norfolk?
    *Norfolk.* A good direction, warlike sovereign.
This found I on my tent this morning.    [*Giving a scroll.*
    *King Richard.* 'Jockey of Norfolk, be not too bold,  305
For Dickon thy master is bought and sold.'
A thing devised by the enemy.
Go, gentlemen; every man to his charge:
Let not our babbling dreams affright our souls;
Conscience is but a word that cowards use,        310
Devis'd at first to keep the strong in awe:
Our strong arms be our conscience, swords our law.
March on, join bravely, let us to 't pell-mell;
If not to heaven, then hand in hand to hell.


*His oration to his Army.*

What shall I say more than I have inferr'd?        315
Remember whom you are to cope withal:
A sort of vagabonds, rascals, and runaways,
A scum of Bretons and base lackey peasants,
Whom their o'er-cloyed country vomits forth
To desperate adventures and assur'd destruction.        320
You sleeping safe, they bring you to unrest;
You having lands, and bless'd with beauteous wives,

---

300 **puissance**: force.        301 **winged**: flanked ('having horse-
men for wings', Holinshed).        302 **This**: this is my plan.        **to
boot**: to help us in addition.        303 **direction**: order of battle.
305 **Jockey**: Jacky = Jack (John Howard).        306 **Dickon**: Dick
=Richard.        **bought and sold**: betrayed.        313 **pell-mell**:
vigorously, recklessly (from French).        315 **inferr'd**: (already)
alleged (cf. III. v. 74).        316 **cope withal**: deal with.
317 **sort**: company.        318 **lackey**: (only fit to be) servants.
319 **o'er-cloyed**: overfull.        321 **You ... safe**: when you might
be safely sleeping.

They would restrain the one, distain the other.
And who doth lead them but a paltry fellow,
Long kept in Britaine at our mother's cost?          325
A milksop, one that never in his life
Felt so much cold as over shoes in snow?
Let's whip these stragglers o'er the sea again;
Lash hence these overweening rags of France
These famish'd beggars, weary of their lives          330
Who, but for dreaming on this fond exploit,
For want of means, poor rats, had hang'd themselves:
If we be conquer'd, let men conquer us,
And not these bastard Bretons; whom our fathers
Have in their own land beaten, bobb'd, and thump'd,          335
And, on record, left them the heirs of shame.
Shall these enjoy our lands? lie with our wives?
Ravish our daughters?                    [*Drum afar off.*
            Hark! I hear their drum.
Fight, gentlemen of England! fight, bold yeomen!
Draw, archers, draw your arrows to the head!          340
Spur your proud horses hard, and ride in blood;
Amaze the welkin with your broken staves!
            *Enter a* Messenger.
What says Lord Stanley? will he bring his power?
  *Messenger.* My lord, he doth deny to come.
  *King Richard.* Off with his son George's head!          345
  *Norfolk.* My lord, the enemy is pass'd the marsh:
After the battle let George Stanley die.
  *King Richard.* A thousand hearts are great within my
      bosom:

323 **restrain**: keep from you.   **distain**: stain, defile.          325
**Britaine**: Brittany [N].          326 **milksop**: soft, no soldier (H.'s
word).          329 **rags**: odds and ends, worthless people (cf. I. iii. 233).
331 **fond**: foolish.          335 **bobb'd**: drubbed.          336 **on recórd**:
as is recorded.          341 **in blood**: passionately *or* in the blood
drawn by your spurs.          342 **Amaze the welkin**: frighten
the sky.          344 **deny**: refuse.

Advance our standards! set upon our foes!
Our ancient word of courage, fair Saint George,                    350
Inspire us with the spleen of fiery dragons!
Upon them! Victory sits upon our helms.          [*Exeunt.*

### *Scene IV.* ANOTHER PART OF THE FIELD

*Alarum: Excursions. Enter* NORFOLK *and Forces;*
*to him* CATESBY.

*Catesby.* Rescue, my Lord of Norfolk! rescue, rescue!
The king enacts more wonders than a man,
Daring an opposite to every danger:
His horse is slain, and all on foot he fights,
Seeking for Richmond in the throat of death.                    5
Rescue, fair lord, or else the day is lost!

*Alarum. Enter* KING RICHARD.

*King Richard.* A horse! a horse! my kingdom for a
    horse!
*Catesby.* Withdraw, my lord; I'll help you to a horse.
*King Richard.* Slave! I have set my life upon a cast,
And I will stand the hazard of the die.                    10
I think there be six Richmonds in the field;
Five have I slain to-day, instead of him.—
A horse! a horse! my kingdom for a horse!          [*Exeunt.*

*Alarums. Enter from opposite sides* KING RICHARD *and*
RICHMOND, *and exeunt fighting. Retreat and flourish.*
*Then re-enter* RICHMOND, STANLEY, *bearing the crown,*
*with divers other Lords, and Forces.*
*Richmond.* God and your arms be prais'd, victorious
    friends;

351 **spleen:** anger.          1 **Rescue:** come to the rescue.          3 **an**
**opposite:** any opponent.          **every danger:** mortal combat.
9 **set . . . cast:** risked everything on this one battle [*N*].          10 **die:**
singular of 'dice'.

The day is ours, the bloody dog is dead.                    15
   *Stanley.* Courageous Richmond, well hast thou acquit thee!
Lo! here, this long-usurped royalty
From the dead temples of this bloody wretch
Have I pluck'd off, to grace thy brows withal:
Wear it, enjoy it, and make much of it.                    20
   *Richmond.* Great God of heaven, say amen to all!
But, tell me, is young George Stanley living?
   *Stanley.* He is, my lord, and safe in Leicester town;
Whither, if you please, we may withdraw us.
   *Richmond.* What men of name are slain on either side? 25
   *Stanley.* John Duke of Norfolk, Walter Lord Ferrers,
Sir Robert Brakenbury, and Sir William Brandon.
   *Richmond.* Inter their bodies as becomes their births:
Proclaim a pardon to the soldiers fled
That in submission will return to us;                    30
And then, as we have ta'en the sacrament,
We will unite the white rose and the red:
Smile, heaven, upon this fair conjunction,
That long hath frown'd upon their enmity!
What traitor hears me, and says not amen?                    35
England hath long been mad, and scarr'd herself;
The brother blindly shed the brother's blood,
The father rashly slaughter'd his own son,
The son, compell'd, been butcher to the sire:
All this divided York and Lancaster,                    40
Divided in their dire division,
O! now, let Richmond and Elizabeth,
The true succeeders of each royal house,
By God's fair ordinance conjoin together;

16 **acquit**: acquitted.    17 **royalty**: the crown.    31 **ta'en
the sacrament**: sworn (cf. I. iv. 208) [*N*].    32 **the white rose
and the red**: the badges of the houses of York and Lancaster [*N*].
35 i.e. any hearer who does not say 'amen' is a traitor to England.
40–44 i.e. let Richmond and Elizabeth unite this realm hitherto
divided in its loyalties between York and Lancaster.

And let their heirs—God, if thy will be so,—                45
Enrich the time to come with smooth-fac'd peace,
With smiling plenty, and fair prosperous days!
Abate the edge of traitors, gracious Lord,
That would reduce these bloody days again,
And make poor England weep in streams of blood!        50
Let them not live to taste this land's increase,
That would with treason wound this fair land's peace!
Now civil wounds are stopp'd, peace lives again:
That she may long live here, God say amen!        [*Exeunt.*

48 **Abate the edge**: blunt the sword.        49 **reduce**: bring
back.

# COMMENTARY

*s.d.* = stage direction(s).
   F = first Folio (1623).
   Q = first Quarto (1597).
*O.E.D.* = *Oxford English Dictionary* (full edition).
D.W. = J. Dover Wilson in the new *Cambridge Shake-*
      *speare.*

Where other editors or critics are mentioned by name, the names of
their books will usually be found beneath quotations from them in
the Select Criticism.

References to other plays of Shakespeare are to the *Oxford
Shakespeare.*

Textual notes and a few other more advanced points are enclosed in
square brackets thus [ ].

## ACT I, Scene I

The play follows chronologically straight after the end of the Third
Part of *Henry VI.* Henry VI was murdered in the Tower on 21 May
1471, and was buried two days later. The Lancastrians had been
finally crushed at the battle of Tewkesbury 'some three months'
earlier in the same year, and Edward IV, who had become king in
1461, was henceforth secure on the throne till his death in 1483.

The first scene is devoted to the establishment of the positions of
Richard, Duke of Gloucester, younger brother of the king and of
George, Duke of Clarence. There is no historical evidence for Richard
having contrived the death of Clarence.

The luxuries of peace which he sneers at were very conspicuous at
the court of Edward IV and his Queen; so much so that it provoked
a Bull from the Pope to check it. 'Through the royal chambers,
bright with arras, fresh with strewn flowers and rushes, music was
always sounding' (Kendall, *Richard III*).

Stylistically we can notice at once that the lines are predominantly
'end-stopped', that is to say that there is very commonly a pause in
grammar and sense at the end of a line, and hence often a stop, as
opposed to the more frequent 'run-on' lines of Shakespeare's later
dramatic poetry. On the other hand there are many lines with an

extra syllable at the end, often called double endings (e.g. lines 4, 7, 8, 11, and 12), and even one with two extra syllables (1. 16), making what is called an 'Alexandrine'.

**2. this sun of York.** Pronunciation suggests the pun, which was common, on 'son'. Edward IV was the son of Richard Plantagenet, Duke of York, who began the Yorkist cause by claiming the throne in 1455, during the reign of Henry VI.

Contrast the absence of sun near the end of the play and of Richard's life (v. iii. 283).

**6. monuments** not necessarily on tombs in churches, but in the halls of great houses.

**7–13.** Notice the series of contrasts, or antitheses, in these lines— even more marked by double alliteration in 1. 8. A strong influence on the early Shakespeare was Lyly whose famous book *Euphues* carried this sort of thing to its greatest extreme. In one of his plays, *Campaspe*, he has the same antithesis as this : 'measures in a dance ... order for a march', and also the phrase 'barbed steeds'.

**15.** The adjective 'amorous' is strictly appropriate to a person, but is transferred to the thing, as is common in poetry of all ages. Something similar is seen in the use of 'lascivious' in 1. 13.

**17.** [The word 'ambling' apart from its context hardly has the force given in the footnote; so that it is not unlikely we should hyphen the two words 'wanton-ambling' and give an adverbial force to the first, which is quite in Shakespeare's manner, 'walking in an alluring way'.]

**20.** In this account of Richard's appearance the dramatist closely follows Holinshed, who himself followed More : see Introduction.

**22.** Where two adverbs come together Shakespeare sometimes uses only the adjective in one case, omitting the adverbial termination. Cf. iii. iv. 48 'cheerfully and smooth'. The word 'unfashionable' was doubtless suggested by the applicability of 'made up' to the work of a tailor.

**33. drunken.** In Holinshed we read only of 'a foolish prophecy'. If the dramatist's word implies more it must, presumably, be that Richard had set on someone to feign drunkenness as a cover for making this prophecy 'that after King Edward one should reign whose first letter of his name should be a G'. The Christian name of the Duke of Clarence was George, but, as Sir Thomas Vaughan saw on his way to execution, Richard's title also began with G.

**39–40.** See the Introduction, on the Sources.

**44.** In saying this Clarence is either being sarcastic as to Edward's motive in imprisoning him, or is reproducing an excuse made by the king, who might have alleged that some over-zealous vindicator of the royal safety might attack Clarence in view of the prophecy. (No previous commentator seems to have found any difficulty here.)

50. To those who know what is to come, when Clarence is drowned in a butt of malmsey wine, this is dramatic irony. Shakespeare had almost certainly read in *The Mirror for Magistrates* (cf. Introduction, p. 13) the account of Clarence's end put into his own mouth:

> Howbeit they bound me whether I would or no,
> And in a butt of Malmesey standing by,
> New Christened me, because I should not cry,

and uses the grim quibble at this earlier point.

55. **cross-row.** In the old 'horn-books', from which Elizabethan children learnt to read, the alphabet was preceded by a cross, and was called the 'Christ-cross-row' (hence our word 'criss-cross').

Notice the rhyme from here to 59 which gives a sort of formal, old-fashioned flavour to the lines.

64. **My Lady Grey.** From here to line 83, and in later places, Richard refers in sarcastic or sneering terms to the Queen and her relatives. Her former husband was, indeed, only a Knight, Sir John Grey, who was killed in the battle of St. Albans in 1461, fighting on the Lancastrian side, but she herself was of noble birth, and, as she was only thirty-four at this time, she hardly deserves to be called 'outworn' (l. 81).

Her brother, Antony Woodville, had become Earl Rivers two years before this, on the death of his father, and also had the title Lord Scales through his wife (so that II. i. 68 in F is a confusion). Holinshed describes him as 'a right honourable man, as valiant of hand as politike in counsel'.

65. [This line provides a simple illustration of how the text could go wrong. The first Quarto has the reading here printed. The second word was probably written in an abbreviated form which a later Q misread as 'tempts'. This made a line which did not scan, and the insertion of 'harsh' restored the metre. But the less common word 'tempers' is, by one of the general principles of all textual criticism, more likely to be right, especially when its corruption can be explained. Again in l. 75 F restores metre, but violates natural sense by reading 'was for her delivery'.]

73. **Mistress Shore.** The ordinary form 'Mrs.' for a married woman is really an abbreviation of 'Mistress', the mistress of a house-

hold. Jane Shore was wife of a London goldsmith, and the mistress of the King, using the word in its secondary sense. More gives her a good character, saying that she never abused the King's favour.

**83.** By the word 'our' Richard may be insinuating that people with Lancastrian connexions, as the Queen had, have no place in a Yorkist régime.

**84.** [In view of the corruption which modern textual experts see in this play I have followed the new *Cambridge Shakespeare* in omitting 'I' at the beginning of this line and 'O' at the beginning of 49, and the second syllable of 'kindred' in 95 in order to regularize the metre. But I have not followed Pope in omitting 'a bonny eye' in 94. As it stands that line is a 'fourteener', perhaps a quotation from a song in that favourite old metre.]

**102.** Of course Richard does *not* mean her husband, but if he were to say openly whom he does mean it could be used as a charge against him of libelling his sovereign.

**103.** [The simplest way of restoring regularity to the metre is to read 'I do beseech' with F, and to omit 'and withal', on the assumption that it was an actor's insertion.]

**106.** The literal meaning of 'abject' is something thrown away (Latin *abjicio*), but the modern use of the adjective gives the key to Richard's point in substituting it for 'subjects'. Once more the antithesis of 'abject' and 'subject' comes in Lyly's *Campaspe*.

**109.** **widow** instead of wife continues the scorn of 81: 'I will solicit you though it should be at the expense of so much degradation and constraint as to own the low-born wife of King Edward for a sister' (Dr. Johnson).

**122.** This longer form of 'good-day' only survives now when we speak of passing the 'time of day' with someone.

**153.** It is not agreed by the chronicles who killed the young prince. At 1. i. 54 Clarence accuses himself of the deed.

**157–8.** Some interpret this as Anne's wealth; but is it not rather her connexion with the Lancastrians?

# ACT I, SCENE II

This scene is at once preposterous and dramatically effective. The best commentary upon it is Shakespeare's own:

> Was ever woman in this humour woo'd?
> Was ever woman in this humour won? (229–30)

The chroniclers tell us of the removal of the body of Henry from the Tower to St. Paul's, from there to Blackfriars, and finally to Chertsey for burial; but Anne was in concealment with Queen Margaret. There was a story that there had been an earlier affection between Richard and Anne (which is more than probable since for three years they were brought up together), but the dramatist does not allude to this, probably because it would have shown Richard in a more favourable light. The scene he has invented serves well to show Richard's unscrupulousness and self-confidence playing upon the weakness and susceptibility to flattery of a young woman. 'Richard's wooing may be dictated by political necessity, but its prime purpose for the dramatist is to show Richard's insolent virtuosity in persuasion, his delight in the exercise of his mind and will, his pride in attempting the impossible and his triumph in its achievement' (Palmer).

In the long opening speech there are conspicuous examples of the rhetoric and devices which mark Shakespeare's early style, e.g. the repetition and play on words in 15–16. Lines 26–28 furnish an early example of the dramatic irony which is another prominent feature of *Richard III*. This term, or 'Sophoclean Irony', is used to describe words and sentences which bear one meaning for the characters who hear them spoken, but a further or deeper meaning for the readers or spectators who have some inkling of what is to come. In this case Anne is herself to be such an unhappy wife to Richard, and even spectators who do not know the rest of the play might guess from Richard's remarks and character as seen in the first scene, that Anne would not be happy if he married her.

5. **holy.** Henry was, like Edward the Confessor, famous for piety, and is still celebrated as the 'pious founder' of Eton College and King's College, Cambridge.

8. **Be it lawful.** Anne is more or less praying to the soul of the dead king as if he were a canonized saint, and since the Reformation the invocation of saints had no longer been a part of Anglican religion.

10. **Wife.** Cf. I. i. 153. Holinshed says Anne had actually married Prince Edward, others that they were only betrothed when he was killed.

15–16. The Elizabethans did not think puns and word-play unsuitable to tragic occasions. Compare for example the speech of the dying Gaunt in *Richard II*.

26–28. [The text is that of most editors, following Q and F; but it would be made easier and improved in sense by changing with Dover Wilson to:

> More miserable by the life of him
> Than I am by my young lord's death and thee!]

**38.** It is recorded that an actor once spoke the latter part of this line as 'let the parson cough'. This 'Spoonerism' serves to illustrate the sort of error sometimes made in the printing house, which may account for some queer readings in F or Q.

**40. halberd.** This is said to have been a combination of spear and battle axe mounted on a long pole. Perhaps we shall be near enough what was carried by the escort of the funeral if we recall the Yeoman of the Guard on our stage today.

**47–48.** The language harks back to Matthew x. 28, as does that of 63 to Genesis IV. 10, and that of 65 to Numbers xvi. 30. An Elizabethan could hardly avoid familiarity with his Bible; and although the Authorized Version did not come till 1611, earlier versions often have some of the same phraseology.

**50.** To make this line conform to the metrical pattern we must treat 'de'il' as a monosyllable, and slur over the open vowel at the end of 'trouble'. A reader who cares for the metrical feel of the line will gradually become able to make this sort of adjustment for himself, and instances will not always be mentioned in this Commentary.

**54–56.** Compare Mark Antony displaying the wounds in Caesar's body in *Julius Caesar* III. ii. 168–96. This bleeding comes in Holinshed only, not in Hall.

**68.** Much of this scene from here onwards consists of quick interchange between Anne and Richard, speeches of one or two lines, often taking up the form of the previous speaker's sentence. This rhetorical device goes back to Greek drama where it is called 'stichomythia', and came to the Elizabethans through the Roman dramatist Seneca, who had already been translated into English.

**78. diffus'd** is the later Folios' correction of 'defus'd', which would mean 'shapeless', and, presumably, introduce a glance at Richard's deformity.

**92.** In Holinshed Edward IV pushed the young prince away, and then four men, one of whom was Richard, slew him. In *Henry VI*, v. v. King Edward does strike a blow, but subsequently restrains Richard from striking Queen Margaret.

**101.** There is no definite authority for Richard's having killed Henry VI, but More reports it as common rumour.

**103.** The hedgehog's prickles suggest hostility to everyone; and there may also be an allusion to Richard's crest of the hog (cf. I. iii. 229).

**112.** If we choose to treat the words from 'Some' to 'bed-chamber' as one line, we may suppose a pause in the middle.

**143.** In spite of 119, where the word Plantagenets appeared to mean Lancastrians, it is equally applicable to the Yorkists as they were also descended from the father of Henry II, who received the nickname.

**151.** The basilisk's glance was supposed to be deadly. Shakespeare had already made Richard refer to it in *3 Henry VI*:

I'll slay more gazers than the basilisk (III. ii. 187).

**158–61.** Edmund, Earl of Rutland, was the second son of Richard Plantagenet, Duke of York, Edward IV and Richard of Gloucester being his first and fourth sons respectively. Rutland was supposed to have been murdered by Lord Clifford after the battle of Wakefield in 1460. The news of York's death was brought by a messenger (*3 Henry VI*, II. i. 79), not, as here, by Warwick.

**179. the death** has a judicial ring about it, as in Mark vii. 10: 'He that curseth father or mother, let him die the death'.

**181.** No one seems to have asked why love for Anne should have made Richard kill Henry VI. It is, of course a rhetorical exaggeration, but perhaps he means that with Henry out of the way he might have won her away from Prince Edward.

'Richard turns the strong point of Anne's attack, his own inhuman nature, into the basis of his plea—he who never wept before has been softened by love of her' (Moulton).

**203.** Anne means that to accept the ring is not to pledge her hand or heart to him. But the woman who hesitates is lost! Looking back later (IV. i. 78–80) she admits the short time in which

'my woman's heart
Grossly grew captive to his honey words'.

Anne is not convinced, but she is overpowered by the strength of Richard's will.

[F omits the line, but this is much more probably a mistake than a change of mind on the part of the dramatist.]

**205.** There was a proverb: 'The lover is not where he lives but where he loves'; and the idea is a commonplace in lyric poetry of the time.

**213. Crosby-place,** House, or Hall had been bought by Richard, was later inhabited by More and his daughter, and was in 1910 carefully moved from Bishopsgate in the City to the Chelsea Embankment, where it serves as a hostel dining-hall for women from overseas.

228. **White-friars.** Holinshed gives Blackfriars as a stage in the taking of Henry's body for burial at Chertsey. The change is probably accidental. Whitefriars was a house of Carmelite friars who wore a white cloak over their brown habit.

229–30. **humour** refers first of all to Anne's state of mind (cf. I. iv. 119, for this sense), but perhaps also secondarily to Richard's nature. Shakespeare had already hit out a somewhat similar couplet in *Titus Andronicus*:

> She is a woman, therefore may be woo'd;
> She is a woman, therefore may be won (II. i. 82–83),

which is repeated in slightly different form in *1 Henry VI*, v. iii. 77–78. The improbability of the whole situation is only slightly reduced by the substitution of 'three months' (242) for the three weeks which had really elapsed since Prince Edward had been slain. But there is a more extreme case in the medieval romancer Chrétien de Troyes, who depicts a knight wooing the wife of a man he has just killed.

246. More force is given to the words 'no doubt' if we suppose that in soliloquy Richard is admitting the falsity of some slur which had been cast on the birth of Prince Edward.

251. [This line might appear to have twelve syllables, but in both F and Q the last word is spelt as a disyllable, thus reducing it to the much commoner case of one extra syllable. In 255 we could treat the last word similarly or slur it to the monosyllable 'can't' and so remove all abnormality.]

In this soliloquy the dramatist has fully re-established the hypocrisy and callousness of Richard in case any hearer should feel sympathy for his assumed love for Anne. The mood is that of 'the artist's enjoyment of his own masterpiece'. But, 'having shown us Richard at the top of his form' here, Shakespeare 'can do no more than repeat the achievement later' (Palmer).

## ACT I, Scene III

The historical date of this scene would be April 1483, but most of it is invented by the dramatist. So far we have had the character and machinations of Richard built up for us; now we meet the Queen and her kindred, and also the old queen, Margaret, widow of Henry VI, who is to act as the mouthpiece of the Vengeance awaiting Richard. Richard does not attempt to disguise his hostility towards the Queen's party, but now assumes a new pose as the plain, blunt man; as hypocritical in its way as his earlier appearances. He also seeks to enlist the common sympathy for an older aristocracy displaced by *nouveaux riches*. Rivers was Queen Elizabeth's only brother, and Grey and Dorset her sons by her former marriage; but Shakespeare seems to treat Grey as her brother (37 and 67).

9. We must be careful to distinguish this Prince Edward, later Edward V, from Edward, son of Henry VI and short-lived husband or betrothed of Anne; see I. ii. 10.

13. Double negatives are common in Shakespeare, and survived in rustic speech in modern times.

15. Chronicles differ as to when, in fact, Richard was legally proclaimed Protector.

17. **Stanley.** Lord Stanley (strictly a Baron) was created Earl of Derby after the battle of Bosworth at the end of this play, so that it is historically wrong to call him Derby here, as do Q, F, and most editors. The Oxford text follows Theobald in changing Derby to Stanley wherever it occurs, and this will be less confusing to readers. But the inaccuracy is probably Shakespeare's; and 'Lord of Stanley' is surely incorrect for 'Lord Stanley'.

20. The Countess Richmond had some reason for her 'arrogance' (24). She was a great-granddaughter of John of Gaunt, who, by her first marriage to Edmund Tudor, Earl of Richmond, was the mother of the future Henry VII, by her second, aunt of the Buckingham of this play, and by her third, husband of Thomas Lord Stanley. Her personal name Margaret lives in that of the boat-club of the college she re-founded at Cambridge—St. John's.

41. The expression 'at the highest' is the equivalent of our 'at its height', but it derives from the favourite medieval image of the wheel of Fortune.

Forebodings are a marked feature of this play; cf. Clarence's dream and the citizens in II. iii. Richard himself is not subject to them till near his end.

42. Gloucester enters in high indignation, apparently in the middle of expounding his wrongs to his companions.

49. Englishmen of all ages have laughed at the bowings and scrapings and greater freedom of gesticulation of the Latin nations. For

a kindlier, if patronizing expression, recall the song in *H.M.S. Pinafore* which begins 'He is an Englishman'.

**51.** In *King Lear* Kent claims also to be a 'plain' man, and Cornwall comments that such 'plainness' may 'harbour more craft and more corrupter ends Than twenty silly-ducking observants, That stretch their duties nicely'—a comment more applicable to Richard than to Kent.

**71.** The eagle is the royal bird, and Gloucester belongs to the reigning family. He compares the Queen's relations to the small birds who dare to feed where they like and on what they like, or, to vary the metaphor, to make hay while the sun shines.

**101. A bachelor** again hits at the 'widow' he married; see I. i. 81.

**111.** All that Queen Margaret says down to 157 is heard by the audience only, and Richard is not supposed even to see her till then.

**121–3.** This is unhistorical, since Richard was only eight in 1460 when Edward first became king.

**130.** The Lancastrians won the second battle of St. Albans in 1461, which may underly the phrase 'Margaret's battle'; but 'battle' *may* only stand for 'army' or 'forces'.

**155. As** is an emendation for 'A' almost required by the sense.

**158–9** nicely illustrates the difference between metaphor and simile. We might have expected here a simile to the effect that they were like pirates quarrelling over their spoil; whereas they are spoken of as being pirates.

**165.** The literal sense of 'make' suggests the play on 'make' and 'mar'.

**174–8.** All this is described in *3 Henry VI*, I. iv, which should be read if only as a revelation of the savagery of civil war—a savagery less far removed from the twentieth than from the nineteenth century.

**196.** Although Margaret's 'curses' in this form are not historical, they are dramatically most effective, since they will all be fulfilled as the play goes on; and the old queen appears again in IV. iv to point this out.

**228. hog** is not merely general abuse, but has reference to Richard's badge of a white boar. The word 'rooting' is used especially of a pig digging up with his snout.

**230.** There may be an allusion to masters branding their slaves. Nature has branded him with his deformity at birth.

**233. rag of honour.** 'Rag' is several times used as a term of contempt in Shakespeare, and in this play we have 'overweening rags of France' (v. iii. 329); but this phrase is more difficult. Presumably it would have to be analysed as 'a mere rag in respect of honour'.

. 'Richard adroitly slips in the word "Margaret" in place of the intended "Richard", and thus, with the coolness of a schoolboys' small joke, disconcerts her tragic passion in a way that gives a moral wrench to the whole scene' (Moulton).

234 & 236. A play on two senses of the verb 'call'. We may notice at the same time the play on 'duty' in 251–3, and on 'serve' in 251–2.

242. **bottled** is not here used in its modern sense of contained in a bottle, but with reference to the shape of a bottle, swelling out after a narrow neck.

256. Grey had been created Marquess of Dorset in 1475. Margaret is like Richard in resenting the new nobility. The word 'stamp' means the impression put on the coin when still fresh from the fire, and so here the title of honour.

264. An **aery** is first a nest, then a brood, of a bird of prey. The connexion with a cedar tree may well be due to Ezekiel 17. 3.

273. [I have followed Dover Wilson in adopting Alice Walker's change of attribution from Buckingham to Gloucester, since it avoids the awkwardness of Margaret addressing Buckingham in 274 and the others in 275–6 and also makes her greeting to Buckingham in 280 much more natural.]

280. **princely** can have its full force, since Buckingham was directly descended from a granddaughter of Edward III.

309. [Q assigns this line to Margaret, which is absurd, and shows that neither text can be implicitly trusted.]

314. A 'frank' was a stall or sty in which an animal was put for fattening up before being killed, so that the verb combines the two ideas. Clarence's 'frank' was of course the Tower.

324–38. We are now back with the self-confessed villain of the play's beginning.

328. **gulls.** This is the first occurrence known to the *O.E.D.* of the word in its common Elizabethan sense, now archaic, of a fool or simpleton. It is uncertain whether this sense is derived from the dialectical use of 'gull' for a young bird, not particularly a sea-bird. One of the most interesting Elizabethan books is called *The Gull's Horn Book*, and describes the adventures of a simple soul in the capital.

334–8 remind us of Antonio's remark to Bassanio about Shylock that has become proverbial: 'The devil can cite Scripture for his purpose' (*Merchant of Venice*, i. iii. 99).

## ACT I, SCENE IV

This last scene of the first act is the best, and one of the most famous in the play. The pathos of this murder may well be compared with *King John*, IV. i, where, however, Arthur's pleading with Hubert to spare his life is successful. In so far as Clarence recognizes his fate as a fitting punishment for his earlier treachery, there is an anticipation of the main theme of the play in Richard's sin and punishment.

The imagination of Clarence's dream in the early part makes a contrast with the rough realism of the murderers later, and this contrast is reflected in the use of verse and prose. The verse itself is very largely end-stopped and formal, as is usual in an early play of Shakespeare's, but gives a gleam of something more individual in 'the empty, vast, and wandering air' of 39, and in the contrast of outward honour and inward care, which is almost a commonplace with Shakespeare (76–83).

The historical basis for the scene is so small that it may be quoted in full: 'The duke was cast into the Tower and therewith adjudged for a traitor, and privily drowned in a butt of malmesey' (Holinshed). The dramatist also derived a little from Holinshed's account of the murder of the princes in the Tower later, a little perhaps from the dialogue between Leir and the Murderer in the old play of *King Leir* used for his King Lear, and from the Induction and tragedy of Clarence in the *Mirror for Magistrates* (cf. Introduction). The 'Induction' by Sackville (who was also the author of the first blank-verse tragedy *Gorboduc* published in 1563) describes a visit to Hell from which one stanza may be quoted for its parallels to Clarence's dream:

> Herefrom when scarce I could mine eyes withdraw,
> That filled with tears as doth the springing well,
> We passed on so far forth till we saw
> Rude Acheron, a loathsome lake to tell,
> That boils and bubs up swelth as black as hell;
> Where grisly Charon, at their fixed tide
> Still ferries ghosts unto the farther side.

But Shakespeare almost certainly knew also the original in Virgil, *Aeneid* VI (295 onwards). Finally it may just be noted that the differences between F and Q are particularly numerous in this part of the play, but no attempt to recount them can be made in this edition.

10. **Burgundy** was not in those days simply that delightful district in the SE. of France near the Swiss border famous for its vine-

yards, but the most powerful dukedom in France and ruling also in Flanders. Clarence's sister Margaret had married Charles the Bold, Duke of Burgundy, and Clarence himself aspired to the hand of the heiress of Burgundy after his first wife died.

**24–28.** In writing these lines the poet may well have had in mind the ships of the Spanish Armada wrecked round the coasts of Britain in 1588.

> [I have accepted the emendation (first printed in the new Cambridge edition) of 'ingots' for the rather inappropriate 'anchors'. The word ingot is used by Shakespeare in *Measure for Measure*, III. i. 26 meaning 'heavy riches'.]

**29–33.** The idea recurs more beautifully and less gruesomely in Ariel's song in *The Tempest* (I. ii. 394–400): 'Those are pearls that were his eyes'. If we are to give much force to the words 'woo'd' and 'mock'd' 'we must think of the skulls with their false eyes as glancing round like a capricious lover' (D. W.), but Shakespeare uses 'woo' rather loosely in *Romeo and Juliet*, I. iv. 100.

**45–47.** The ultimate source of this journey into the kingdom of the dead is the journey of Aeneas to his father in the infernal regions in *Aeneid* vi. The present editor has long been of opinion that Shakespeare knew the second, fourth, and sixth books of the *Aeneid* in the original Latin, probably from having read them at Stratford-on-Avon Grammar School. There are many reminiscences of these books, especially in his earlier plays, and a particular touch here, not previously noted, which suggests knowledge of the Latin.

> [In 46 the Quarto text has the rather conventional epithet 'grim' for Charon, but the Folio has 'sour', used metaphorically of his temper, but almost certainly an unconscious reminiscence of the adjective 'cruda', which means literally 'unripe', applied by Virgil to his fresh and vigorous old age (*viridis ac cruda senectus*).]

Another English play, only a year or two earlier than *Richard III*, Kyd's *Spanish Tragedy*, begins with the Ghost of Andrea describing his descent at death to the same Hades, also mentioning Acheron, Charon, Avernus, &c., more fully than Shakespeare here.

**54.** [The reading of Q 'squeak'd' is at least as likely to be original, since ghosts were thought of as having thin voices. The soul was often conceived as a sort of essence or very fine substance, as in 36–41 above, and the appropriate voice might well squeak.]

**57.** Furies were the Latin *Furiae* or *Dirae*, corresponding to the Greek *Erinyes*, supernatural beings who exacted vengeance for wrong both in this world and in the next.

72. Clarence's wife, Isabella Neville, had in actual fact died in December 1476, before the time of his imprisonment.

This line, like 46, 51, and 68, has the extra syllable at the end, which is so common in this play, although the verse is in other ways rather stiff. Notice also the rhyme in 82–83.

84. Can any clear distinction be drawn between the characters of the two Murderers in the rest of the scene ? With the humour which dilutes the horror of the situation may be compared the drunken porter in *Macbeth* (II. iii).

94. **guiltless of the meaning.** Editors naturally compare what Macbeth says to his wife when she asks him 'What's to be done' about Banquo :

> Be innocent of the knowledge, dearest chuck,
> Till thou applaud the deed (III. ii. 45–46).

108. **remorse.** In earlier English the word was applied not only to some future feeling of regret after a deed, but to 'pity' generally, such as might forbid a deed that would breed remorse.

125. **'Zounds** is short for '(By) God's wounds', an oath which the Folio text tones down to 'Come', since by that time an act had been passed against profanity on the stage. This accounts for a number of differences between F and Q, not only in this play.

138–9. Cf. 'Conscience does make cowards of us all' (*Hamlet*, III. i. 83).

**shamefast** is the correct form of the word 'shamefaced', since it is formed from the Anglo-Saxon 'scamu' (= shame) and the adjective 'faest' (= fast or firm). The confusion arose because shame is commonly expressed in the face.

147–9. The easier explanation is that of the footnote. But if we do *not* identify the devil here with conscience, but prefer to oppose him to conscience, then 'him' and 'he' must be 'conscience', which had hitherto been spoken of as 'it'.

155. **Malmsey** was a kind of wine from Napoli di Malvasia in the Morea, a part of Greece.

170. Verse replaces prose as Clarence wakes up properly.

185–95. The distinction is between private vengeance and public, the latter delegated by God to the Law (cf. III. v. 40–42). But, in fact, a hasty process of law *was* carried through against Clarence ; and modern tyrannies only too frequently make the law the servant of their policies.

187. **quest:** 'a body of persons appointed to hold an inquiry' is one meaning of the Latin *quaestio* from which 'quest' is derived; but I suspect the word may have come into the poet's mind from the *Mirror for Magistrates* where it is used apropos of Clarence's condemnation (l. 352).

206. This language probably reflects the dramatist's own day, in which the reformed Anglican church insisted on the actual reception of the sacrament of Holy Communion as against attendance at Mass before the Reformation. (No one seems to have raised the point hitherto.)

213. Shakespeare uses the adjective 'dear' in all sorts of contexts where the modern meaning is inappropriate. Sometimes the meaning is nearer 'dire', as when Richard II speaks to Norfolk of 'the dateless limit of thy dear exile' (I. iii. 151), and here. In fact the *O.E.D.* treats this as a separate adjective from the O.E. *deor*. But at least there has been confusion between the two adjectives. When, for example, Milton in *Lycidas* speaks of 'sad occasion dear' do we not sense a touch of affection as well as disaster in the adjective?

218–22. The distinction is not now, as in 185, &c., between public and private vengeance, but between punishment inflicted by man as God's minister and directly by God Himself. Hence it seems probable that 'indirect' in 221 does not mean so much 'unlawful', as it is usually glossed, as 'through the agency of others', i.e. men.

224. **gallant-springing** is another case of the rather common device in this play by which two adjectives are used where the first has to play the part of an adverb qualifying the second; cf. 'childish-foolish' (I. ii. 142). The metaphor comparing a young man growing up to the growing time of the year is set out more fully apropos of Rutland in *3 Henry VI*, II. vi. 48–50.

226–7. **brother's** is in the first case an objective, in the second a subjective genitive, to use a clear distinction of the Latin grammars. But besides this ambiguity there is the nicer irony by which the Murderer uses the word 'love' instead of 'hate', and thinks of Richard where Clarence had Edward in mind.

Irony is again conspicuous in 234–5 and 239, since Clarence's idea of why the Murderers should go from him to Richard is very different from their's.

244. **kind** here has very nearly its modern sense, but still with a touch of its original sense of natural affection, as of brother for

brother; it is this which enables the Murderer to use it of what is natural.

248–50. This enlarges on the description given at I. i. 114–16. In cases like this we may either assume that Shakespeare has forgotten exactly what he had said before, or that he deliberately improves on it by giving more detail.

252. Cf. I. i. 118–19.

258–9. Bolingbroke speaks in the same vein at news of Richard II's murder (v. vi. 38–40), and Henry is reported to have repudiated the murderers of Becket.

261–71. [The text here, as in most editions, follows a re-arrangement first suggested by Tyrwhitt. A slightly different order is adopted in the new Cambridge edition.]

# ACT II, Scene I

This scene takes place at the approaching death-bed of the king, Edward IV, and provides a startling contrast between his piety at the prospect of leaving this life so soon and the jocularity, feigned simplicity, and gross hypocrisy of his brother. The source of the scene lies in two passages from Holinshed. The first describes the reconciliation of Hastings and Dorset only, 'who joined their hands together when (as it appeared after by their deeds) their hearts were far asunder'. The other, which occurs earlier in Holinshed, speaks of Edward's remorse for Clarence's death: 'When any person sued to him for the pardon of malefactors condemned to death, he would accustomably say and openly speak, "O unfortunate brother, for whose life not one would make suit".' (Spelling modernized.) Shakespeare after his manner makes the latter sentence live by inventing Stanley's plea for his man.

3–6. 'A penitent Edward and a despairing Richard may turn to Jesus with a prayer for mercy; but Christ is not otherwise nor at other times a part of their universe' (H. B. Charlton).

7. [This line furnishes a good example of where F is certainly wrong. For it reads 'Dorset and Rivers', who, being both of the Queen's party, did not need reconciling. So also in 45 below.]

34–39. There is here dramatic irony for those who know the subsequent fate of Buckingham; just as there is in 43–44 even for those who have only heard or seen the play so far as this.

56. [If the words 'or in my rage' were omitted metre would be restored since the present half line 55 would coalesce with 56. Dover Wilson

omits the words, arguing that Richard would not admit to flying into a rage.]

**64. cousin** could be used very freely; but in fact Buckingham's grandmother and Richard's mother were sisters.

**66.** For Lord Rivers see the Commentary at I. i. 64. Our line 68, which is absent from Q, is clearly due to a misunderstanding, probably a hasty reading of Hall's 'Lord Antony Woodville Earl Rivers and Lord Scales', as if it referred to three separate persons and not one. The use of 'all' in 67 of only two people may also proceed from some disturbance of the text at this point.

**73.** [**humility** is explained in Dover Wilson's Glossary as 'humanity' on the strength of one quotation (made by Furness in the Variorum) from an alphabet book of 1552 which says that 'humility is a gentleness of the mind, or a gentle patience without anger or wrath'. It is true that this sense suits well here and in III. vii. 17 and is possible in other places of Shakespeare cited by Wilson. But it may be that the quotation from Huloet is less of a definition than a description of the result of a humble frame of mind; while the failure of the *O.E.D.* to identify the sense claimed must cause hesitation in accepting it definitely.]

**74.** It is easy to see from this example how a 'holy day' kept to celebrate some happy event passes into the modern word 'holiday'.

**82.** [This line is here given to Rivers as in Q, not, as in F, to the King. Then the slower reaction from the sick man comes in 87. Again in 93 the 'but' of Q seems rather more pointed than the 'and' of F.]

**92–95.** Richard means that the Queen's kindred are more disloyal to the King than Clarence was, but, as so often, the actual expression is dictated by the desire to play on words.

**99.** [I have restored the F 'requests' for the full but almost unpronounceable 'request'st'. There are no parallels for the simpler form.]

**105.** Cf. *Measure for Measure*, v. i. 451–5. We can often find in this and other early plays thoughts which the dramatist developed later.

**112–13.** This is invented by Shakespeare; and the Earl of Oxford was in France at the time of the battle of Tewkesbury.

**124.** Man is spoken of as made in the image of God in Genesis i. 27; and so he may be spoken of as (made in) the image of the Son of God, Christ, who according to Christian belief died to redeem man. The religious language ascribed to Edward here (cf. l. 4) may be regarded as dramatically appropriate without involving Shakespeare's belief; but the warmth of the language on the same topic in *Measure for Measure*, II. ii. 73–75 seems to come from the writer's heart.

128. **speak.** Rowe's change to the past tense 'spake' is attractive, but the present is made more natural if we carry on the 'would' from the previous clause.

134. Hastings was Lord Chamberlain, and would therefore naturally be called upon. The words 'poor Clarence' are metrically outside the line, and F (not Q) prints them as a separate line

# ACT II, SCENE II

One of the distinguishing features of our play is the prominence of children. They have more to say for themselves than the children in later plays like *Coriolanus* and *The Winter's Tale*; are, in fact, too wise for their years. These two are the children of Clarence and Isabella Neville, daughter of the Earl of Warwick, and their names were Edward and Margaret. They were later beheaded in, 1499 and 1541 respectively. Richard was really in the North when he received the news of Edward's death; but the dramatist uses the occasion to show his deceit from a new angle. Buckingham's advice in the later part of the scene does come from Holinshed. Much of the style in this scene is conventional, particularly the artificial balance in 72–78 (cf. I. ii. 62, &c.).

2. The Duchess of York was the wife of Richard Plantagenet, third Duke of York, of whom we heard in I. ii. 157.

14. The Boy gives a sinister and prophetic echo to his uncle's words just above (II. i. 139).

24. **pitied me.** [Q reads here 'hugg'd me in his arm', which sounds more vigorous, but spoils the metre. It was probably transferred by memory from I. ii. 251.]

30. The word 'dugs' was not so much confined to animals in the sixteenth century as later.

33–34. The F stage direction instead of 'distractedly' is 'with her hair about her ears'—the conventional state of mourning for women from classical times.

38–39. **scene** and **act** should be given their full force as references to the stage, of which Shakespeare is fond, and not weakened, as they now are, to worn-down metaphors. For 'make' there is a recent and attractive conjecture 'mark'.

46. The F reading, restored in our text, seems more likely than the conventional 'perpetual rest' of Q; especially when we remember

how frequent such pagan language is in dramatists like Kyd, who influenced the early Shakespeare so much.

81. **parcell'd.** The noun 'parcel' originally meant a portion, and this survives in the phrase 'part and parcel of . . .'; so the verb here means 'divide up'.

92. The slight awkwardness of metre can be overcome by slurring 'unwillingness' into three syllables instead of four.

118. **splinter'd** must not be taken in its modern sense, to which 'broken' in the previous line would incline a hasty reader. The sense required is well illustrated by *Othello*, II. iii. 330–2: 'This broken joint between you and her husband entreat her to splinter'.

121. **Ludlow** is a town in Shropshire near the Welsh border to which Prince Edward had been sent to keep an eye on 'the Wild Welsh-men' (Hall). Later on Milton wrote *Comus* for presentation in the great Hall of the Castle, which still survives.

123–6. Buckingham and Richard (cf. 150–1) want only a small train because they want to get control of the Prince, and also to get into their own power such of the Queen's party as should be with him. Both sides here pretend that they desire to preserve the friendship to which the dying king had bound them.

127 is an overlong line; so that we may suspect 'green and' has crept in from 135.

142. [F here and in 153 has 'London', which is obviously wrong; while Q had omitted 123–40; so that neither can be taken as a secure guide.]

148. **Index** was first of all used of the finger pointing to something important, and then to a summary of contents prefixed to a book; so here, 'prelude'. We are to suppose that Richard and Bucking-ham had already discussed plans against the Queen's party, while pretending unfeigned friendship with them.

## ACT II, SCENE III

The main purpose of this little scene is to show us how the King's death affects the man in the street. It is not for him to scramble for the spoils, or aspire to increase his own power, but rather to fear a time of greater anarchy. The varying tempers of men are showing in the differing degrees of pessimism of the three citizens.

Once more Shakespeare gives dramatic form to what he found in Holinshed and More:

'Yet began there some manner of muttering among the people as though all should not long be well, though they neither wist what they feared, nor wherefore; were it that before such great things men's hearts of a secret instinct of nature misgive them; as the sea without wind swelleth of himself sometime before a tempest.'

**8. The while** is usually an adverbial phrase meaning 'at the present time', as in III. vi. 10 of this play; but here it could equally well be an instance of 'while' in its original part of speech as a substantive meaning 'time'; hence 'God help our present situation.'

**11.** The original of this warning is in the Bible (Ecclesiastes x. 16), and it was quoted in Langland's *Piers Plowman* of the fourteenth century. But Shakespeare probably took it from the speech of Buckingham in Holinshed, when a little later on than this he puts forward Richard's claims to the throne.

**12–15.** The sense of these lines must be clear to anyone, but the syntax is confused. The poet has tried to say in one sentence what would have been better in two, viz. that their hopes must rest on good government by the council while he is young, and by the King himself when he is older.

**16–17.** In fact Henry was proclaimed King of France in Paris in 1422, but not crowned there till he was nine years old, in 1430.

**19. famously.** This usage might be illustrated from a rather colloquial use, surviving even in the present editor's lifetime, whereby it meant 'well' or 'excellently'. Where we might say 'he did me proudly' of our host, a Victorian novelist might have written 'famously'.

**46.** 'To give evidence, I suppose, or serve on the jury in the court of the local J.P.s, or of the justices of assize' (D. W.). But the essential thing was to provide a reason for the citizens to walk off the stage when there was no curtain.


# ACT II, Scene IV

One purpose of this scene, as of its predecessor, is to cover a lapse of time while the young prince travels from Ludlow towards London. It also serves to increase fear and dislike of Richard, when the audience learn that even his own mother does not defend him, and that a child seems to have an almost instinctive dislike of his uncle.

More's account of the Queen taking sanctuary is among his most vivid passages. When she heard that the young King was in Richard's hands, and that her brother and son had been arrested 'she gat herself in all the haste possible with her young son and her daughters out of the Palace of Westminster in which she then lay into the Sanctuary, lodging herself and her company there in the Abbot's Place.' When the Archbishop came to Westminster before daybreak next morning: 'He took the Great Seal with him, and came yet before day unto the Queen. About whom he found much heaviness, rumble, haste and business, carriage and conveyance of her stuff into Sanctuary, chests, coffres, packs, fardels, trusses, all on men's backs, no man unoccupied, some lading, some going, some discharging, some coming for more, some breaking down the walls to bring in the next [nearest] way. . . . The Queen herself sat alone alow on the rushes all desolate and dismayed.' (Spelling partly modernized.)

1–3. The reading here given is that of Q, which raises no difficulties, except for the rather unnatural accentuation of Nórthampton. Stony Stratford is on the London–Holyhead road, Watling Street, about fifty miles from London. Northampton is fifteen miles further away from London.

> [F has Stony Stratford in the first line, and in the second line 'And at Northampton . . .', which both scans more easily and may preserve the rather complicated facts of Richard bringing back the young prince. (See Appendix III in A. H. Thompson's Arden edition, 1907.)

13. [great weeds. It seems at least probable that Shakespeare wrote 'ill weeds', since there was a proverb 'ill weeds grow apace', and that a reporter or printer substituted the familiar antithesis of 'great' to 'small'.]

37. The proverb was 'Little pitchers have wide ears', where the ears are in the first instance the 'handle of a pitcher or drinking vessel' (O.E.D.). The proverb enshrined the quickness with which some children pick up words dropped by their elders which they are not supposed to hear, or, at least, to understand.

44–45. Richard coming from the North and Buckingham from the West had met at Northampton, and there arranged to arrest Rivers and the Queen's party.

51. jet is the same word as 'jut' in origin, as we speak of a cliff jutting out. The present sense is well illustrated in Titus Andronicus (ii. i. 64), 'to jet upon a prince's right'.

59. It is a noticeable trick of Shakespeare's style to join two nouns and verbs in this way, which have to be re-arranged in thought, i.e. here to joy their gain and weep their loss.

3. [This line can, with some difficulty, be scanned as an Alexandrine, i.e.

a line of twelve syllables instead of ten; but it would be made a little easier by the omission of 'O', perhaps an actor's addition: and even regular if we also read 'self to self' with Dover Wilson.]

**66. Sanctuary.** All readers of the play will have come across somewhere the primitive idea, surviving in the middle ages, that criminals could escape from the hand of justice or vengeance by putting themselves under the protection of a deity in a sacred place. The 'Abbot's Place' (see introduction to this scene) stood south of the Abbey, and is incorporated in College Hall, where Westminster School boys have their lunch.

**71.** The Great Seal of the Realm was in the keeping of the Lord Chancellor, who was at the moment Rotherham, Archbishop of York. By delivering it to the Queen 'for the use and behoof of your son' (More), he showed his recognition of the lawful successor, and his fear of Richard.

# ACT III, Scene I

The historical date of Prince Edward's arrival in London was 4 May 1483. He is depicted as melancholy and apparently full of foreboding, as well he might be, since on his way he had been parted from all those by whom he had been surrounded, especially his uncle Rivers, who had superintended his government of Wales. His character, or at least his mood, is in contrast with the pertness of his younger brother, who is summoned to meet him. Hazlitt condemned part of the scene as 'the fantoccini exhibition [i.e. marionettes or puppets] of the young princes bandying childish wit with their uncle'; to which it has been replied (by J. Palmer):

'The scene itself is excellent stagecraft. What could be more *theatrically* effective than Richard's playful gift of his dagger to York and the boy's pert allusion to his uncle's deformity? What could be more *theatrically* moving than young Edward's instinctive mistrust of the Lord Protector, his premonitory recoil from the Tower, his pathetic exhibition of a mind already alert and inquisitive and of a spirit which aspires to fame: "An if I live . . .'' &c. (91–93).'

**1. chamber.** London is called *Camera Regis*, or the King's Chamber, in More and Holinshed, and Camden in 1610 says the use began after the Norman Conquest.

**2.** I suspect that the dramatist intended irony in this phrase. At first hearing it suggests that Edward was the object of all his uncle's solicitude, but we are intended to understand that all Richard's thoughts are set upon preventing the Prince becoming King in fact.

**6.** The Prince finds Clarence removed; but the plural will include Rivers, his true uncle, and Dorset and Grey, his half brothers but much older than he was, who might at least have arrived just before him.

**37.** This line is an Alexandrine, and even then the last two syllables have to be slurred into one. The same is true of 39.

**44–56.** We are in a better position than commentators of the last century to appreciate this kind of sophistical argument; for we have heard murder called 'liquidation' often enough, and that those who oppose, or even are thought unsympathetic to, a prevalent régime have set themselves outside the rights of trial by law. It is obvious that in so far as the sanctuary should protect anyone it was equally valid for children. Buckingham really means that politicians of his age did not respect such old-fashioned religious scruples, if it did not suit them. In fact 'grossness' becomes on his lips here equivalent to freedom from prejudice.

**52.** [Metre is easily restored by the omission of 'And'; as it would be in 71 if we could suppose that Shakespeare wrote 'rebuilt', for which another word with the same meaning 're-edified' was at some stage substituted.]

**69–71.** The tradition that Julius Caesar had begun the Tower was questioned even before Shakespeare's time by the antiquary Stow. Its beginning is now ascribed to William the Conqueror.

**79.** There was a proverb: 'Too soon wise to live long.' This sort of aside marks the 'stagy' villain, beloved of unsophisticated audiences.

**82–83.** The so-called Morality plays, which reached their height in the early sixteenth century, usually had a buffoon-like character called the Vice, who might, like comic characters in pantomimes, indulge in puns and double *entendres*. Shakespeare refers to the Vice in several places, notably in *Twelfth Night* (IV. ii. 134), and when Prince Hal calls Falstaff 'that reverend Vice, that grey iniquity' (*1 Henry IV*, II. iv. 199).

**85–86.** Caesar 'set down' his conquests in the famous *Commentaries* on the Gallic War and the Civil War.

**110–11.** It has been pointed out that two kinds of irony can be seen here: first the unconscious irony of York asking for what he will have only too much of when murdered in the Tower, supposedly at his uncle's instigation; and secondly the conscious irony which we may read into Richard's 'with all my heart'.

**114.** [As it stands this line is an Alexandrine; but it can be made normal by the omission of the unnecessary 'And' at the beginning, since then 'being' is easily read as one syllable metrically.]

121. [I cannot see why Dover Wilson paraphrases this as 'I shouldn't think much of it, even if . . .'. This seems unnecessarily rude even as a secondary meaning to that in my footnote.]

129–31. It is usually supposed that York intends an allusion to the hump on his uncle's shoulder (hence 'scorn' of 133). Apes and bears are associated elsewhere in Shakespeare, and in Elizabethan times a bear was often taken about with a monkey on his shoulders. But men could also be 'ape-bearers', as we learn from *The Winter's Tale*, IV. ii. 102.

148. The Prince is still thinking of his uncle Rivers, so recently put to death.

157. Catesby was a lawyer of undistinguished birth who moved from the service of Hastings to that of Richard, and rose to be Speaker of the Commons in 1484.

We may suspect the word 'hither' to be a natural addition by actors or reporters, since it spoils the metre.

160. History does not record that Richard had as yet imparted his designs to anyone else, although he had held councils on his way to London.

165. Holinshed and More speak of the affection between Edward IV and Hastings. After the King's death Hastings became the lover of the King's mistress (cf. 185).

179. Holinshed, using More, says that while a council was being held in one place about the coronation of the prince as Edward V 'as fast were they in another place contriving the contrary, and to make the protector king'.

191. [As in 114 the first word is unnecessary and upsets the metre; so that it may well be regarded as what has been called 'Actor's connective'.]

194–6 prepares for a sequel in IV. ii. 87, &c., where Richard's mood is very different. Buckingham claimed the earldom of Hereford in virtue of his descent from Thomas of Woodstock (a son of Edward III), who married the coheiress of Humphrey de Bohun, Earl of Hereford, &c. The lands of Hereford had gone to the younger coheiress, and had later passed to the Crown.

# ACT III, SCENE II

In this scene we have the contrast of the misgivings of Stanley, who is beginning to fear Richard, and the self-confidence of Hastings.

Stanley's dependence on Hastings (cf. l. 168 of the previous scene) is now demonstrated. The optimism of Hastings as against *our* knowledge of his insecurity permits some of the strongest 'dramatic irony' in Shakespeare, in 20–33, 57–61, 67–68, 97–103, and 118.

The material for this scene is almost all in More, Hall, or Holinshed (often in all three), but has been re-grouped by the dramatist.

**10–33.** Contrast the straightforward account of this dream and then its explaining away with the imaginative appeal of Clarence's dream in I. iv.

**33.** The word **kindly** seems to hold a double irony: first the dramatic irony referred to above, and secondly the fact that the word itself could be taken also in its etymological sense of after his kind or nature, which would in this case mean 'cruelly'.

**77.** [The omission of 'My Lord' as an actor's interpolation would restore the decasyllabic pattern; otherwise this line is an Alexandrine.]

**82. London:** is commonly thought to be a mistake of F and Q for Ludlow, as it certainly is in F at II. ii. 142, perhaps through the use of 'L' as an abbreviation; but Shakespeare may have been nodding, or have assumed that not all the lords in question had gone to escort the Prince to London.

**88.** The phrase would naturally suggest the end of a day, especially in view of the Biblical echo from 'the night is far spent and the day is at hand'; but dinner is yet to come (119), let alone supper, so that the expression must be used because of the early hour at which the day had started for some (5); unless the dramatist is writing carelessly.

**92.** Perhaps **wear their hats** suggests not merely being alive but the position of those in authority who do not doff their hats to superiors.

**108. Sir** was the title of a priest who had taken a bachelor's degree; cf. Sir Christopher Urswick in IV. v. 1. The purpose of introducing a priest here is to prepare for III. iv. 86.

**111.** In introducing Buckingham Shakespeare has departed from his source which merely has 'a knight'.

## ACT III, Scene III

At first sight this short scene would seem of no importance, except to make more vivid to an audience the fact that Richard had the relations of the Queen executed. But in fact, coming as it does exactly at the middle point of the play's length, it may be said to mark the turning-point, in so much as it shows the beginning of the accomplishment of Margaret's curses, which will end with the ruin of Richard himself. Lines 13–16 take us back to I. iii. 210–14, where the word 'standers by' was used which is picked up by 'standing by' here.

1. **Ratcliff,** knighted at Tewkesbury, 1471, was a servant of Richard, destined to fall with him at Bosworth, who was at this time governor of Pontefract (= Pomfret) castle, in Yorkshire. He is described by Shakespeare's sources as 'bold in mischief, as far from pity as from all fear of God'.

23. **expiate** properly is to 'pay for' a crime or the like. Possibly because this brings the whole matter to an end, the verb once or twice takes on the sense of 'bring to an end', as in Sonnet XXII, 'Then look I death my days should expiate.'


# ACT III, Scene IV

The setting for this scene is supposed to be the upper room of the White Tower, which was formerly the Council chamber. Dramatically its chief interest is the continuation of the dramatic irony of Hastings's over-confidence which began in the previous scene but one; here especially in 51–53, 56–57, and 65. Shakespeare draws very closely from his source, Holinshed, who himself is following More, even in the incident of the strawberries, which More must have had from the lips of Morton, Bishop of Ely; but the part of Buckingham is enlarged, as at the close of scene ii, where he was substituted for 'A Gentleman'.

Ratcliff and Lovel are not mentioned in Holinshed, and we have already heard that the former was at Pomfret; so that something has gone wrong when both are mentioned in the text at 77. Either the dramatist was careless, or some doubling of parts by actors has affected the text.

4–5. **It is** is not the natural answer to 'all things'. Perhaps Shakespeare wrote 'all thing', which was an earlier form of our 'everything'.

10–12. For once editors, keen enough on parallels, do not appear to have quoted Duncan's 'There's no art To find the mind's construction in the face' (*Macbeth*, I. iv. 11–12).

13. Buckingham guilefully leads Hastings on. So in 26–27 he makes the worst of the situation for him.

**19.** It was not uncommon for the Lord Chamberlain to speak for the King; so there is less presumption than we might suspect in this offer.

**23.** The time was about 9 a.m. (More).

**26–27.** The 'cue' is the last words of an actor's speech, after which another character takes over. The stage metaphor is continued by 'part', and is especially appropriate here when Richard and Buckingham are going to pretend to fear Hastings.

**31.** An Ely Place still remains to recall the London house of the Bishops of Ely. Hatton Garden is on the site of their palace garden, but takes its name from a later occupant, Sir Christopher Hatton.

**32–33.** Richard's apparently irrelevant request was intended, presumably, to confirm his happy mood to all present; and Shakespeare must have retained it to make a greater contrast with what follows after 57, when he is reported by More as returning 'with a wonderful sour angry countenance, knitting the brows, frowning and fretting, and gnawing on his lips'.

**47** is prose. If Shakespeare wished to put the homely remark into verse he had only to reverse the order, and begin with 'these'.

**55.** The Q reading 'likelihood' is a commoner word, but for that very reason less likely to be the original.

**67–68.** In *3 Henry VI*, III. ii. 156 Richard had spoken of Nature shrinking his arm up like a withered shrub, as well as of his deformed shoulder. But, since *this* affliction was nothing new, it has been suggested that Richard was subject to the rash brought on in some people from eating strawberries, and that this was what he displayed on this occasion.

**75–76** are almost word for word from More; but would have seemed more probable if Shakespeare had mentioned the men-at-arms who had been brought in.

**83.** A **foot-cloth** was an ornamented covering for a horse hanging down on each side; and the only point of the epithet here must be to suggest that it was a horse suitable for processions, &c., and not a spirited charger, which took fright, and so gave a bad omen.

## ACT III, Scene V

Richard now has to defend his hasty and illegal execution of Hastings, and for this purpose he pretends to be going in fear of his life

(14–19 and 40–45). Almost all the material of this scene comes in More, Hall, or Holinshed—usually in all three; but Shakespeare makes the Mayor here and the London citizens in scene vii less intelligent, and easier dupes of Buckingham and Richard.

5. Shakespeare has many references to the stage, of which the longest is the opening of *Hamlet*, III. ii. There may be, but need not be, some reference here to the acting of Burbage, who actually took the part of Richard, or, if the account is too uncomplimentary for that, to Alleyn of a rival company.

20. **Ratcliff**; cf. III. iv. 77 and Commentary at beginning of that scene.

24. Both here and in 32 one superlative form covers both adjectives, just as in other places we have found one adverbial ending covering a second adjective.

33. This short line should probably be omitted, with D. W., as an unauthorized addition.

40–45. Richard shows himself conscious that due processes of law mark a Christian and civilized nation as opposed to despotisms of the Orient. The collocation of Turks and infidels is probably due to unconscious remembrance of the Prayer Book collect for Good Friday.

49–50 [are given to Buckingham in F, which is at least as likely as the Q attribution here printed.]

54. **prevented** could be taken in its modern sense if we make the antecedent of 'which' not just 'his end' but the whole of line 52. If the hasty execution of Hastings was against Richard's meaning, it was certainly not against his wishes. But we remember from the case of Henry II and Becket, among others, that those who have got their servants to murder their enemies often find it convenient to repudiate those servants.

74. See III. vii. 4–5 and Commentary there. In those days a contract of marriage, or 'troth-plight' was regarded as binding from the legal point of view. If Edward, therefore, had been 'contracted' to Lady Lucy his children by Elizabeth might be regarded as illegitimate. The lady confessed that Edward had seduced her, but no evidence of a formal contract was alleged. Lady Lucy was Lady Eleanor Butler, a daughter of the Earl of Shrewsbury.

75–77. The 'citizen' was named Burdet, and the case comes in Hall, but not in Holinshed.

85–93. Shakespeare slightly elaborates a story taken from More and Holinshed.

97. **Baynard's Castle** was a house on the north bank of the Thames near the present Blackfriar's Bridge. It belonged to Richard till his death, and in Shakespeare's day to William Herbert, Earl of Pembroke.

102–3. **Shaw** was brother of the Mayor, **Penker** provincial of the Augustine friars, 'both great preachers, both of more learning than virtue, of more fame than learning' (More).

# ACT III, Scene VI

This short scene allows time for Richard and Buckingham to get to Baynard's Castle; but it also serves to underline the haste and irregularity of the proceedings against Hastings. The underling who has had the job of hurriedly engrossing the condemnation complains that it was prepared some time before the victim was even accused or suspected.

3. Just as much business which we should regard as secular was done inside old St. Paul's, so proclamations would be read there.

10–12. When Richard tried to make the citizens think the execution necessary, 'every man', says More, 'answered him fair as though no man mistrusted the matter, which of truth no man believed', one citizen observing that the document 'was written by prophecy'.

# ACT III, Scene VII

This highly dramatic scene is a climax of Richard's hypocrisy as seen by Shakespeare. To a modern sophisticated reader it may seem almost farce, but it is the sort of situation which has given this play its popularity on the stage. In the first half of the scene the dramatist is following his sources pretty closely; after that he expands. The 'brace of bishops' flanking Richard do not come in More or Holinshed but in Hall (1548) and in Grafton's continuation of Hardyng's verse chronicle (1543).

Historically there was a lapse of ten days between the execution of Hastings and the speech of Buckingham here reported; compression of this sort is common to most of the historical plays.

4. It is not being suggested that Edward's children were not his, but

that they were borne to him by a woman who was not his lawful wife. When he was about to marry Elizabeth, his mother, the Duchess of York, alleged that he was under contract to marry Elizabeth Lucy (see 177–9). It was partly on this ground that Parliament settled the crown on Richard, and that the princes in the Tower could be regarded as bastards.

**6.** According to Holinshed, just before Edward fell in love with Elizabeth Grey, Warwick had been sent to Louis XI, the King of France, to ask for the Queen's sister, Bona, for Edward. But when Edward found that he could not have his way with Elizabeth Grey without marrying her, Warwick was made to look foolish; whereupon he deserted the Yorkist cause.

**25.** An expedition against Scotland in 1482 won Berwick for England.

**26. statuas** is a hybrid form, half Latin and half English printed by most editors here and in *Julius Caesar* (II. ii. 76), where the metre requires a trisyllable; it is also found in Bacon.

**50.** There was a proverb 'maids say nay, and take it', and the coyness suggested by the simile admirably suits the part Richard is assuming.

**70–76.** Note the series of antitheses in the manner of *Euphues* and such works, imitated in Shakespeare's early plays.

**80. Marry** appears to count as a single syllable metrically, as in II. iii. 46 and III. iv. 56.

**135.** The syntax of this sentence is a little loose. In 132–3 the string of nouns were in apposition to 'you'; but the phrases here are in apposition to 'the charge . . . land'.

**144.** The abstract 'ambition' is put for the concrete 'I, being ambitious but tongue-tied'.

**158. poverty of spirit** may be said to support the *ordinary* meaning for the 'humility' ascribed to himself by Richard in II. i. 73 (q.v.).

**179.** When Edward undertook to marry Lady Grey, his mother tried to break the engagement by asserting that her son was already pledged to Lucy (cf. III. v. 74).

**182–3.** Elizabeth met the king when she came to petition him that she might keep the lands of her husband; see I. iii. 128. In 184–5 Buckingham disparages her, just as Richard had done in I. i. 81; see the Commentary on I. i. 64. In fact she had only two sons— hardly enough to destroy her beauty in the days when domestic help was not rare!

188. If we had only the text before us we should assume that the 'bigamy' consisted in Edward's marrying Elizabeth when already engaged to another woman (178); but in view of More's use of the word of marriage to a widow it is probable that it had this sense here. Church law condemned such marriages, perhaps because of the advice of St. Paul that widows should remain so, and the Duchess of York in More, followed by Hall, uses the word of Edward's marriage to Elizabeth.

213–16. This is a master-stroke of guile in Buckingham. We may be sure that the citizens had not contemplated such a thing.

218. [For this line the Q has 'Come, citizens: 'zounds! I'll entreat no more.' followed by the delicious hypocrisy of 'O! do not swear, my Lord of Buckingham.'
    This could hardly *not* be Shakespeare's; but F, on which the Oxford text is based, pruned away the oath by God's wounds in accordance with a statute against profanity, and the next line had to go with it.]

242. The coronation of Richard really took place eleven days later; but the dramatist must speed things up.


# ACT IV, SCENE I

As often, the fourth act is quieter than the third. After the plans and guile of Richard comes the sufferings of his victims, first of the two queens, Elizabeth the late queen who should be queen-mother, and Anne about to be crowned queen, but none the happier for that. The material of the scene is mainly invented, apart from the reference to Richmond.

7. [whither can count as one syllable for metrical purposes, like 'whe'r' in 227 of the last scene, which itself was printed 'whether' in F.]

33–35. Women of Shakespeare's day, and long after, indulged in tight corsetting which pulled their figure into the desired shape, but seemed not to give them room to breathe in moments of emotion. Even Cleopatra is made to tell her maid Charmian to cut her lace; see *Antony and Cleopatra*, I. iii. 71.

40. Elizabeth's other son, Lord Grey, had already been put to death, at Pomfret (III. 3).

42. Richmond had fled to Brittany after the battle of Tewkesbury. His mother, the Countess of Richmond (I. iii. 20), had taken Stanley as her second husband (49).

52. Perhaps the reason for the Duchess speaking of a 'wind of Misery' when she wants to bewail the evil of the times is that the

thought of sailing overseas suggested wind to the dramatist's half-conscious mind. Anyhow a prevailing wind is a natural image for a state of affairs.

60. There may be an allusion here to an old method of punishment which fastened a crown of red-hot iron on the criminal's head.

61. The new queen would of course be anointed with oil as part of the coronation rite inherited from Old Testament times, and it is this oil which she wishes might be poison to end her unhappy life.

64. Elizabeth realizes that Anne would suppose her to be jealous of a new queen who was not the wife of her own son, the rightful heir.

65–80. If we compare this passage with Act I, scene ii, we shall find that there is some enlargement on what is said there. Shakespeare is seldom content to reproduce exactly what he wrote earlier.

83. Shakespeare elsewhere, and other Elizabethan poets, call 'sleep' golden; but it is particularly in keeping with his rich store of metaphor that this should be combined with an image which suggests freshness rather than richness. We do not need to think of 'golden dew' as an entity in itself.

85. Warwick had deserted the Yorkist for the Lancastrian side; see Commentary at III. vii. 6.

91–96. Notice the rhetorical balance, repetitions, and rhymes in these lines.

95. The Duchess was in fact sixty-eight, but exaggeration may be allowed to her and the poet.

97–103. [These lines are absent from Q, but could ill be spared.]


# ACT IV, Scene II

Richard, now crowned king, has reached the summit of ambition, but 'uneasy lies the head that wears a crown', and the more so when the true heir still lives. This moment also marks the beginning of Richard's decline, since his cruel murder of the princes would lose him more sympathy than the execution of Hastings, with whom he might be thought to have had a legitimate quarrel. Richard now ceases to exercise his wit.

Nearly all the material for this scene may be found somewhere in the usual sources, but the dramatist has altered the time and place of some incidents for concentration, and invents the consultation with Buckingham as to the proposed murder. In Holinshed, following More, Richard at this point asks Brackenbury to dispose of the princes, and the breach with Buckingham only comes over the dukedom of Hereford.

8. Certain kinds of stone when passed over gold cause discoloration if the gold contains alloy; so Richard will test the genuineness of Buckingham's devotion to him.

10–17. Richard expects Buckingham to be able to take a hint from the mere reminder that 'Young Edward lives', and to reply with words something like 'But in him nature's pattern's not eterne'. Compare King John talking to Hubert about Arthur in *King John*, III. iii.

27. Richard's habit of gnawing his lip had been noted by More at an earlier point; see Commentary on III. iv. 32–33.

31. Does this line contain a hint that Buckingham, who was of princely rank, is beginning to think who is to rule the country if Richard makes himself too odious?

36. This conversation with the page actually took place at Warwick a little later, and is an example of the displacements referred to in the introduction to this scene. Historically, also, Tyrrell (spelt Tyrel in F) had been previously employed in offices of trust, and was by no means an unknown person.

46–47. [It looks from the metrical irregularity in both F and Q as if something has gone wrong here. Regularity could be restored by the omission (with D. W.) of 'what's the news?', which might well have been added by an actor.]

50–51. Holinshed explains that Richard's object in starting this rumour was to see whether the people would impute it to him or to fortune; so that, in the latter case, he could safely get rid of her.

53–55. In a fever of intellectual activity Richard is thinking of how to dispose of all who might be considered his rivals for the throne. Margaret was only ten now, and later became Countess of Salisbury. The boy, another Edward, is said to have been weak-witted from having been kept in close confinement from his earliest years.

56. Catesby may be supposed to be dumbfounded at the suggestions he hears.

63–64. It is impossible not to quote *Macbeth* (III. iv. 136–8):

> I am in blood
> Stepp'd in so far that, should I wade no more,
> Returning were as tedious as go o'er.

But we may also note how the poet improves on himself. In view of the many parallels in plot as well as in language between these plays, written at an interval of about ten years, it is all the more fruitful to study their differences as tragedies.

**78. By this token:** Presumably he hands Tyrrell a ring, or something else which will gain him admission to the Tower.

**91–92.** In Holinshed Richard tells Stanley to keep his wife in a secret place and not allow her to communicate with anyone.

**98–115.** [This is the only important passage in the play absent from F. The reason for this omission is not known, but it has been suggested that the lines might have been objectionable to George Villiers, the Duke of Buckingham contemporary with the play, who was very important at Court when F was printed (see the *Review of English Studies* for July 1937).]

**102–6.** Richard visited Exeter in 1483, after the failure of Buckingham's rebellion and Richmond's first expedition; so we have another example of Shakespeare re-arranging material. But the 'bard of Ireland' is his own invention. The pronunciation of Richmond and Rougemont might be made to sound more alike than they look on paper.

**113–14.** The general sense is not in doubt, but it is not certain whether 'keep the stroke' means 'go on striking' or 'keep time', both of which meanings can be extracted from *O.E.D.* A 'Jack' is a human figure which strikes the bell in many old clocks, of which an example may be seen in Wells Cathedral. 'Jack' was always a term of contempt.

**121.** Brecknock is another form of the county and town of Brecon, where some of Buckingham's estates lay. Fragments of the Norman castle remain, and one portion is called the Ely Tower because Buckingham there made a compact with his prisoner Morton, Bishop of Ely, to overthrow Richard.

# ACT IV, Scene III

The murder of the princes in the Tower, so important in arousing the ultimate detestation of Richard, is not shown even by the dramatist who allows the blinding of Gloucester on the stage. If it had been a Greek drama we might have heard the shrieks of the victims off stage; but the description is enough to raise the fullest pity. The dramatist adds to his sources when he makes the murderers feel remorse. The chroniclers mark the murder as the end of any peace

of mind for Richard. But Shakespeare does not treat Richard as
he does Macbeth.

**6. Albeit** scans as a disyllable. The word 'flesh'd' (taken over from
More) properly applies to a dog or falcon given the flesh of its first
prey, and came to be used of anyone inured to slaughter.

**9–13.** The description suggests a reminiscence of 'The Babes in the
Wood' story, perhaps prompted by the name Forrest (forest =
wood). But the epithet 'alabaster' refers rather to sculptured
tombs in churches with marble for flesh.

**16.** The sentence should have continued with something like 'came
over me', but the breaking off is intended to suggest the horror of
the recollection.

**29–30.** Holinshed says that the chaplain died soon afterwards without revealing where they had been buried.

**31.** The use of 'after-supper' as a composite idea justifying a hyphen
seems proved by *M.N.D.* v. i. 33: 'Between our after-supper and
bed-time'. To give 'soon at' the meaning of 'towards' seems less
necessary here.

**34.** Those who have been baptized in the Church have been declared
'inheritors of the kingdom of heaven', which is not intended to
refer only to a future state. Shakespeare always seems to use the
word of coming into possession of, and not only being future heir
to, something.

**37.** This scheme (cf. IV. ii. 54) was not realized. This 'last of the
Plantagenets' as Holinshed calls her, became Countess of Salisbury, and was cruelly beheaded by Henry VIII in 1541.

**39.** Anne died in 1483, whether from unhappiness or poison is left
open by the chroniclers.

**40–42.** Shakespeare has of course the advantage of knowing what
actually happened to bring about the union of the two houses of
Lancaster and York; but in 1483 Richmond at Rennes in France
swore to marry Elizabeth if he obtained the throne of England.

**51–57.** In the first four lines of this passage we are given a series of
abstract nouns, more or less personified, to the general effect that
if a man delays where quick action is demanded he comes to ruin.
In the last four lines the two rhymed couplets give an effect of
'wise saws and modern instances' to the whole. Mercury was the
herald of the gods and had winged feet.

## ACT IV, SCENE IV

This scene of 530-odd lines is one of the longest in Shakespeare. More than half of it is pure talk—some of this in the classical manner called *stichomythia* (a transliterated Greek word for a feature of Greek drama)—but the lamentation of the three queens has a certain theatrical effectiveness. It recalls many scenes of lament in Greek tragedy, and in fact one late-Victorian critic felt that 'the unhistorical but grandly classical conception of Margaret, that Cassandra prophetess, the Helen-Ate of the House of Lancaster . . .' could only have been due to the more classically minded Marlowe. Queen Margaret never really returned to England after her departure to France in 1476; and the rest of this scene is equally the dramatist's invention. But the confrontation of the two aged women, Margaret and the Duchess of York, is a fine invention, since by it the whole civil war is epitomized. Dowden thought that the 'statuesque composition' of the three women in the same position and actuated by the same passion had a 'Blake-like terror and beauty', similar to some of Blake's illustrations to the Book of Job.

'The common sorrow which the three women feel and share is lent emphasis and made most effective precisely by means of that symmetry of the sentences. . . . Admittedly, this [IV. iv. 82–90] is a conventional pattern; it is still far from being the language of spontaneity. But we cannot fail to note how closely this rapid sequence of bold phrases corresponds to the pattern of the whole scene and to the desperate scorn of Queen Margaret, who seeks in her speech for ever more appropriate symbols for Queen Elizabeth' (W. H. Clemen).

**5.** The choice of the word 'induction' may be due to the use of the heading in *The Mirror for Magistrates*, e.g. Sackville's Induction and Tragedy of Buckingham (cf. 'tragical' in 7).

**15.** Margaret means that it is the sequence of blood shed by one side that has provoked revenge from the other all through the feud of the houses. It is only a question of 'right for right', or the morality of vengeance of the O.T. and most Elizabethan drama. Buckingham at the end of v. i calls it more appropriately 'Wrong hath but wrong'.

**26–30.** This kind of antitheses, oxymorons, and playing with words always had some appeal for Shakespeare, but is more a mark of his early style, influenced by contemporary fashions. Pope put the lines in his margin as unworthy to be accounted Shakespeare's.

49. In *3 Henry VI*, v. vi. 75 Richard says of himself at birth:

> The midwife wonder'd, and the women cried
> O Jesu, bless us, he is born with teeth.

56. This is a unique use of the word 'carnal' in the sense of carnivorous required by the context here (and accepted by *O.E.D.*); but the use of 'flesh'd' in l. 6 of the previous scene helps to cover the transition from the normal sense of 'fleshly'.

61. **Revenge** was a favourite subject in pre-Shakespearian drama as in the plays of Seneca which was one of its main sources. *Hamlet* shows us what Shakespeare could make of it, but all its crudities come up again in the later Elizabethan dramatists, such as Tourneur.

65. **boot:** in Old English meant profit, advantage (as 'bootless' still means 'useless'), and it came to have the flavour of something thrown in as an added advantage, examples of this use occurring from late fifteenth to earlier eighteenth century in *O.E.D.* Cf. *Winter's Tale*, IV. iv. 600: 'What a boot is here with this exchange!'

68. Metaphors or similes from drama are common in Shakespeare; e.g. III. iv. 26–27. So are legal terms, e.g. 77 and 127 of this scene; but we are not bound to conclude that Shakespeare had worked in a lawyer's office.

72. **their:** the plural is used in referring to (the powers of) Heaven or Hell, perhaps out of awe; cf. I. iii. 219.

92–96. Here is a variation of the 'Ubi sunt' theme in which poets, particularly those of the Middle ages and Renaissance, draw attention to the mortality of man and his works. Among the best-known examples is Villon's 'Où sont les neiges d'antan ?', 'Where are the snows of yester-year ?'

98–104 furnishes perhaps the longest example of rhetorical repetition of the same phrase that Shakespeare affords. This kind of device, more rhetorical than poetic, is a mark of his early work.

105. Cf. 'Thus the whirligig of time brings in his revenges' (*T.N.* v. i. 388).

128. Precise sense is sacrificed to antithesis. Apparently the thought is that when the happier periods of a person's life have been succeeded by sorrow the only compensation lies in wordy ('airy') expression of it.

136. Richard did in fact at this time make an expedition against Buckingham; but Shakespeare has not yet come to Buckingham's revolt.

173. Richard behaved thus towards Clarence; and there may be a sort of pun in the word 'kind' since it is derived from the same root as the noun 'kind' and suggests natural conduct between those who are akin to one another. (Cf. Hamlet's 'a little more than kin and less than kind'.)

176. There is no certain explanation of *Humphrey Hour*. To 'dine with Duke Humphrey' meant to go hungry, since some who could not afford a dinner lounged about a part of St. Paul's Cathedral connected with him; and so the phrase may have been used for a time when people wanted a meal. Could the point be that the first time she had a comfortable hour was the hour after she had borne him?

188-91. The curse of the Duchess of York anticipates what Richard's victims will say to him before the battle of Bosworth.

200. Her still living son, Dorset, was not of royal blood.

216. [Lo! The change of this word to 'No!' proposed by Pope and adopted by D. W. improves the pointedness.]

223. **cozen'd** is probably derived from 'Cousin' through the sense of claiming kinship for advantage; but the *O.E.D.* does not regard the derivation as certain, since the transition is not well illustrated.

232-5. It seems likely that the rather unexpected language of a ship wrecked on the rocks for the Queen hanging on to Richard while she scratches his eyes out originated from the word 'anchor'd' in 232; but the word 'bay' in 233 was probably suggested by the idea of a 'desperate' animal turning on its pursuers 'at bay'. The picture of the 'bark' unequal to the sea had been foreshadowed at III. vii. 161; and shipwreck in Clarence's dream at I. iv. 21-33.

251-2. Richard may only be suggesting that Elizabeth *swallows* her remembrance of wrongs in her angry soul, as the spirits in Virgil's underworld drank forgetfulness of their former lives (*Aeneid*, VI. 713-15); but Shakespeare in another allusion ('May this be wash'd in Lethe and forgotten', *2 Henry IV*, v. ii. 72), and some contemporaries, seem to have thought rather of *immersion* in Lethe.

289. Richard had used this excuse in wooing Anne (I. ii. 122-5); and some have blamed Shakespeare for the repetition. But perhaps we are meant to see the decline in Richard marked by his attempt to do the same thing again, whereas now he himself is, as we shall see, tricked by the Queen. Q omits 289-345, perhaps to shorten.

292. [**Look, what** could pass with us since it is a common modern col-

loquialism to begin a sentence with 'look!'; but it has been held
recently that the true meaning was 'whatever'; and similarly with
'look when' 'as soon as' (I. iii. 290). In that case omit the comma,
with D. W.]

**303. mettle** was the same word as 'metal', and the modern distinction of spelling between literal and metaphorical sense was
not made. The word is usually explained here as 'temper' or
'disposition', but I think better sense is given in this context by
the original sense of stuff or substance, primarily that brought out
of a mine. Cf. the words of Macbeth to his wife:

> Thy undaunted substance should compose
> Nothing but males (I. vii. 73).

**305. bid.** This is a very rare form, probably only here in Shakespeare, but he uses the present tense in *Twelfth Night* (II. iv. 304):
'There is no woman's sides Can bide the beating of so strong
a passion.'

**312.** Dorset had been advised to go abroad at IV. i. 41; but in
historical fact he did not go till after the defeat of Buckingham.

**323. orient** properly means 'eastern', since pearls first came from
the east, but the association of the rising sun (Lat. *oriens*) may
have added brightness to its connotation.

**333.** It may be a mark of Richard's decline that he now abuses as
dull the man he had once called 'deep-revolving' and 'witty'
(IV. ii. 42).

**344-68.** In this passage of dialogue in alternate lines, the grammar
often carries on from one speaker's line to the next, as it did in
Greek tragedy.

**349.** [vail of F gives a stronger sense than the 'wail' of Q; while, on the
other hand in 356 the 'love' of Q, adopted by D. W., is perhaps more
pointed than the 'low' of F followed by our text.]

**355. likes of it,** instead of 'likes it' may have arisen from the impersonal construction 'it likes me of . . .'.

**367.** The **George** is a small enamel figure of St. George attached to
the collar worn by Knights of the Garter, the highest order of
English knighthood, founded in the fourteenth century. A fine
coloured illustration of the Garter itself will be found in the
*Encyclopaedia Britannica* (11th ed.) under 'Knighthood'.

**381. brothers**; cf. I. iii. 37. Shakespeare seems to have treated
Grey as well as Rivers as her brothers.

**392. The children** would refer particularly to Clarence's children.

**425–6.** The metaphor is taken from the fabulous Arabian bird, the phoenix, out of whose ashes when dead, a new phoenix was supposed to arise. The finest use of the myth in poetry is in Milton's *Samson Agonistes*, 1688–1707.

**427–32.** Richard thinks that he has repeated his success with Anne, whose wooing is so often recalled by what we have just read; but he is to be deceived, and the 'changing woman' will change once more. Hall had remarked in his narrative that 'surely the inconstancy of this woman were much to be marvelled at'. The reader or spectator is left to decide whether Elizabeth is merely weak, or whether she is deliberately deceiving Richard.

**434.** The historical facts are that shortly after the defeat of Buckingham in 1483 Richmond sailed against England, but met with storms, and was not able to invade England till two years later, in 1485. Shakespeare has telescoped history to give more dramatic unity.

**465. White-liver'd runagate.** The liver was thought of as the seat of courage, and its redness would depend on the amount of blood in it, denoting courage. Cf. *Merchant of Venice*, III. ii. 83: 'How many cowards . . . have livers white as milk.' **runagate is** connected with 'renegade' and may mean a deserter; but it was also used as a vague term of abuse like our 'vagabond', e.g. in the P.B. version of Psalm lxviii (which Shakespeare would have known): 'letteth the runagates continue in scarceness'.

**468. Morton** after the Council at the Tower had been sent to Brecon (see Commentary on IV. ii. 121).

**472.** Richard ignores the daughter of Edward IV whom he proposed to marry, and the children of Clarence who had been attaindered.

**477. the Welshman.** Richmond's grandfather was Owen Tudor, a Welshman.

**479.** Stanley already feared 'the boar' in III. ii; and we shall soon see that Richard's suspicions of him were fully justified.

**485.** The lands of the Stanleys have always been in Lancashire and Cheshire, Knowsley Park being the chief seat of the Earl of Derby.

**496.** This George Stanley married the heiress of a Lord Strange and thus brought into the family the title of the patron of the company which produced this play. After the death of Lord Strange in 1594 the company became the Lord Chamberlain's men.

**508–9.** The cry of owls was thought to portend death (cf. *Macbeth*,

II. ii. 4). Richard's treatment of the messenger, held responsible for his news, anticipates that ascribed to Cleopatra in *Antony and Cleopatra*, and shows Richard's loss of confidence and self-control.

512–14. Buckingham, unable through the floods to cross the Severn and join the Courtenays, fled up the Severn and took refuge near Shrewsbury with an old servant, who betrayed him for the reward of a thousand pounds.

519. Dorset did in fact come out of sanctuary to join the revolt of Buckingham, and did not go abroad till after this. Contrast IV. iv. 312–13.

527. The attempted ruse of Richard's men to lure Richmond ashore is historical. But the future Henry VII was nothing if not wily.

532. Between this line and the next an eighteenth-century adapter of the play for the stage, Cibber, inserted the line that became famous:

'Off with his head! So much for Buckingham!'

533–end. It may be well to remind the reader again how freely Shakespeare has telescoped history in bringing together the revolt and capture of Buckingham of 1483 and the landing by Richmond in 1485.

## ACT IV, Scene V

The purpose of this little scene, although it is not very carefully written, seems to be to show how Richard was deceived both by the Queen and Stanley. The chroniclers describe Elizabeth as inconstant, but the dramatist leaves it open for us to decide whether she has changed her mind over her daughter or whether she was merely humouring Richard. Shakespeare continues to combine events of 1483 with those of 1485.

1. **Christopher** Urswick was chaplain to Margaret Beaufort, the Countess Richmond of I. iii. 20 (see Commentary there). He was, in fact, already a doctor not a bachelor, and master of a Hall at Cambridge, and was to hold various high ecclesiastical offices in the reign of Henry VII.

7. This line is an Alexandrine with an extra syllable at the end; but the Q version (placed later in the scene) scans easily: 'Tell him the Queen . . .'.

13. **Sir William Stanley** was the brother of Lord Stanley.

14. **Oxford** was the earl of that title who had rebelled against Edward IV, and **Pembroke** was the Earl of Pembroke, Jasper Tudor, Richmond's uncle.

20. Stanley is called by Holinshed 'a wily fox', which he had to be to keep his own head and his son's on their respective shoulders. He eventually brought an army south, but remained aloof from the final battle till he could safely declare himself.

## ACT V, Scene I

The execution of Buckingham might more naturally have been added to the previous act. Probably the length of the previous act led the F printers to make a new act here. The date was 1483, whereas the rest of the act belongs to 1485. Once more Margaret's curses are recalled, and the inevitability of Divine punishment for sin; 'Vengeance is mine, saith the Lord; I will repay' (Romans xii. 19 but based on Deuteronomy xxxii. 35 and other O.T. passages). After his betrayal at Shrewsbury (see Commentary on IV. iv. 512–14) Buckingham was brought to Richard at Salisbury, where he hoped, by a full confession of his plot, to get access to Richard, either to plead with him or to murder him, say the chronicles.

## ACT V, Scene II

This scene confronts us with the real matter of the last act, in bringing the rivals close together. Richmond, coming from the north-west, down Watling Street (now A5) is in the neighbourhood of Tamworth which lies just north of that road. Stanley is at Atherstone, a little further along Watling Street towards London; while Richard has moved from Nottingham to Leicester, where he arrived on 20 August 1485. From here he marched due west to near Market Bosworth and prepared for battle.

5–6. The **lines** will be those mentioned at the very end of Act IV, but the chroniclers record a *meeting* between Stanley and Richmond at Atherstone.

8. The past tense of **spoil'd** probably makes the line refer to the murder of the princes. Vines are not usually cultivated in England, but the image is probably taken from Psalm lxxx, where a wild boar is said to root up a vine.

13. **Tamworth** is about 13 miles from Bosworth, but about twice as far from Leicester.

## ACT V, Scene III

In this scene the dramatist gives us on the same stage alternating glimpses of the two sides in the battle. Nothing shows more clearly that the Elizabethan theatre did not aim at the realism common on the modern stage. The 'boards' had to do duty as the right place for whatever business might be depicted on it, now for Richard's tent, now for Richmond's, or for both at once. In the Prologue to *Henry V* Shakespeare tells his audience that war cannot be reproduced on a stage, and that they must use their imaginations.

**2. Surrey** was Thomas Howard, the eldest son of John Howard, first Duke of Norfolk, here present. Surrey lived to win fame under the Tudors and appears as Norfolk in *Henry VII*. His son was the poet Surrey, translator of Virgil.

**19–21.** This rather formal poetry, typical of Shakespeare's early style, is introduced to mark the time of day. The 'car' of the sun-god driven across the heavens is a conventional piece of classical mythology.

**48.** Q reads 'six o'clock' instead of 'nine', which would certainly be a more usual supper-time; but Richard has been marching to this position.

**49.** This is a short line, which comes naturally enough as Richard thinks of one thing, then pauses and thinks of another. But there are so many other examples of metrical irregularity hereabouts (e.g. 72, 75, 79) that it is probable that the text has been disturbed.

**63.** It would be just possible to take **watch** in its common sense of 'sentries' but that this comes in 77, and would be normal practice anyhow.

**64.** The chroniclers mention that Richard rode a great white charger from Leicester. Shakespeare gives the horse a name.

**68. Northumberland** no doubt looked 'melancholy' because his heart was not in the cause. In fact he took no part in the battle.

**70. cock-shut** used to be derived from a large net spread at twilight to catch (shut in) woodcock; but the *O.E.D.* prefers to explain it as either the time at which fowls are shut up for the night, or the time at which woodcocks shoot through a wood so as to be able to be caught in the net.

**109.** This speech will remind those who know it of Henry's speech before the battle of Agincourt (*Henry V*, IV. i. 309–25). Richmond's words have a beauty rather unexpected in this play, especially in their close, but the dramatist has given his later hero a humbler note of penitence.

117. **the windows of my eyes** for eyelids is recalled by the more concise 'Downy windows close' of *Antony and Cleopatra*, v. ii. 319.

119, &c. See the passages from Tillyard and Moulton quoted in *Select Criticism*. The chronicles only tells us that Richard saw 'diverse images like terrible devils'. The dramatist particularizes them.

120–1. The stabbing occurs in *3 Henry VI*, v. v; and Anne's lamentation for him in I. ii of this play.

174. The interpretation in the footnote gives a better sense than to take 'for hope' as 'for lack of hope', although there is parallel for this sense apart from the context.

177. The Ghosts have appeared to Richard in the order in which his crimes were committed; and it would be more appropriate for each ghost to disappear after speaking to the sleeper than for them all to be visible up to this point. I have therefore excised, with D. W. the *s.d.* invented by eighteenth-century editors 'The ghosts vanish'. D. W. adds a *s.d.* 'vanishes' for each ghost in turn, not found in F or Q.

178–207. This speech has been described as 'the weakest passage in the play', and we have only to think of some of the famous soliloquies of Hamlet to realize that Shakespeare was not born with his genius full-blown.

178. Richard has dreamt that Surrey has been killed under him; as was, in fact, to happen.

181. It was a superstition of the time that candles burnt blue in the presence of apparitions. So when the ghost of Caesar appeared Brutus exclaimed 'How ill this taper burns!' (*Julius Caesar*, IV. iii. 275).

The 'dead midnight' reminds us of Hamlet seeing his father appear 'in the dead waste and middle of the night (I. ii. 198).

184. **I am I**: rather a weak phrase, but an echo of Richard's assertion 'I am myself alone' in *3 Henry VI*, v. vi. 83, where also it is in the context of 'love'.

187. [I have omitted from the text the word 'what' after 'revenge' since it upsets the metre, while the omission improves the sense. He goes on to regret that self-love would prevent him punishing himself worthily. In the following line the word 'wherefore', and at the beginning of 210 'Ratcliff' have also been omitted to restore the metre.]

192. **I am a villain.** Richard can now say that his determination of
I. i. 30 has been achieved!

194. There was a proverb 'Conscientia mille testes', a man's own
conscience could be a thousand witnesses against him as a perjured
murderer.

205–7. These lines come in awkwardly here, and would be more
appropriate after 212.

228–32. The material of these lines is Shakespeare's own.

237–8. **s.d.** The headings here and at 314–15 are an exceptional note
in Q and F, perhaps to cover the abruptness of the transition.
Both orations are based upon Holinshed and Hall, from whom
even many of the slightly unusual words or uses are derived, such
as 'homicide', 'sweat', 'cold' ground.

251–2. **foil** is a thin sheet of metal placed underneath a jewel to set
it off; hence its common metaphorical use. 'set' here literally
means seated, but with a play upon the other sense of a jewel
mounted on something else.

270. **[boldly** might well have been originally 'bold', which would preserve
the metre, while the use of adjective for adverb in such a combined
phrase is found elsewhere.]

272. Richard and Ratcliff must be supposed to be discussing what
they overheard when eavesdropping (222).

291–302. The matter of this speech also and some of the words
(e.g. 'foreward') are from Hall and Holinshed.

299–300 are metrically very irregular, but not easily amended.

310–11. The sentiment is as old as Plato, who made a speaker in his
dialogue, the *Republic*, put forward the view that Justice was
invoked as a means of protecting the weaker from the stronger.
Edmund in *Lear* voices the same sort of 'natural' rights of the
strong found in the proverbial

> That they should take who have the power
> And those should keep who can.

The discussion of 'Conscience' is a backward link with that by
Clarence's murderers in I. iv.

325. **mother's** is a mistake in the second edition of Holinshed, which
Shakespeare must have been using, for 'brother's' of the first
edition. The brother was in fact the Duke of Burgundy, who, by
marrying Richard's sister Margaret had become his brother-in-
law; see Commentary on I. iv. 10.

**346. the marsh** lay between the armies, and in advancing Richmond kept it on his right to protect that flank.

## ACT V, SCENE IV

The rest of our play, continuous in Q and F, is divided after 13 in many editions.

Nearly all the material for the scene comes from the chronicles. They do not mention the loss of Richard's horse, but it is recorded that a light horse was brought him on which he might have escaped; and, since a charger could not be brought on the stage, it is a good invention that his horse should have been killed under him, as Shakespeare implies. Holinshed says that Richard was held at bay by Richmond for some time, until he was overwhelmed by a large force under Sir W. Stanley and died fighting manfully. It is not clear whether Richard's death was depicted on the stage, as the F stage direction says, or whether this took place off stage, as in *Macbeth* (v. vii). Richard II died as bravely as Richard III, although in his case the bravery was less to be expected from the earlier part of the play. But the attention of the Elizabethan audience, who were nearer the Wars of the Roses than we are, would have been concentrated on the first Tudor monarch, who has the last word. The poetry is not remarkable and the sentiments are conventional, but 'he gets everything right and refers to all the things an Elizabethan audience cared about' (Tillyard).

**5. the throat of death** is a metaphor of the vigorous sort not too often vouchsafed us in this early play. Cf. Tennyson's 'Into the jaws of death rode the six hundred'.

**7.** This best-known line in the play may derive from the lamer 'A horse, a horse, a fresh horse' in the *True Tragedy* of 1594; while Shakespeare's own line was often imitated later. In a Cambridge 'show' of 1597, discovered in 1964, we find 'A nose, a nose, a kingedome for a nose'.

**9–13.** 'No actor has ever done the curious recovery by Richard of his old gaiety of heart in the excitement of the battle.... He is again the ecstatic prince of mischief of the "Shine out, fair sun till I have bought a glass" phase, which makes the first act so rapturous. All Nietzsche is in the lines: "Conscience is but a word . . . swords our law." And after all the pious twaddle of Richmond his charging order is delicous: "Let us to't pell-mell." The offer of a kingdom for a horse is part of the same thing: any means of keeping up the ecstasy of the fight is worth a dozen kingdoms.' (From a letter of G. B. Shaw to the actor Forbes-Robertson.)

22. [Pope inserted 'first' after 'me' to restore the metre.]

31. Richmond had sworn at Rennes to marry Elizabeth if he gained the throne.

32–44. We might compare the peace promised to the country by the ending of internal faction with the peace promised to Verona by the ending of the feud between the houses of the Capulets and the Montagues in *Romeo and Juliet*.

37–38. Among the characters introduced in *3 Henry VI* are 'A son that killed his father' and 'A father that killed his son' (ii. v. 53 and 78).

48–end. These lines would have a strong topical appeal to an Elizabethan audience.

# SELECT LITERARY CRITICISM
## General Impression of the Play

(*The extracts under each sub-heading are arranged in chronological order*)

THIS is one of the most celebrated of our author's perform-ances; yet I know not whether it has not happened to him as to others, to be praised most when praise is not most deserved. That this play has scenes noble in themselves, and very well contrived to strike in the exhibition, cannot be denied. But some parts are trifling, others shocking, and some improbable.

JOHNSON, edition of *Shakespeare*, 1765

THE play itself is undoubtedly a very powerful effusion of Shakespeare's genius. The groundwork of the character of Richard, that mixture of intellectual vigour with moral de-pravity in which Shakespeare delighted to show his strength, gave full scope as well as temptation to the exercise of his imagination. The character of the hero is almost everywhere predominant, and marks its lurid track throughout.

HAZLITT, *Characters of Shakespeare's Plays*, 1817

*Hamlet* is great literature; *Richard III* a big, black, gross, sprawling melodrama, writ with infinite spirit but with no refinement or philosophy by a man who had the world, him-self, mankind and his trade still to learn.

R. L. STEVENSON, letter of 19 Jan. 1891

WITH *Richard the Third* Shakespeare completes his nonage. It is a masterpiece, but a masterpiece from the same hand which contributed, to how small or great an extent it is impossible to tell, but in any case prentice-wise, to the final shaping of those typical dramas of a pre-Shakespearian epoch, the three parts of *Henry the Sixth*. It resumes the past rather than preludes the future; and, although the continuity of development is never broken, you shall hardly trace the lineaments of the creator of Macbeth and Iago in those of the youngest and most brilliant graduate in the school of Marlowe and Kyd. To say that there is nothing of Shakespeare's personality in *Richard the Third* would be a paradox, for assuredly his sign-manual is upon scene after scene . . . but at most it affords his individual variation upon a traditional manner of the English stage, which had its roots in the miracle-plays and moralities, and had already been brought to a high state of elaboration by his immediate predecessors.

E. K. CHAMBERS, *Shakespeare Survey*, 1925

IT is not a tragedy of the same order as the great four . . . *Richard III* fails to create the inevitability of its own organic structure. But one may also ask whether the frame of mind that it excites in the audience is fittingly to be called tragic emotion. For, while the witnessing of Richard's life might have induced in the audience the imaginative fears of exposure in real life to such devilish workers of cruelty, the sight of his death must have been balm and comfort, strengthening a firm joy in their fortune to exist in a universe whose police system is so palpably efficient in the arrest of evil-doers and whose penal code adjusts the punishment so exquisitely to the crime. It seems a misuse of words to call this sentiment tragic. For some such reason Aristotle refused to admit the tragedy of mere villainy. . . . It would content the audience, as *Richard III* abundantly has done; but it would not be tragedy. If by tragedy we mean the ideal tragic form which Aristotle sought, or the particular forms in which Shakespeare embodied his greatest tragedies, then *Richard III* is not great tragedy.

H. B. CHARLTON, *Shakespearean Tragedy*, 1949

LAMB'S appreciation of *Richard III*, which would now be accepted as just by most critics, but was something new in 1802, must be set down partly of course to Lamb's genius, but partly also to the fact that few before him had been in a position to view the play in its historical perspective, seeing that the earliest attempt to establish the chronological order of the

plays had been published by Malone only twenty years before.
. . . Thus Lamb was able to appraise *Richard III* for what it
was at the time of its original production without wronging it,
as some critics are still apt to do, by deprecating it in comparison with the later tragedies. With ethics almost as conventional as its structure is formal, of shallow depth, and
devoid of tenderness—except for the rather sugary picture of
the two dead princes in the Tower, which the murderers indulge in once the deed is safely accomplished, and which
Hazlitt strangely picks out for special commendation—*Richard
III* shows us little or nothing of 'the mighty Poet of the
human Heart' [Keats]. Yet Londoners, to whom in 1594
tragedy meant Senecan tragedy, e.g. *The Spanish Tragedy, The
Jew of Malta* (in which Barabas is brought in, as Lamb notes,
'with a large painted nose to please the rabble') . . . must have
found Shakespeare's dramatization of More's *History* almost
incredibly brilliant. Nor is it possible even today to name any
other drama as consummate as *Richard III* in its own kind,
a kind that having brought it thus to perfection Shakespeare
never again essayed. It is indeed this very perfection which
has blinded many to the play's true character. For the kind
in question is not rightly tragedy, but melodrama; the melodrama of genius, yet all the more melodrama for that.

J. DOVER WILSON, edition of the play in the (*New*) Cam-
*bridge Shakespeare*, 1954

## The Moral Theme

IT is the God of the Old Testament that must be supposed to
rule in such a moral order as Shakespeare here depicts, but it
is a moral order. The justice is that of an eye for an eye, a
Prince of Wales for a Prince of Wales. Prayers that are offered
as curses by those with hatred in their hearts are answered by
a divine justice without pity. The stage should indeed be hung
with black for the presentation of this play. But it was a play
that rounded out the cycle of history by which the crown was
snatched from the House of Lancaster by unruly Yorkist hands
only to be lost by the third heir to the importunate Richmond.
Holinshed explained:

And as it thus well appeared, that the House of York showed itself more bloody in seeking to obtain the kingdom, than that of Lancaster in usurping it: so it came to pass, that the Lord's vengeance appeared more heavy towards the same than towards the other, not ceasing till the whole issue male of the said Richard duke of York was extinguished. For such is God's justice to leave no unrepentant wickedness unpunished, as especially in this caitiff Richard the third, not deserving so much as the name of a man, much less a king, most manifestly appeareth.

Thus Shakespeare pictured the dominating sins of the play as perjury and murder, sins against the moral order. He portrayed and analyzed the passion of ambition that caused Richard to sin and the passion of fear that at the same time punished him for his sins and forced him to wade still further in blood. He inserted non-historical scenes developing the Elizabethan philosophy of revenge. He used the supernatural to enhance the horror of the play and to contribute to the impression of a divine vengeance meting out punishment for sin. He showed God's revenge exacted through the agency of the evil Richard, who was nevertheless held to account for his evil-doing. He made use of pathos in the death of the royal children. These are the common methods of Shakespearean tragedy, and they justify those who hold *Richard III* to be a tragedy.

L. B. CAMPBELL, *Shakespeare's Histories*, 1947, U.S.A.

## The Construction of the Play

THESE four Nemesis Actions, it will be observed, are not separate trains of incident going on side by side; they are linked together into a system, the law of which is seen to be that those who triumph in one nemesis become the victims of the next; so that the whole suggests a 'chain of destruction' like that binding together the orders of the brute creation which live by preying upon one another. When Clarence perished it was the King who dealt the doom and the Queen's party who triumphed: the wheel of Nemesis goes round and the King's death follows the death of his victim, the Queen's party are naked to the vengeance of their enemies, and Hastings is left to exult. Again the wheel of Nemesis revolves, and

Hastings at the moment of his highest exultation is hurled to destruction, while Buckingham stands by to point the moral with a gibe. Once more the wheel goes round, and Buckingham hears similar gibes addressed to himself and points the same moral in his own person. Thus the portion of the drama so far considered yields us a pattern within a pattern, a series of Nemesis actions woven into a complete underplot by a connecting-link which is also Nemesis.

R. MOULTON, *Shakespeare as a Dramatic Artist*, 1885

FURTHERMORE in the structure of this play, unlike that of almost all plays before Shakespeare, there are no loose threads. Each motive of the action, once it has been introduced, each minor character and each detail is never lost sight of but taken up again at a later moment and made use of in connection with the major issue. This is all the more admirable as Shakespeare has not achieved this tightness of construction by restricting, as the early English classical tragedies had done, the number of persons and events to be covered in his play but by retaining the large number of characters and incidents which usually figured in a chronicle play. This elaborate and well-considered construction of the play is generally attributed to Shakespeare's superior dramaturgical skill. But it is more than that. Shakespeare has given it a deeper significance by reflecting through this well-planned action Richard's intellectual superiority in planning and scheming, his immense power of will, his clarity of purpose. Richard is the secret agent of the action, and all its threads eventually converge in his hands even if he is not on the stage. Again this is different from Tamburlaine's role in Marlowe's play. For in *Tamburlaine* the whole action is a kind of façade for Tamburlaine's conquering advance and the repetition of parallel episodes of victory over different sets of enemies in their lack of interconnectedness is epic rather than dramatic. In Shakespeare's play we can see how it is Richard who cunningly and secretly watches the movements and actions of his enemies to weave them into his spider's web before they are aware of it and then to wait for the advantageous moment at which he can overcome them. Thus the movements and indeed even the words and thoughts of Richard's victims are made use of by him for his diabolical intents, are integrated into his plans. . . . *Tamburlaine* is indeed a play round a super-human figure who overrides and overshadows all his enemies and all other characters; for these are only feeble foils to serve as interchangeable material for the illustration of his victorious passage. This however we cannot say of *Richard III*. Far more than in *Tamburlaine* we are allowed to enter the mind and world of his victims, not only in that scene for which Shakespeare found no foundation in his source, Clarence's dream and murder, but also in several other scenes.

W. H. CLEMEN, *The Shakespeare Quarterly* (U.S.A.) for 1954

THE play itself is also a symphonic structure which I can only describe in terms of music: a rhetorical symphony with five movements. . . . The first movement employs five 'subjects': Richard himself, his own overture; the wooing theme (to be repeated in the fourth movement); Richard among his enemies (repeating the duplicity with which he has fooled Clarence); Margaret's curse; and the long dying fall of Clarence. It occupies the whole of Act I.

The second movement includes Act II and scenes i–iv of Act III. It begins with the King's feeble peace-making—in which Buckingham invites his curse—and its other subjects are: a lamentation after the King's death (repeated in the fourth movement); the fall of the curse on Rivers, Grey and Vaughan (when the curse is remembered), and on Hastings (the curse briefly recalled again). The future subject of Richard's moves against the Princes is introduced betweenwhiles.

The third movement cuts across the Act-divisions and runs from III. v to IV. iii. Its main subject is the Gloucester–Buckingham plot for the crown, with the magnificently sardonic fooling of the London *bourgeoise* with a crisis-scare, a brace of bishops, and the headline story that here is a highly respectable unlibidinous monarch for decent England. On its success Anne is called to be Queen, and thus to meet the curse she herself called on Richard's wife before he wooed her in that humour and won her (the first movement is here caught up). Buckingham now makes himself one of Richard's future victims by showing reluctance for the plot against the Princes, and Richard throws him off with a snub. The Princes are dealt with (the account of Forrest and Deighton echoing that of the murderers of Clarence, one of whom had a temporary conscience); and Richard concludes with a brisk summary and prospectus: [IV. iii. 38–39 quoted] and so, since Richmond plans to marry 'young Elizabeth, my brother's daughter', 'To her go I, a jolly thriving wooer' (Richard's last jocularity). The movement ends with the first murmurs of Richmond. Previously there has been slipped in the trivial-sounding prophecy about 'Rougemount', besides Henry VI's prophecy (IV. ii. 99 etc.). The flight of the Bishop of Ely really troubles Richard.

The fourth movement brings down the curse on Buckingham (. . . the movement runs from IV. iv to v. i inclusive). Mainly it repeats themes heard before: with a long lamentation scene . . .; a repetition of Margaret's curse with the curse of Richard's mother added; the second wooing scene; the subject of Nemesis repeated by Buckingham. In it the sound of Richmond's advance has become clearer; and Richard's self-command and certainty begin to waver.

The fifth movement is all at Bosworth: the fall of the curse on Richard himself. There is the dream-prologue of the procession of contrapuntal ghosts (including all those so qualified from the four previous movements) and, like all ghosts, they are reminiscent and repetitive. The play ends with the epilogue to the Wars of the Roses—spoken by Queen Elizabeth's grandfather—calling a blessing on the English future, and inverting the opening lines of Richard's prologue.

A. P. ROSSITER, *Angel with Horns*, 1961

## The Style of the Play

THE poetry of the play is that of great and high spiritual adventure. There is much that stays in the mind as exquisitely said and beautifully felt. But the wonder of the work is in the greatness of the conception. This is truly great, both as poetry and as drama. The big and burning images do not please, they haunt.

J. MASEFIELD, *Shakespeare* (revised edition), 1912

THE style is uniform throughout. It is a highly mannered rhetorical style, extravagant in utterance, with many appeals and exclamations. There is much violent and vituperative speech; the word 'blood' runs like a *leit-motif* through the play. Epithets, and sometimes nouns, are piled up, in pairs, with or without a conjunction; in triplets or even greater numbers. Types of line-structure tend to recur. One is based on such a triplet; another is the 'balanced' line, of noun and epithet against noun and epithet. A 'clinching' line at the end of a speech is also common. There are 'cumulative' passages of parallel lines with parisonic beginnings or endings. Words or phrases are repeated for emphasis. There is much 'ringing of the changes' on individual words, between line and line and speech and speech. Sometimes this is progressive, as new words are introduced. Sometimes it takes the form of a bitter pun. There is rhetorical structure, in antithesis, antiphon, stichomythia. Some of it is ultimately of Senecan origin. All these features occur individually in pre-Shakespearean plays and recur in later Shakespearean plays with diminishing frequency. But I do not think they are quite so massed and multiplied elsewhere.

E. K. CHAMBERS, *William Shakespeare*, 1930

THE symmetry of *Richard III* is remarkable; it is all-pervading, and extends from the patterning of Richard's character to the design of the dramatic structure and the intricate antiphony of the verse. All that could be done to *Richard III* in the beaten way of 'art', without interfering with the conventional substance of the melodrama, had been done. In that direction, one feels, Shakespeare had reached the limit of possibility. His art was still formal; but in *Richard III* it reached a perfection of formality beyond the compass of any of his contemporaries.

J. MIDDLETON MURRY, *Shakespeare*, 1936

THE verbal technique of the wooing scene in comedy with its quick repartee, its puns and its brilliant dialogue is here transferred to tragedy and suffused with grim pathos and terrible paradox. The figures of rhetoric are here used in their original function, namely as means of persuasion. Moreover Richard slyly characterises himself through this rhetorical dialogue. He who uses these figures like a virtuoso and who enjoys this 'keen encounter of our wits' with such sarcasm and cynical pleasure appeals to us as the kind of man in whose command over words and people we begin to believe, the master-actor who watches himself and applauds himself while acting and talking, a man who can play with words just as he can play with people. This virtuosity in language and the conscious enjoyment of it, through which this great dissembler can adjust himself to very diverse situations and persons gives more credibility, or, shall we say, a more 'organic function' to the use of the 'arts of language' not only in this scene. Richard's rhetoric is effectively set off by the brusque colloquialism of his diction on other occasions. In fact, Richard's peculiar speech seems to be the first example of Shakespeare's characterizing a person through language—another feature of his art which we do not find in the drama before him.

W. H. CLEMEN, *The Shakespeare Quarterly* (U.S.A.) for 1954

THE writing of these early plays is marked by the gradual attainment of true individuality. Shakespeare's early blank verse is appreciably less the expression of an unmistakable personality than that of Marlowe. This observation, however, though true, is only part of the truth. If Marlowe's writing is still more powerful, more emphatic, in its effect, Shakespeare's already shows a wider range, greater resources of imagery, and a closer adaptation to varied dramatic needs. The result is an instrument perhaps less obviously personal, but superior in theatrical possibilities, as may be seen already in a play as early as *Richard III*. The central figure of this historical tragedy, although clearly owing something to the characteristic Marlovian blend of rhetoric and irony, is perhaps the first of Shakespeare's tragic figures to emerge from the conventions of contemporary melodrama with a genuine force of personality. His opening definition of his own character is expressed with a linguistic vigour that is already typical:

[I. i. 13–21 quoted.]

The speech, based though it is on the established dramatic conventions of envious villainy, represents a toning down of Marlowe's rhetorical overtones in the interests of a less grotesque irony and a firmer delineation of character. Although a certain stilted quality survives in the movement of the verse (there is a sense, common in Elizabethan stage heroes and villains, of the speaker playing up to a dramatically acceptable picture of himself), the general effect is remarkably concise and pointed. Richard's state of mind is conveyed primarily through a series of sharp visual touches—the vision of himself as strutting ludicrously before a 'wanton ambling nymph', as being barked at by the dogs as he passes before them, as spying his misshapen shadow in the sun—and through the sustained contrast, implying contempt and repudiation, between the 'sportive tricks' and exigencies of 'these fair, well-spoken days' and his own situation, 'deform'd, unfinish'd', 'scarce half made up', 'lamely' and 'unfashionable'. In this way, by making envy the vehicle for a criticism felt, by its very directness, not to be altogether unjustified, the speaker is humanized, transformed from the abstract incarnation of a traditional vice exploited for melodramatic effect into something like a person whose nature is twisted indeed by his exclusion from 'love's majesty' (the phrase stands out forcibly by contrast with the sneer that follows it), but who retains in the cool, pungent run of his comments a definite human plausibility. . . . In the delineation of motive beyond the limits of convention his language first attained some sense of its full possibilities.

D. A. TRAVERSI, *An Approach to Shakespeare*, 1956

THE man himself [Richard] never rises to the level of great poetry, for he never has feelings that are incommunicable. His deeds create no sense of tragic waste.

M. M. REESE, *The Lease of Majesty*, 1961

## The Imagery

THE omnipresence of the hero. Richard III, is a striking feature
of this drama. We have already said that the whole action
depends upon him. But not only that—we feel his presence
even when he is not upon the stage. Images are partly responsible for this. Again and again, the impression which Richard's
nature makes upon the other characters and which lingers with
them is reflected in their speeches, generally in the form of
animal-imagery. The fundamental image for him is that of the
repulsive dog, an image of which we find traces as early as
the last part of Henry VI (3 Henry VI, v. vi. 53 and 76). In the
great scene of lament in the fourth act Queen Margaret finds
the most impressive formulation of this image . . .

[Clemen quotes IV. iv. 47–50.]

Richard III appears further as poisonous toad, as foul
hunchback'd toad, bottled spider, as hedge-hog, elvish mark'd,
abortive, rooting hog. To the avengers of the murdered princes
Richard appears as a boar; thus Richmond describes him in
the following image . . . [Clemen quotes v. ii. 7–10].

We cannot exaggerate the imaginative value of these revolt-
ing images. Without our becoming conscious of it, the repulsive
figure of the hunchback Richard as we see it upon the stage is
repeatedly transformed into animal bodies conforming to his
nature, and thus his brutal, animal character is illuminated
from this angle too. *Richard III* is Shakespeare's first play in
which the chief character is delineated by symbolical images
occurring as a *leitmotif*.

W. H. CLEMEN, *The Development of Shakespeare's Imagery*,
1951

## The Character of Richard

SHAKESPEARE has not made his Richard so black a Monster as
is supposed. Wherever he is monstrous, it was to conform to
vulgar opinion. But he is generally a man. Read his most
exquisite address to the widowed Queen to court her daughter

for him—the topics of maternal feeling, of a deep knowledge of the heart, are such as no monster could have supplied. Richard must have *felt* before he could feign so well; but ambition choked the good seed. . . . This observation applies to many other parts. All the inconsistency is that Shakespeare's better genius was forced to struggle against the prejudices which made a monster of Richard. He set out to paint a *monster*, but his human sympathy produced a *man*.

C. LAMB, Letter to R. Lloyd, 26 July 1801

THESE old playwrights invested their bad characters with notions of good, which by no possibility could have co-existed with their actions. Without a soul of goodness in himself, how could Shakespeare's Richard the Third have hit upon those sweet phrases and inducements by which he attempts to win over the dowager queen to let him wed her daughter? It is not nature's nature, but imagination's substituted nature, which does almost as well in a fiction.

C. LAMB, Notes, &c., to *Extracts from the Garrick Plays*, 1827

WE have seen the part of Richard lately produce great fame to an actor by his manner of playing it, and it lets us into the secret of acting, and of popular judgment of Shakespeare derived from acting. Not one of the spectators who have witnessed Mr. C.'s exertions in that part but has come away with a proper conviction that Richard is a very wicked man, and kills little children in their beds, with something like the pleasure which the giants and ogres in children's books are represented to have taken in that practice; moreover that he is very close and shrewd and devilish cunning, for you could see that by his eye.

But is in fact this the impression we have in reading the Richard of Shakespeare? Do we feel anything like disgust, as we do at that butcher-like representation of him that passes for him on the stage? A horror at his crimes blends with the effect which we feel, but how is it qualified, how is it carried off, by the rich intellect which he displays, his resources, his wit, his buoyant spirits, his vast knowledge and insight into characters, the poetry of his part,—not an atom of which is made perceivable in Mr. C.'s way of acting it. Nothing but his crimes, his actions is visible; they are prominent and staring; the murderer stands out, but where is the lofty genius, the man of vast capacity,—the profound, the witty, accomplished Richard?

The truth is that the Characters of Shakespeare are so much the objects of meditation rather than of interest or curiosity as to their actions, that while we are reading any of his great criminal characters—Macbeth, Richard, even Iago,—we think not so much of the crimes which they commit, as of the ambition, the aspiring spirit, the intellectual activity, which prompts them to overleap those moral fences.

c. LAMB, 'On the Tragedies of Shakespeare' in *The Reflector*, 1811

THE inferiority of his person made the hero seek consolation and compensation in the superiority of his intellect; he thus endeavoured to counterbalance his deficiency. This striking feature is portrayed most admirably by Shakespeare who represents Richard bringing forward his very defects and deformities as matters of boast. It was the same pride of intellect, or the assumption of it, which made John Wilkes boast, although he was so ugly, he only wanted with any lady ten minutes start of the handsomest man in England. This certainly was a high compliment to himself; but a higher to the female sex, on the supposition that Wilkes possessed this superiority of intellect, and relied upon it for making a favourable impression, because ladies would know how to estimate his advantages.

This play should be contrasted with *Richard II*. Pride of intellect is the characteristic of Richard. . . . Shakespeare here, as in all his great parts, developes in a tone of sublime morality the dreadful consequences of placing the moral in subordination to the mere intellectual being. In Richard there is a predominance of irony, accompanied with apparently blunt manners to those immediately about him, but formalised into a mere set hypocrisy towards the people as represented by their magistrates.

COLERIDGE, *Lectures on Shakespeare*, 1811–12 and 1818

THE CHARACTER OF RICHARD

THE Richard of Shakespeare is towering and lofty; equally impetuous and commanding; haughty, violent, and subtle; bold and treacherous; confident in his strength as well as in his cunning; raised high by his birth; and higher by his talents and his crimes; a royal usurper, a princely hypocrite, a tyrant, and a murderer of the house of Plantagenet.

> But I was born so high:
> Our aery buildeth in the cedar's top,
> And dallies with the wind and scorns the sun.

The idea conveyed in these lines is never lost sight of by Shakespeare, and should not be out of the actor's mind for a moment. The restless and sanguinary Richard is not a man striving to be great, but to be greater than he is; conscious of his strength of will, his power of intellect, his daring courage, his elevated station; and making use of these advantages to commit unheard-of crimes, and to shield himself from remorse and infamy.

HAZLITT, *Characters of Shakespeare's Plays*, 1817

THE character of Richard the Third . . . is the picture of a demoniacal incarnation, moulding the passions and foibles of mankind, with superhuman precision, to its own iniquitous purposes. Of this isolated and peculiar state of being Richard himself seems sensible when he declares: 'I am myself alone'. From a delineation like this Milton must have caught many of the most striking features of his Satanic portrait. The same union of unmitigated depravity and consummate intellectual energy characterises both, and renders what would otherwise be loathsome and disgusting, an object of sublimity and shuddering admiration. . . . The task, however, which Shakespeare undertook was, in one instance, more arduous than that which Milton subsequently attempted; for, in addition to the hateful constitution of Richard's moral character, he had also to contend against the prejudices arising from personal deformity, and yet, in spite of striking personal defects, which were considered also as indicatory of the depravity and wickedness of his nature, the poet has contrived, through the medium of the high mental endowments just enumerated, not only to obviate disgust, but to excite extraordinary admiration. One of the most prominent and detestable vices indeed in Richard's character, his hypocrisy, connected, as it always is, in his person, with the most profound skill and dissimulation, has, owing to the various parts which it induces him to assume, most materially contributed to the popularity of this play, both on the stage and in the closet. He is one who can 'frame his face to all occasions', and accordingly appears during the course of his career, under the contrasted forms of a subject and a monarch, a politician and a wit, a soldier and a suitor, a sinner and a saint; and in all with such apparent ease and fidelity to nature that while to the explorer of the human mind he affords, by his penetration and address, a subject of peculiar interest and delight, he offers to the practised performer a study well calculated to call forth his fullest and finest exertions.

N. DRAKE, *Shakespeare and His Times*, 1817

[Those who are interested in the comparison of Satan with the villain-hero in Elizabethan drama should be sure to read H. Gardner's essay 'Satan and the theme of Damnation in Elizabethan Tragedy' in *English Studies* for 1948.]

RICHARD, like Edmund, like Iago, is solitary; he has no friend, no brother; 'I am myself alone;' and all that Richard achieves tends to his own supremacy. Nevertheless, the central characteristic of Richard is not self-seeking or ambition. It is the necessity of releasing and letting loose upon the world the force within him (mere force in which there is nothing moral), the necessity of deploying before himself and others the terrible resources of his will. One human tie Shakespeare attributes to Richard; contemptuous to his mother, indifferent to the life or death of Clarence and Edward, except as their life or death may serve his own attempt upon the crown, cynically loveless towards his feeble and unhappy wife, Richard admires with an enthusiastic admiration his great father:

Methinks 'tis prize enough to be his son.

And the memory of his father supplies him with a family pride which, however, does not imply attachment or loyalty to any member of his house.

E. DOWDEN, *Shakspere, His Mind and Art*, 1875

EXACTLY in this consists Shakespeare's personal variation upon the stock Machiavellian theme. His Richard is a monster, like Barabbas or Aaron, and not merely an example of ordinary human frailty. He makes evil his good; but, as I read him, it is not so much for the sake of the evil itself, as for sheer joy in the technique of villainy, in the contriving of the nice adjustment of springs and wires whereby evil comes about. He does not really want the crown, but he does want the world to bustle in; and, scene after scene, he goes off the stage last, twisting his misshapen body in glee, not at the fruit but at the success of his machinations. What a roll his triumphs make! . . .

E. K. CHAMBERS, *Shakespeare Survey*, 1925

## The Stage Popularity of Richard

THE ordinary playgoer, whose reactions in such cases are infallible, has never doubted the political veracity of Shakespeare's Richard. What is strange—and yet not strange at all—is that the ordinary playgoer has not only believed but delighted in him:

> Off with his head! Now, by St. Paul I swear,
> I will not dine until I see the same.

This is after the unregenerate heart of a public which covertly admires a man who comes straight to the point without fear, scruple or procrastination. These are high politics with the gloves off, the foils unbated, and the mask removed. Richard is not a good man. But when was a good man popular? He is not a merciful man. But when was mercy esteemed in public life? And though he is neither good nor merciful, he is every endearing thing else. He is brave, witty, resourceful, gay, swift, disarmingly candid to himself, engagingly sly with his enemies. Above all, he has no conscience to trouble him—not till he sleeps. It is uncommonly refreshing for those who feel the restraint of conscience some fourteen hours a day to see a man upon the stage entirely free of it. On this subject of conscience we are disposed to sympathise with the Second Murderer:

[I. iv. 136–46 quoted.]

Richard, turning his conscience out of doors, promises his audience a moral holiday, and the promise is kept to such good purpose that those who are most refreshed with his heathen villainies leave the theatre thanking God most fervently for their Christian virtues.

J. PALMER, *Political Characters of Shakespeare*, 1945

[The same critic provides a useful conspectus of Richard's part in the *Henry VI* play, too long for quotation here; see pp. 106–74.]

ONLY by realizing that Shakespeare expects us at once to enjoy and to detest the monstrous Richard can we fully appreciate the play he wrote about him.

J. D. WILSON, *op. cit.*, 1954

## Richard and Macbeth

VILLAINY is not a tragic theme even when raised to the level of genius. It can only contribute to tragedy when it so ruins a soul as to reveal the moral foundations which, but for the catastrophe, might have remained unseen. Beside the thick-coming fancies of Macbeth the ghosts of Richard's victims are a melodramatic addition. Compared with the melancholy grandeur of Macbeth's features, worthy of the fallen archangel himself, Richard's are those of a light-hearted fiend. But this is after all a portrait from the artist's youth. If it lacks depth when compared with the masterpieces of his maturity, its energy is superb and worthy of its subject.

P. ALEXANDER, *Shakespeare's Life and Art*, 1938

[A detailed comparison of Richard and Macbeth by Whateley will be found in Furness's 'Variorum Shakespeare' of *Richard III*, pp. 549–52.]

## *The Lamentation Scene* (III. iv)

IN this great static scene, until Margaret leaves the stage, we have as it were an orchestration of grandeur which only a rhetoric so formal could achieve. It is brought about by the repetition of *motifs*, the alternation of reproaches, the similarity of the complaints, the parallelism of the situations and the depth of the personal feelings, which are first opposed to each other and then join forces. The grand speech of Queen Margaret—expert in curses, as Queen Elizabeth calls her—is the perfection of this proud, haughty, nostalgic and strictly balanced style in which, under the almost impersonal character of the traditional themes (the theme, for example, of 'mais où sont les neiges d'antan' ['Where are the snows of yester-year?']), a personality is expressed beyond that of Queen Margaret herself, the personality of Shakespeare.

H. FLUCHÈRE, *Shakespeare* (translated), 1953

## *The Ghosts' Scene* (V. iii)

THEN comes night, and with it the full tide of Nemesis. By the device of the apparitions the long accumulation of crimes in Richard's rise are made to have each its due representation in his fall. It matters not that they are only apparitions. Nemesis itself is the ghost of sin: its sting lies not in the force of the blow, but in the close connection between a sin and its retribution. So Richard's victims rise from the dead only to secure that the weight of each several crime shall lie heavy on his soul in the morrow's doom. This point moreover must not be missed—that the climax of his fate comes to Richard in his *sleep*. The supreme conception of resistance to deity is reached when God is opposed by God's greatest gift, the freedom of the will. . . . Richard can to the last preserve his will from faltering. But, like all the rest of mankind, he must some time sleep: that which is the refuge of the honest man, when he may relax the tension of daily care, sleep, is to Richard his point of weakness, when the safeguard of invincible will can protect him no longer. It is, then, this weak moment which a mocking fate chooses for hurling upon Richard the whole avalanche of his doom; as he starts into the frenzy of his half-waking soliloquy we see him, as it were, tearing off layer after layer of artificial reasonings with which the will-struggles of a lifetime have covered his soul against the touch of natural remorse. With full waking his soul is as strong as ever: but meanwhile his physical nature has been shattered to its depths, and it is only the wreck of Richard that goes to meet his death on Bosworth field.

R. MOULTON, op. cit.

THE scene of the ghosts of those Richard has murdered follows immediately on Richmond's solemn prayer. It is essentially of the Morality pattern. Respublica or England is the hero, invisible yet present, contended for by the forces of heaven represented by Richmond and of hell represented by Richard. Each ghost as it were gives his vote for heaven, Lancaster and York being at last unanimous. And God is above, surveying the event. The mediaeval strain is continued when Richard, awaking in terror, rants like Judas in the Miracle plays about to hang himself. The scene, like Richmond's prayer and his last speech, is very moving. It may have issued from Richard's official self, from Shakespeare identifying himself with an obvious and simple phase of public opinion. But the identification is entirely sincere, and the opinion strong and right, to be shared alike by the most sophisticated and the humblest. The scene becomes almost an act of common worship, ending with Buckingham's assertion:

> God and good angels fight on Richmond's side;
> And Richard falls in height of all his pride.

And just because he participates so fully, because he holds nothing of himself back, Shakespeare can be at his best, can give to his language the maximum of personal differentiation of which he was at the time capable. This differentiation he achieves, not as in some of the other great places of the play by surprising conjunctions of words or new imagery but by subtle musical variations within a context of incantation. He seems indeed to have learnt and applied the lessons of Spenser.

At the same time the substance of what each ghost says is entirely appropriate to the speaker and by referring back to past events in the tetralogy serves to reinforce the structure of the plot. There may be better scenes in Shakespeare, but of these none is like this one. Of its kind it is the best.

E. M. W. TILLYARD, *Shakespeare's History Plays*, 1944

## *The principle of order and the final scene* (v. iv)

THE greatest bond uniting all four plays is the steady political theme: the theme of order and chaos, of proper political degree and civil war; of crime and punishment, of God's mercy finally tempering His justice, of the belief that such had been God's way with England.

I noticed that in each part of *Henry VI* there was some positive, usually very formal or stylised, reference to the principle of order. In *1 Henry VI* there was the scene of Talbot doing homage to his king, in *2 Henry VI* the blameless conduct of Iden and his perfect contentment with his own station in life, in *3 Henry VI* Henry's pathetic longing for the precisely ordered life of a shepherd. In *Richard III* Shakespeare both continues this technique by inserting the choric scene of the three citizens . . ., and at the end of the play comes out with his full declaration of the principle of order, thus giving final and unmistakable shape to what, though largely implicit, has been all along the animating principle of the tetralogy. His instrument, obviously and inevitably, is Richmond; and that this instrument should be largely passive, truly an instrument (hence likely to be overlooked or made little of by the modern reader), was also inevitable in the sort of drama Shakespeare was writing. In the tremendous evolution of God's plans the accidents of character must not be obtruded. Every sentence of Richmond's last speech, today regarded as a competent piece of formality, would have raised the Elizabethans to an ecstasy of feeling. Richmond gets everything right and refers to all the things they minded about. He is conventionally pious, his first words after the victory being, 'God and your arms be prais'd, victorious

friends'; just as Talbot after his capture of Rouen had said,
'Yet heavens have glory for this victory'. Then he thinks of the
immediate problems and asks about the dead. Hearing of them
he begins his last speech,

> Inter their bodies as becomes their birth,

and thereby implies: after thanks to God, the keeping of due
degree on earth. And again he duplicates Talbot, who, in the
same scene, after thanking God, said,

> let's not forget
> The noble Duke of Bedford late deceased,
> But see his exequies fulfill'd in Rouen.

Then, after degree, mercy:

> Proclaim a pardon to the soldiers fled
> That in submission will return to us.

And lastly an oath, taken with full religious solemnity and
duly observed, and the healing of the wounds of civil war, with
an insensible and indeed very subtle transfer of reference from
the epoch of Bosworth to the very hour of the play's per-
formance, from the supposed feeling of Richmond's supporters
to what Shakespeare's own audience felt so ardently about the
health of their country. The reference to father killing son and
son killing father served at a single stroke to recall the battle
of Towton and to take the audience out of the Wars of the Roses
to the wider context of civil wars in general: to Israel, France
and Germany; to the writers of chronicles and the Homilies;
to what they had heard endlessly repeated on the subject by
fireside or in tavern. . . .

> [lines 31 to end quoted].

An Elizabethan audience would take the dramatist's final
amen with a transport of affirmation.

E. M. W. TILLYARD, *op. cit.*

# APPENDIX I

## *A Note on Metre*

'METRE' comes from a Greek word *metron* meaning 'measure', and denotes any pattern or repeated arrangement of syllables by number, length or stress, used to give form to poetry. The poetry of European nations has almost universally till quite recent times been in metrical form, and it is only the *regular* recurrence of some pattern which distinguishes poetry from prose, since prose also has rhythm and may be so impassioned as to be called 'poetic'. It is just this regular recurrence of the same pattern (even with minor variation) that dictates the writing or printing of poetry in lines, and often in verses, or stanzas, as well.

A reader new to the study of metre might be inclined to ask, 'Why trouble about it at all?' The final answer is that without a feeling for the metre much of the pleasure of poetry is missed. But a more limited and severely practical answer might be given, that if a student does not understand the metre of a poem or play, he will not easily quote phrases or lines in a form that the poet could possibly have written; whereas an implicit feeling for metre, especially for that in which all Shakespeare's plays are written, will enable us to memorize more easily and to reproduce correctly the dramatist's lines, and even to see why one form of words is more likely than another in some of the cases where two versions have come down to us, or why the first printed form has been corrected by editors. Nothing looks more illiterate to an examiner than to come upon lines of poetry that manifestly do not 'scan' (i.e. preserve the metre), or are even written as prose!

Metre in classical Greek and Latin poetry is based on the number of syllables and their 'quantity' (i.e. long or short), made up into a certain number of units to a line, called 'feet'. English poetry from the time of Chaucer onwards, and to some extent before that, has a certain number of feet to a line and of syllables to a foot, but instead of scanning by long and short syllables it depends on accent or stress of the voice. Thus we may take as an example the place name 'Liverpool': the first syllable has a short vowel and would be called short by the rules of classical scansion, but an English-speaking person lays the main stress on this syllable, with a minor stress on the last syllable; whereas a French-speaking person not familiar with the name might be heard to stress the middle syllable. A poet of course takes his stress from the normal pronunciation of his day, and, as we get more familiar with the metre of Shakespeare, we shall sometimes be able to say with confidence that such and such a word must have been pronounced in a different way in the poet's day from that now normal. Or again we can let the dramatist tell us how to pronounce a name he uses which is unfamiliar to us. The name 'Theridamas' in Marlowe's *Tamburlaine* often defeats a reader, but the places where it occurs in verse show that we should pronounce it with accents on the second and the last syllables—'Therídamás'.

Most English poetry between Chaucer and Shakespeare had been written in rhyme, usually in the case of longer poems or plays in some sort of rhyming couplets, though sometimes even in long poems in a stanza form, like Chaucer's *Troilus and Criseyde*. But in his last work, the *Canterbury Tales*, Chaucer used a line of five feet and ten syllables rhyming in couplets, commonly called the 'heroic couplet'. A little before the time of Shakespeare plays began to be written in lines of this length *without* rhyme; and, although any lines devoid of rhyme could be called 'blank', the term 'blank verse' is now only used of this particular length of line. English verse has often been described in terms borrowed from those used for the classics; and in that terminology the line is an iambic pentameter, that is five (Gk. *pente*) measures or feet, of which the most common foot is an iambus (or iamb), a short syllable followed by a long, marked thus ∪ —. But, since English verse is a matter of stress and not of quantity, it is better to avoid the use of long and short marks, and simply put an acute accent on the syllables where the voice stress naturally falls, and to describe the line as decasyllabic (Gk. *deka*, ten). Blank verse, then, consists of

unrhymed lines of five feet, each foot being composed of ten
syllables with a strong stress on the second syllable of each
foot. Here is an example from *Richard III* of an absolutely
regular line:

> This noble isle doth want his proper limbs

in which the feet and accents may be shown thus:

> This nó|ble iśle | doth wánt | his próp|er límbs.

There are far more regular lines like this in an early play like
*Richard III* than in Shakespeare's mature work. But even here
there are many variations, which can be classified as (1) excess
or defect in the number of syllables or (2) excess or defect in
the number of accents.

(1) The commonest position in which extra syllables occur is
at the end of a line, where it is called a 'double ending'; as, for
example, the twelfth line of the play:

> $\overset{1}{\text{He ca}}$|$\overset{2}{\text{pers nim}}$|$\overset{3}{\text{bly in}}$ | $\overset{4}{\text{a la}}$|$\text{dy's}$ $\overset{5}{\text{cham}}$|ber;

and it is surprising that there are no less than six of these
extra syllables or overrunning lines in the first eighteen lines
of the play, and a higher proportion than we should have
expected in the play as a whole. Where there are two extra
syllables, or a whole foot, the line is often called by its French
name, an Alexandrine (most of these are pointed out in the
Commentary), e.g.

> $\overset{1}{\text{I, that}}$ | $\overset{2}{\text{am rude}}$|$\text{ly}$ $\overset{3}{\text{stamp'd,}}$ | $\overset{4}{\text{and want}}$ | $\overset{5}{\text{love's maj}}$|$\overset{6}{\text{esty}}$
>
> (i. i. 16)

(where also the stress on the first syllable illustrates one of the
commonest variations in accentual pattern).

Another fairly common surplusage of syllables is a foot of
three instead of two syllables, e.g.

> Having God, her conscience, and these bars against me (i. ii. 236)

where we can almost slur the two syllables of 'having' into one
and scan thus:

> $\overset{1}{\text{Having God,}}$ | $\overset{2}{\text{her con}}$|$\text{science and}$ | $\overset{3}{\text{these bars}}$ | $\overset{4}{\text{against}}$ | $\overset{5}{\text{me.}}$

Another example of a trisyllabic foot is found in the Q at III. vii. 3, where our text has the F's

> The citizens are mum, say not a word,

but Q reads

> The citizens are mum, and speak not a word.

If Shakespeare wrote this line, the three last syllables make a trisyllabic foot.

(2) But variation in the number of *syllables* is far less common and important than variation of *accent*. If we read the verse as we should, that is by the sense, we shall find that there are few lines in which there are five equally strong accents, each on the second syllable of a foot. Often there will occur feet with two strong accents or none, and still more frequently two or three of the accents will be strong and clear, while it will be more or less a matter of taste as to whether we consider some of the other syllables in the accented position to be bearing a stress at all. When the angry Richard answers saying

> They do me wrong, and I will not endure it (I. iii. 42),

it is pretty clear that the strongest voice stress falls on the words 'wrong' and the second syllable of 'endure' (which of course includes 'it'); and the stresses on 'do', 'I' and 'not' are subordinate stresses (some people in fact might prefer to stress 'will' instead of 'not'); but this does not in any way destroy the clear pattern. Again in the next line

> Who are they that complain unto the king?

the second foot has either no accent, or a weak one on 'they', and the fourth foot has no accent on 'unto'. Five lines further down we have a good example of reversed accent in the first foot, one of the most effective variations:

> Smile in men's faces, smooth, deceive and cog.

The reader of Shakespeare needs to try and get the basic pattern of the metre so well into his mind that he is aware, almost subconsciously, of many variations as he goes along, and is only held up by an occasional line where the poet has exercised exceptional licence, sometimes for a dramatic purpose, such as a pause. Where no such purpose is discernible, and where the irregularity is not one of those commonly occurring, such as the extra syllable(s) at tne end of a line, it is permissible to suspect textual corruption.

The most common and important variation in blank verse, that of the pauses dictated by grammar and sense (and therefore marked by punctuation) is not strictly a matter of metre. When the verse of an early play like this is called 'stiff' it is chiefly because the pause comes so much more often at the end of the line than in its course.

Although the metre of all Shakespeare's plays is basically *blank* verse, there is always a certain proportion of rhymed couplets. These usually have the kind of clinching or semi-proverbial sound, and in most plays are commonest at the end of scenes or speeches. In *Richard III* there is a good example of the proverbial, almost sing-song, effect in the prophecy

> which says, that G Of Edward's heirs the murderer shall be

(I. i. 39–40), and the same rhyme is prolonged at 55–59.

A fairly long speech by the Duchess of York (IV. iv. 184–96) is suitably rounded off by a rhyming couplet:

> Bloody thou art, bloody will be thy end;
> Shame serves thy life, and doth thy death attend.

The Ghosts addressing Richard in V. iii several times use rhymed couplets, such as might make their words more memorable.

An example of rhyme at the conclusion of an episode is the last words of the First Murderer which end Act I.

# APPENDIX II

## The Life of William Shakespeare

(condensed from Sir Edmund Chambers's *William Shakespeare*)

WILLIAM SHAKESPEARE was born of middle-class parents at Stratford-on-Avon, a provincial market town of some importance, at an uncertain date between April 24, 1563, and April 23, 1564. His parents were natives of Warwickshire. His father, John Shakespeare, whose principal business was that of glover, rose high in civic life, becoming alderman in 1565 and bailiff in 1568, but later fell on evil days. His mother was Mary Arden. Shakespeare was educated at King Edward VI's Grammar School, Stratford, where he must have learnt a fair amount of Latin, if little or no Greek. He married in 1582 Anne Hathaway, and his first child, a daughter, was baptized in May 1583, to be followed in February 1585 by twins, Hamnet (died 1596) and Judith, who survived her father.

We have no certain information as to Shakespeare's life between 1584 and 1592. There is an early tradition that he stole deer from Sir T. Lucy of Charlecote. We know Shakespeare was in London by 1592 but not when he went there. During these years Shakespeare must have acquired the varied knowledge and experience of life shown in his plays.

The mention of Shakespeare in a death-bed letter of the playwright Greene in September 1592, shows that as a writer for the stage Shakespeare was just becoming a serious rival to the university wits—Marlowe, Peele, Nashe, and Lodge. The years when the theatres were closed on account of plague gave time for the poems *Venus and Adonis* (1593) and *Lucrece* (1594), both dedicated to the Earl of Southampton. By March 1595 Shakespeare was a shareholder in the acting company of the Lord Chamberlain's men, who divided with the Admiral's men the command of the London stage from about 1594 to 1603. For this company, which later became the King's men, Shakespeare seems to have written during the rest of his career. After

1599 most of his plays were performed at the Globe Theatre. Shakespeare probably wrote his *Sonnets* between 1595 and 1600, but they were not printed till 1609.

In 1596 Shakespeare obtained a grant of arms; in 1597 he bought New Place, a substantial house and garden at Stratford, but he is still found living in London in 1597, 1599, and 1604. Shakespeare occasionally appeared as an actor himself, chiefly before 1598.

About 1610 Shakespeare retired to Stratford, and he wrote no more after 1613. He took no part in civic life, and died on 23 April 1616. There is no reason to reject the report that he died of fever contracted from drinking too hard at a merry meeting with Drayton and Ben Jonson. The family is extinct.

## TABLE OF APPROXIMATE DATES OF SHAKESPEARE'S PLAYS

**1590–1**
  *2 Henry VI*
  *3 Henry VI*

**1591–2**
  *1 Henry VI*

**1592–3**
  *Richard III*
  *Comedy of Errors*

**1593–4**
  *Titus Andronicus*
  *Taming of the Shrew*

**1594–5**
  *Two Gentlemen of Verona*
  *Love's Labour's Lost*
  *Romeo and Juliet*

**1595–6**
  *Richard II*
  *Midsummer-Night's Dream*

**1596–7**
  *King John*
  *Merchant of Venice*

**1597–8**
  *1 Henry IV*
  *2 Henry IV*

**1598–9**
  *Much Ado About Nothing*
  *Henry V*

**1599–1600**
  *Julius Caesar*
  *As You Like It*
  *Twelfth Night*

**1600–1**
  *Hamlet*
  *Merry Wives of Windsor*

1601–2
*Troilus and Cressida*

1602–3
*All's Well That Ends Well*

1603–4
————

1604–5
*Measure for Measure*
*Othello*

1605–6
*King Lear*
*Macbeth*

1606–7
*Antony and Cleopatra*

1607–8
*Coriolanus*
*Timon of Athens*

1608–9
*Pericles*

1609–10
*Cymbeline*

1610–11
*Winter's Tale*

1611–12
*Tempest*

1612–13
*Henry VIII*
*Two Noble Kinsmen*

PRINTED IN GREAT BRITAIN
AT THE UNIVERSITY PRESS, OXFORD
BY VIVIAN RIDLER
PRINTER TO THE UNIVERSITY